The Hardest Year

A Love Story in Letters During the Vietnam War

CAROLE AND WILLIAM WAGENER

The Hardest Year: A Love Story in Letters During the Vietnam War

© Copyright 2023 Carole and William Wagener

ISBN: 978-1629672588

Library of Congress Control Number: 2023907145

www.CaroleWagener.com

All rights reserved. No part of this book may be reproduced in any form or by any electronic or mechanical means, including information storage and retrieval systems, without written permission from the author, except in the case of a reviewer, who may quote brief passages embodied in critical articles or in a review.

Trademarked names may appear throughout this book. Rather than use a trademark symbol with every occurrence of a trademarked name, names are used in an editorial fashion, with no intention of infringement of the respective owner's trademark.

The information in this book is distributed on an "as is" basis, without warranty. Although every precaution has been taken in the preparation of this work, neither the author nor the publisher shall have any liability to any person or entity with respect to any loss or damage caused or alleged to be caused directly or indirectly by the information contained in this book.

v23-7.25

Praise for *The Hardest Year*

"This book was as revealing as it gets for a couple. Carole and Bill held nothing back in their letters. What a ride, what raw emotions, what daily stress they shared with each other, so many insecurities of youth, of young love, of a marriage she questioned from the beginning for a variety of reasons. I couldn't put it down and found myself grateful for the honesty these two young people shared."

Grace Tiscareno-Sato, Reviewer,
Military Writers Society of America

"Carole and Bill's *The Hardest Year* is one for the history books. Carole and Bill's correspondences exemplify the raw emotions, new and fleeting love, and moral injury that soldiers endure. Bill's heroic time at war and Carole's tumultuous encounters on the UW-Madison campus during the riots and protests parallel each other as they maneuver through the infancy of their marriage. This book is a true transportation into the Vietnam era both from a civilian and a military lens."

Laura Naylor Colbert, Iraq War Veteran,
author of *Sirens: How to Pee Standing Up*

"*The Hardest Year* is a memoir of young love, the Vietnam War, and the heartache of newlyweds spending their first year apart halfway around the world from each other. Their dialogue through distance is a love story, a war story, and a poignant reminder of a time in history that should never be forgotten."

Annette Langlois Grunseth, Wife/Sister of a Vietnam Veteran,
author of *Campus and Combat: Writing through War*

"This book chronicles the struggle of a newly married couple separated almost immediately by the husband's deployment to fight a war. During their one year apart, the couple's emotions and relationship are on a continual roller coaster. Will the separation bring them closer or tear them apart? The heartfelt letters written by Carole and Bill contain several meaningful lessons for any couple facing the same circumstance."

Patrick Sturm, retired Lieutenant Commander, U.S. Navy, president of Coastal Dunes California Writers Club

This book is dedicated to the families of our country's veterans, especially those who served in Vietnam, and to all the women who took on the tremendous responsibility of telling their stories.

"The Vietnam War—a war that she had never served in or been to—was the single most important event of her life."

~ Andrew Wiest, *Charlie Company's Journey Home: The Forgotten Impact of Vietnam on the Wives and Families of Veterans*

TABLE OF CONTENTS

AUTHOR'S NOTES i
ACKNOWLEDGEMENTS iii
INTRODUCTION v
PART I 7
    CHAPTER 1 - August 1968: Decisions, Decisions 9
    CHAPTER 2 - One Ugly Man 17
    CHAPTER 3 - Running Out of Time 31
    CHAPTER 4 - Becoming a Physical Therapist 37
    CHAPTER 5 - September 1968: Is She or Isn't She? 43
    CHAPTER 6 - Pete, Pot, Panthers, and Pigs 57
    CHAPTER 7 - October 1968: Henry vs Helen 67
    CHAPTER 8 - November 1968: Island Fever 87
    CHAPTER 9 - December 1968: A Full Moon, Empty Arms 103
PICTURES 121
PART II 137
    CHAPTER 10 - January 1969: Unhappy New Year 139
    CHAPTER 11 - February 1969: All Hell Breaks Loose 151
    CHAPTER 12 - March 1969: Rolling in the Muck 167
    CHAPTER 13 - April 1969: Geez, Louise 181
    CHAPTER 14 - May 1969: Into the Shadows 193
    CHAPTER 15 - June 1969: All of War's a Stage 205
    CHAPTER 16 - July 1969: A Million Angels' Wings 215
    CHAPTER 17 - August 1969: A Solemn Warning 227
PART III 235
    CHAPTER 18 - The Hardest Journey Home 237
    CHAPTER 19 - September 1969: *Di Di Mau!* 245
    CHAPTER 20 - October 1969: We Don't Want
                              Your Goddamn War! 253
EPILOGUE 263
Glossary of Terms 267
Endnotes 271

AUTHOR'S NOTES

This memoir is based on handwritten letters, cards, and newspaper clippings sent between Carole and Bill Wagener from September 1968 to August 1969. The vernacular is accurate to that time, using words that are no longer politically correct. The letters, based on actual events, may have been compressed. Please note there was a time lapse between these letters due to a lag in the mail. Some names and identifying characteristics were changed to protect privacy, and some dialogue was recreated. The remainder of the book is based on Carole and Bill's memories to the best of their recollection over time. Because this is a war story, some chapters are very graphic and may not suit those with posttraumatic stress disorder (PTSD) or other trauma related disorders. In addition, the book contains some offensive language and sexual references. Finally, there are several military terms, and various German, French, and Vietnamese phrases mentioned in this book. These terms are defined in the glossary.

ACKNOWLEDGEMENTS

by Carole Wagener

I wish to thank everyone who has made this book possible, especially my friends at the Coastal Dunes California Writers Club in Nipomo, California, who helped me birth this book. Also, thank you to the Word Wizards Critique Group in Santa Maria, California, and my fellow students in the Life Story Class at Cuesta College in San Luis Obispo, California, for their input.

Thank you, Peter Dunne, writer/producer of *Eight is Enough,* and *Dr. Quinn, Medicine Woman,* for giving me the encouraging feedback I needed at the California Writers Conference and telling me this book would be "Fantastic." A special thanks to the editors, Judythe Guarnera, Sara Roahen, Eldonna Edwards, and Daniel Siuba, and to all of my beta readers, including Tom Avitabile, book coach and author of *Forgive Us Our Trespasses* and *Give Us This Day.*

To my four exceptional friends, Karen, Renee, Danne, and Viviana, thanks for all your truthfulness, support, and encouragement. Thank you to my husband and our children for bearing with me through seven years of writing, editing, and burning dinners. Thanks to my sister, Cheryl, and my best friend in college, Jayne, for being there for me.

To all our readers, I hope you'll better relate to military veterans after you've read *The Hardest Year.* To all veterans and their families, I sincerely wish you obtain the healing this book may provide as Bill and I share our unique wartime experiences. Finally, to all those currently serving in the military, "Thank you for your continued service, and God bless."

INTRODUCTION

Like seeds in young people's lives, the first year of marriage sprouts the stalks for couples striving to maintain their union. Over time, memories become unconsciously embellished, leading to silent disagreements. Letters establish the authenticity of two intertwined lives. The Wagener's notes recorded intimate, personal moments and provided a historical eye-opener. The Vietnam War placed an ocean between Carole and Bill, a distance bridged by hope and prayers that carried them through *The Hardest Year*.

~ Renee G., a friend

Map of South Vietnam

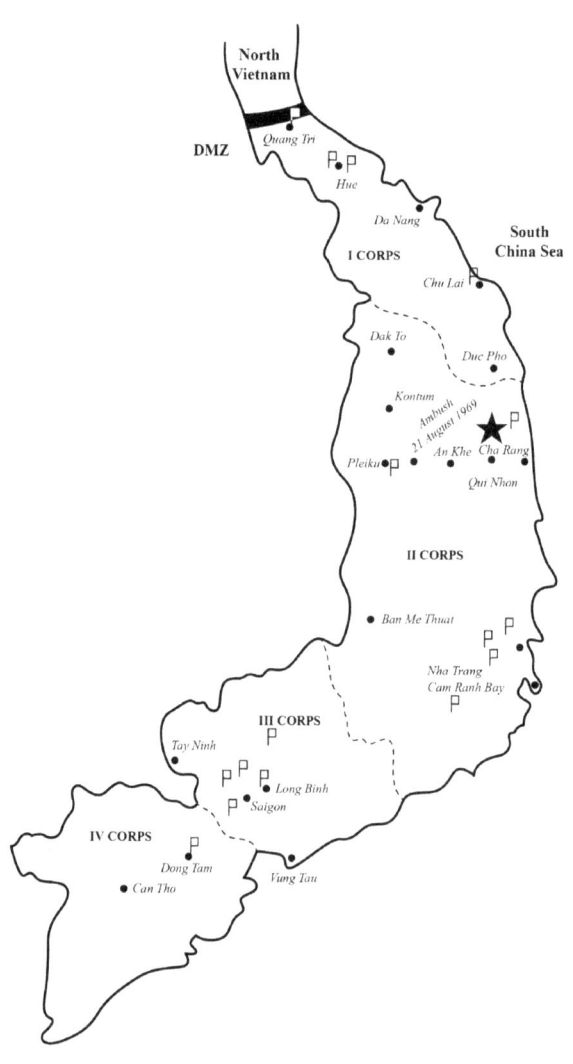

PART I

CHAPTER 1 - AUGUST 1968: DECISIONS, DECISIONS

The cinnamon from Mom's freshly baked apple pie battled with the tangy scent of my first attempt at making *kummel klops*, German meatballs. While lighting the two white tapered candles on the dining table, I struggled with a dreaded feeling. Glancing up at my parents' wedding picture on the mantle next to my great-grandmother's clock, I heard its familiar *bong, bong, bong* for the sixth time and panicked.

He's late.

Specialist 4 Bill Wagener had only two weeks left of his military leave from the U.S. Army before deploying to Vietnam. On his first morning home, he asked me, "Carole, will you marry me before I leave?"

I answered, "Maybe."

Tonight I wanted to butter up my boyfriend of two years so he'd be amendable to a year-long engagement instead of rushing into marriage. So, after a romantic dinner, I hoped we could slow dance together, where I would bring up the topic.

Billy took dance lessons as a teen and was teaching me. My sister, Cheryl, and I practiced to the music on the *American Bandstand*, but sometimes I still stepped on her toes. Earlier, I set the record player up in the living room to play my favorite romantic song, "You Send Me," by Sam Cooke.

Meanwhile, flipping on my transistor radio in the kitchen, I adjusted its antenna to find some music other than Wisconsin polka bands on the local stations. It was a good night when the rock and roll station, WLS-Chicago, could be heard all along Lake Michigan to my small hometown of Alaska, Wisconsin.[1]

I switched the burner of the electric stove on, set a big pot of water on top, and then fine-tuned my transistor to 94.7. I cranked up the volume to "Brown Eyed Girl" and danced around the kitchen to its Jamaican beat, relieving the stress that simmered inside me like the water in the pot. Finally, I threw the egg noodles in and stirred. In ten minutes, dinner would be ready.

I wondered, *Did Van Morrison write his song just for me?* I'd inherited big brown "Obry" eyes from Dad's family, and Billy told me they were my best feature. But my worse feature was my Titanic nose. Unfortunately, my nose was like Ma's, adding to my self-consciousness.

My self-esteem always sank when the girls on the playground bullied me about my nose. Finally, one day I'd had enough of it and worked up my courage to talk to the fifth-grade teacher.

"Mrs. Jenerjohn, I don't like it when Debbie and Cindy don't play with me and call me Pinocchio-nose."

"You tell those mean girls that I let my nose grow long because I don't go around poking it into other people's business."

Most likely, the mean girls' parents received a phone call from my teacher the night before. The next day, I did as told, and to my relief, the name-calling immediately stopped.

But for good reasons, my family nicknamed me "Spilly Carole." I rushed into the bathroom and slipped Ma's checkered gingham apron over my head, tying it around my slender waist to protect my pink and white crepe dress. Then, measuring my appearance in the mirror, I quickly whipped up my reddish-orange hair into a ponytail, put on pastel blue eyeshadow, and applied frosted pink lipstick. A blast of August heat fried my hair and frazzled my nerves as I walked back into the steamy kitchen to drain the egg noodles.

Dinner's ready. Bill better get here soon.

My parents had a six o'clock reservation at the Alaska Supper Club, just up the road from our store. They could no longer wait to greet Billy as it was getting late. Just as they were leaving, I heard the deep-throated rumble of a motorcycle pull up and stop.

Billy waltzed in the store's front door just as my folks walked out. He greeted them and kissed me on the cheek. I put up the CLOSED sign and locked the door to prevent unwanted customers from intruding on our intimate dinner. I didn't want anything to get in the way of my plan.

Billy followed me back into the kitchen, sniffed the air, and smiled. "Carrot, it sure smells good in here."

"Billy, stop calling me Carrot." That Summer Blonde Hair Lightener with the promise to "be a summer blonde all year long" had turned me into a bright redhead.

"Just kidding, Carole. Do you always have to be so sensitive? And by the way, I don't appreciate being called Billy. Hearing 'Billy' is like nails grating on a chalkboard."

"Okay, but if you call me Carrot again, I'll keep calling you Billy."

Bill embraced me from behind, and I tensed but continued slowly stirring the meatballs, not wanting to burn the sauce. He hovered over my right shoulder as I added the sour cream to the mixture. I broke out in a light sweat when he nuzzled my neck with his chin.

"What's cooking?" he asked.

"Grandma Obry's special meatball recipe." Feigning being slightly miffed, I uncoiled from his embrace and inquired, "Why were you late? I was afraid something horrible happened to you on that motorcycle."

Bill ran on his own schedule and threw up both hands, laughing. "The only time I arrived early for dinner was on Thanksgiving Day in 1945, the day I was born. I upset the family's Thanksgiving meal, and I've been upsetting the family ever since. Anyway, it's a bad habit of mine. Mother told me that if I don't change, I'll be late for my wedding."

I chuckled, thinking next time I'd tell Bill to arrive fifteen minutes earlier than planned. Meanwhile, Bill glanced toward the living room.

"Okay, if I watch TV? The Democratic National Convention is on."

"I wasn't planning on watching TV." My smile dropped. "I'm not really into politics." Politics was the last thing I wanted to discuss tonight.

Bill settled into Dad's comfortable chair in front of the television without acknowledging what I said. "Mind if we eat in here?"

"I guess…" I turned on the Motorola and handed him the remote. "Here, you find the channel."

I angrily rattled the folded TV trays and set them up in the living room. My romantic evening shattered after slaving the entire afternoon preparing my first landmark meal. Grandmother's proverb, "The best way to a man's heart is through his stomach," was now in question.

I did my best to cook a fine meal, but it wasn't enough to get Bill's attention. Of course, throughout my youth, Mother said I could do better, but this meal had turned out perfect, leading me to think, *Was it something about me that wasn't quite good enough for Bill? Or was he just preoccupied with the day's politics?*

Crestfallen, I slowly walked back into the kitchen, blew out the candles, and turned off the radio. Carrying our plates into the living room and setting them down on the cold metal trays, I felt more like a waitress than Bill's girlfriend. How could I talk to him with the TV blaring the world's concerns?

So far, 1968 proved to be a turbulent, troubling year for our country. On January 31, U.S. involvement in Vietnam escalated during the Tet [Chinese Lunar New Year] Offensive. Two months later, President Johnson announced he wouldn't seek re-election. Riots broke out in early April after James Earl Ray assassinated Dr. Martin Luther King in Memphis. The nation reeled again on June 6 when Sirhan Sirhan assassinated Robert F. Kennedy in Los Angeles after RFK secured the presidential primary nomination for the California Democratic Party. These events set the stage for the current Democratic National Convention held in Chicago in a nation with an already tense vibe.

My parents were Republicans, so I knew nothing about the Democratic Party. *I'm not even old enough to vote,* I thought, plopping down on the sofa to eat dinner and watch TV. Nevertheless, I wanted this special night with Bill to be memorable—dominated by the irresistible food on his plate and for him to pay proper respect to my cooking without the rest of the world intruding.

But the unprecedented black-and-white world had already entered the living room. During the four-day convention, thousands of protestors, led by somebody called Tom Hayden,[2] camped out in nearby Grant Park. Bill and I ate in stunned silence and watched while, outside the convention hall, police broke up antiwar protests on the streets of Chicago.

The camera switched coverage to the inside of the International Amphitheatre on the South Side of Chicago, where Democratic delegates battled on the convention floor about the party's stance on the Vietnam War. It was unbelievable. Men fought with one another and violently overturned tables and chairs. Then, back in the streets, protesters fled as law enforcement officers in riot gear tear-gassed them.

I asked, "Why's this happening?"

"People are very divided over this war in Vietnam," Bill answered without taking his eyes off the TV.

I went to the kitchen to prepare dessert. Bill's eyes finally popped when I served him a mammoth slice of apple pie á la mode, but back on the convention floor, a plainclothes security officer punched a young reporter, Dan Rather, in the stomach.

"What the hell! Did you see that?" Bill stood up, pointing at the TV.

Newscaster Walter Cronkite remarked, "I think we've got a bunch of thugs here, Dan."

"I can't watch anymore of this big city problem. That couldn't possibly happen here."

I gathered our plates and hurried off to the kitchen. My parents arrived home just as I finished putting the dishes away. I rushed my father into the living room, pointing at the TV.

"Dad, you need to see this."

"History in the making," Bill excitedly said as he offered Dad the Lazy Boy chair.

With the violence on TV, Bill's single-minded focus, and my dad joining him, he wasn't paying any attention to me. I was disappointed the opportunity to talk about Bill's proposal of immediate marriage never arose. It also troubled me that he would be leaving on September 12 for an increasingly unpopular war. Feeling overwhelmed with defeat, I excused myself and kissed Bill good night on the cheek.

I went to bed but couldn't sleep. My thoughts swirled in my mind while the TV blasted outside the door of my room.

"Dad, can you turn it down?" I shouted, rolled toward the wall, hugged my old blue stuffed cat for comfort, and thought about marriage.

If I say "yes" to Bill, will Mom and Dad continue to pay my college expenses? Does my family approve of me marrying a Catholic? Does Bill's family approve of him marrying a Lutheran? What if Bill's killed in Vietnam? Who'd want to marry me then, a war widow?

Instead of fearing the future, I thought about what first attracted me to Bill. I saw everything in him that I wasn't—he had a fierce streak of independence, a well-rounded education, and a quick wit. In addition, he wasn't afraid to speak his mind, always willing to enter into a debate to prove his point, and he liked to win, whether it was a discussion, a card game, or chess. I usually felt uneasy around men, but not around Bill.

Even though his facial features were a bit effeminate, with a small Romanesque nose and thin lips, I thought he was handsome with his French-Canadian mother's thick black hair and his English-German father's straight teeth. In addition, he'd proved his masculinity by becoming a high school wrestling champion and a leader in the Boy Scouts.

Meanwhile, I lead such a sheltered, naïve life. But because of Bill, I learned to swim, ride horses (well, sort of), and could name the constellations in the night sky. It also impressed me that Bill could paddle a canoe across the lakes in the Northwoods of Canada or navigate his dad's tugboat on the Great Lakes without getting lost. So that gave me hope he could find his way walking through a Vietnam jungle.

While walking to the University of Wisconsin-Green Bay campus every day, I saw a cute red motorcycle parked in front of an apartment complex, which I found out later was where Bill lived. That's the kind of small bike I'd been saving for from my waitress job. But Mother told me "No," and her word was final. She hated motorcycles, saying they were unsafe. But the few times I was on the back of one with the wind blowing in my face, I enjoyed the freedom, the thrill, and the need for speed.

I had a gut feeling, though, that Ma disapproved of Bill. Maybe she thought he wasn't "good enough" for me. But the harder she tried to push me away from him, the tighter my grip became.

So, who is good enough for me? Some farm boy from down the road she picks out? A life of milking dairy cows and making jams. Really, Mom? That's not for me!

I wanted to be part of the Wagener clan of doctors, lawyers, and sea captains and not remain a country bumpkin. I was getting along well with Bill's family. His mother even predicted our children would be beautiful if we married, and Bill wanted to have a dozen of them.

In June of 1968, against my parents' wishes, I flew out to visit Bill at Fort Belvoir for a one-week vacation and to tour Washington, D.C. I stayed on the military base in a two-dollar-a-night room.

Bill had classes during the weekdays but joined me in the mess hall for lunch. Afterward, I hung out in the cafeteria, drank coffee, and read a book. Then, one afternoon, a nice-looking GI approached and asked to join me.

"So, I hear you're not engaged." He said and sat next to me.

"That's correct."

He flirted and kept repeating, "but you're not engaged," as if that made it okay to hang out with me. When class let out, I was still the only girl in the chow hall, and soon a handful of other soldiers flocked around me like flies to honey. Bill soon arrived and shooed them all away.

"Hands off, guys. She's my girl."

Even though I'd never been in love before, I thought Bill loved me and was the right guy for me. With a promising future ahead of us, why did this war have to get in the way of our courtship, forcing me to make a hurried decision? God knew I wasn't good at making quick decisions.

It was late when Dad finally turned off the TV, and I heard Bill's motorcycle leave. I said my bedtime prayers and dozed off, thinking about how we first met.

CHAPTER 2 - ONE UGLY MAN

Two years earlier, when Bill and I attended the UWGB (Deckner campus), he volunteered to be the "ugly man" for his service fraternity, Alpha Phi Omega. Looking like an escapee from the set of *Frankenstein's Planet of the Apes*, Bill wandered around the hallways seeking charitable donations. His goal was to collect as many pennies as possible throughout the day as each counted for a vote. But he looked so frightening that most students scurried away like mice before he could even ask for coins.

Bill's most significant competitor was a sports jock from Green Bay, a high school football player named Bear. Bear didn't dress up scary but took a different tactic. By setting up a table at the entrance of UWGB, he allowed the voters to come to him.

Bear, wearing his high school letter jacket, sat relaxed at the table. One of his friends taped a sign on it reading "Support Bear for the Ugly Man Contest." Two other guys removed jars from a box underneath and placed them on the tabletop. I heard them commenting about having their mothers' clean and save jars for them all week.

Attracted to one of Bear's tall, dark, and handsome friends who wore black-rimmed glasses, I walked up and asked, "What's this Ugly Man Contest all about?" He didn't answer but remained focused on lining up the jars in a straight row down the center of the table.

Is he too shy to speak or just not interested?

Sexy-looking Bear, with his dark-brown slicked back hair, sat at the head of the table with his muscular arms neatly folded on top of his textbooks. He leaned forward and shot me one of his million-dollar smiles.

"Carole, I'm collecting pennies for my favorite charity, the Newman Center. Can I have all your pennies, please?"

I met Bear earlier that semester while studying in the library with Janet. Since switching her major from nursing to physical therapy, Janet and I quickly became best friends. I understood why Bear gave her his high school class ring to wear—Janet was perfect, from her cute button-shaped nose to her brunette bouffant hairdo, making her look like Jackie Kennedy. And, ooh, those mod outfits she wore, even though they were hand-me-downs from her older sister. There was no point in me competing for Bear's attention and losing Janet's friendship.

"Here you go, Care Bear." I emptied my coin purse into one of the empty containers and hurried off to class. A scary-looking creature walked past me, carrying an empty Mason jar.

Who's that?

Bear laughed and said, "So, Bill, you think you're gonna beat me by wearing that creepy outfit? And with only one jar of pennies? Here, take one of mine." Bear handed Bill an empty jar knowing full well that if he collected the most pennies by the end of the day, Bill would need to surrender all of his coins to Bear's favorite charity.

I looked back at the gruesome guy wearing thick makeup consisting of pointy ears, raccoon eyes, and a long row of stitches embossed on his right cheek. He had a blackened front tooth and, of all things, a broken pencil protruding from his left nostril. His raven hair matched the ape-suit jacket he wore.

For the rest of that day between classes, I avoided the creature that was Bill. His Lurch-like gait grossed me out as he strolled down the hallway, and if I saw him coming toward me, I turned and walked in the opposite direction. But later that afternoon, Bill finally caught up with me and my new friend Dixie, who shared the same math class with him.

We returned to Dixie's locker to pick up something she'd forgotten, as she was prone to do. My voice caught in my throat as the dark creature snuck up behind my pixie-headed friend, poking inside her locker. Dixie spun around, let out a blood-curdling scream, and almost fell back into the locker. Instead, I grabbed her arm and steadied her.

"Bill Wagener, is that you? You half-scared the crap out of me," Dixie yelled at her would-be attacker.

Bill laughed unmercifully. "I'll go away if you give me some pennies."

Dixie scrounged through her purse and tossed a few pennies on the floor. Bill looked miffed but bent over to pick them up and dropped them into his half-filled jar. Then, finally, he looked up at me with pleading brown eyes.

"How about your friend here? You got any pennies?"

"Sorry, but I'm fresh out of change. Bear has all of my votes."

Bill hung his head and sulked away. Dixie clutched the class ring she wore on a chain around her neck.

"Bill keeps asking me out, but I'm already going steady. How about you, Carole? We could all go on a double date to the movies."

After the initial shock of meeting the ape-like man, I reflected on those big brown eyes. "Maybe, but I'd sure like to see him without makeup."

Bear won that fundraiser by collecting ten thousand pennies to Bill's one thousand. But Bill won a date with me, and in November, we finally went to a movie with Dixie and her boyfriend. I was just eighteen, and Bill was twenty-one. While we watched *Romeo and Juliet*, he slid his arm around my shoulder, making me uncomfortable. A shy teen, I hadn't dated in high school.

Bill continued to woo me. Finally, on our third date, he tried to kiss me while saying good night outside my apartment. I slipped away and ran up the staircase like a frightened Cinderella. The next day, when Bill visited, I had my roommate tell him I was asleep. I stared out my bedroom window, reluctantly watching him walk away. But the truth was, I was afraid of being in an intimate relationship with any man.

Over time, Bill took a softer approach with me. We became better acquainted at school, and I looked forward to his frequent visits to the language lab, where I worked part-time on campus.

"*Wie geht es Ihnen heute?*" [How are you today?] he asked.

"*Sehr gut, danke. Was wollen Sie?*" [Very good, thanks. What do you want?]

Bill visited the language lab often to listen to audiotapes, practice his German-speaking ability, and fulfill his German 101 requirement. He was always the last student to come in before closing. He usually asked me out for a twenty-five-cent hamburger at the new McDonald's restaurant, walked me back home to my apartment, or gave me a ride on his Honda Super Sport 90 motorcycle.

Our friendship grew that spring semester, but Bill's grades fell because he worked nights as a busboy at a Bob's Big Boy restaurant and didn't have time to study. When the semester ended, UWGB placed Bill on academic probation. Afraid of losing his student deferment and being drafted, he spoke to his eldest brother, Rod, who'd served in the U.S. Army in Germany as a physician. Dr. Rod advised him that as far as the military went, "Those in the know take two years and get out!"

Bill ultimately decided that, rather than be drafted, he'd enlist in the Army for two years and signed up for helicopter training. He didn't want to be like his roommate, Bernie, who freaked out when his draft number came up. The police found Bernie sitting on a park bench where he spent the night, holding onto his draft notice, still dazed and unable to speak. Bernie didn't snap out of it and was committed to a psych hospital.

On October 21, 1967, one day before he left for Basic Training at Fort Polk, Louisiana, Bill asked his mother to give him a military haircut. He didn't want to pay an Army barber for the satisfaction of shaving off all his hair. I cried for the first time that warm autumn day as the hair clipper buzzed outdoors in the backyard. Bill's curly locks swirled to the ground in the breeze, piling up like blackened leaves, until his mother achieved the desired "chrome dome" look.

After his departure, the reality of our separation sank in. We tried to carry on a long-distance relationship via mail and infrequent phone calls. But it was a lonely time for me, not seeing Bill roaming the campus halls as I continued my sophomore year at UWGB and waited for him to come home on leave.

Bill wrote that Basic Training was rough, as some nights he'd only received four hours of sleep. In addition, one of his fellow GIs died of meningitis, and another went AWOL. On November 15, 1967, Bill wrote:

"What bothers me the most is the drill sergeant's gross language, always addressing us as cocksuckers, dicklickers, and dumbasses. He picks on enlisted men because they are 'fucking dumb shitheads' for joining. I would be a millionaire if I had a penny every time he said the F-word. Sometimes, I almost regret enlisting but am told it will be different after Basic. I hope I don't go insane if it doesn't get better."

On his authorized Christmas leave home, Bill arrived, very ill, at my apartment in Green Bay. Worried because he had mononucleosis the year before, the next day, I drove him up to Sturgeon Bay to visit his brother for a check-up. Bill was diagnosed with extreme exhaustion. He recuperated with proper rest at his father's home, returned to Louisiana to finish Basic Training, and graduated on January 12, 1968.

Three days later, Bill entered the Warrant Officer Candidate training program at Fort Wolters, near Mineral Wells, Texas, to study to become a helicopter pilot. Unfortunately, after completing all the bookwork, he didn't sign out properly to attend a Catholic mass, so on February 25, 1968, the Army issued him an Article 15.[3]

In his letter, Bill wrote:

"I will be eliminated, dammit, on my last day of preflight. So close, and I failed! Defeated again. I guess you should have picked a winner. Instead, I'm a full-time loser, a total failure."

Washing out of that program was disappointing to him but was a blessing to me because, on the news, helicopters were constantly being shot down in the jungles. Proficient in playing the trumpet in high school, Bill tried out for the 328th U.S. Army Military Band, playing the French horn for eight weeks.

He continued dating other girls during this time and encouraged me to date, also. He wrote: "Carole, enjoy the man or boy you're with, and don't try to pretend it's me. Appreciate him for who he is, but control your thoughts and limit your desires."

Taking his words to heart, that year, I met Jake. He was new to Green Bay, a year younger than me, but he wasn't attractive. If I was standing at the bus stop, Jake pulled his car over, picked me up, and gave me a ride to college. He was a perfect gentleman, though, even opening the car door for me. We chit-chatted on the fifteen-minute drive, and about once a week, he asked me if I'd heard from Bill. Maybe Jake wanted to know if Bill and I were still dating, but I'd already clarified that I just wanted to be Jake's friend.

While Bill was gone, I dated one guy named Tom. I attended summer school, taking an English class while working part-time at the Fiesta Restaurant on East Mason Street. One day while on break reading *Moby Dick*, I heard the door chime, looked up, and couldn't believe my eyes.

"Hey, Carole, remember me?"

How could I forget you? I sat behind you in chemistry all last year, looking at the back of your big head. When I said "Hi," you mostly ignored me, so I talked to Jake instead.

I pretended to keep reading until Tom slid into my booth and sat across from me. "You ought to buy some *Cliffs Notes* for that book."

I set the book down. *What about tall, dark, and handsome men turned me on? Was it from watching Christopher Lee in* Dracula *movies as a kid, seeing all the beautiful young ladies allowing themselves to be seduced by him?*

I folded my arms over my chest, feeling a ring of sweat forming under my armpits. "Oh, really, Tom? Isn't that like cheating?"

But reading about Ahab taking revenge on a white whale who'd bit off his leg bored me out of my gourd. How would I ever finish it in time to write an essay and then start on the other four books I was supposed to read?

"Where can I get one?" I asked eagerly.

Tom leaned in close, giving me a whiff of his 007 cologne. "They should carry it at the University Bookstore."

I handed Tom a menu. "Ready to place an order?"

Tom studied the menu while I examined his jet-black Beatle haircut framing his face, distinguished-looking eyebrows, and dark black eyes. With a last name like Des Jardine, he had to be of French-Canadian descent like Bill.

He finally asked, "How's the chili?"

"Our cook makes the best Mexican chili in all of Northeastern Wisconsin." I bragged, but it was true because we were the only Mexican restaurant in the area.

On many afternoons when we weren't busy, instead of reading, I sat in the kitchen watching Rosa prepare her homemade chili con carne. As she cut up peppers and large chunks of pork and beef and added her authentic seasonings, she shared her religious beliefs and taught me a few words of Spanish.

"Magnifico. Nothing like my mother's chili. Want to try some?" I asked.

Tom nodded. I rushed off to the kitchen and asked Rosa to prepare a large bowl of chili and tried to tell her in my limited Spanish, "Look who's here—*aqui, aqui.*"

I pointed to the dining area. Rosa smiled, handed me the chili, and motioned me to go. I grabbed some crackers and a glass of water on my way out of the kitchen.

"It's a little spicy," I warned, setting the bowl in front of him.

Tom took one bite of the chili and coughed. "Wowee! Hot." He grabbed the ice water.

"You should have a tall glass of milk with that to cut the chili peppers." I rushed back into the kitchen and returned, setting the milk in front of him. Tom gulped it down, finished his meal, and then stood and stared at me as I prepared his tab.

Looking up at him, I said, "I'm not charging you for the milk," and handed him his bill.

"Carole, I wonder if you'd like to go out with me Saturday night."

Say what? I stepped back from the counter. "Oh, yeah, for sure. I'd like that."

I wrote my phone number on a napkin and handed it to Tom. I had no idea what he'd planned for us.

"Why don't you surprise me?"

"Pick you up at 6:00?"

"I'll be waiting for you."

I gave Tom a little smile as he walked out the door. Then, when he was out of sight, I danced into the kitchen to the music of *Cielito Lindo* and told Rosa of my good fortune. Or was it going to be bad fortune?

Did he purposely come into the restaurant to ask me out, or am I just an afterthought? I hoped for the former, but Tom had been so mysterious and elusive in the past. *What changed?*

Saturday night, Tom took me to Shakey's Pizza Parlor & Ye Public House, Green Bay's "in" pizza place. Shakey's served beer and had live 1920s jazz music with a banjo and piano player who wore old-fashioned straw hats and red-striped vests.

Before we ordered our food, Tom asked if I liked anchovies.

"I've never had anchovies before." I wasn't sure what they were and was too embarrassed to ask.

"Oh, you'll absolutely love them," he said, requesting anchovies on the entire pizza and adding, "No garlic, please."

"You're allergic to garlic?"

"Yes, garlic."

At least we had one thing in common. Checking out my vampire theory further, I asked, "Are you allergic to sunlight, too?" But Tom didn't answer me as he carried our drinks to the table.

While we waited for our order, we sat at an indoor picnic table, covered with a red and white checkered tablecloth, sipping our beer and singing along to "Wait 'till the Sun Shines, Nellie." I was hungry and looked forward to tasting the anchovies.

The pizza finally arrived, and I eagerly took a big bite. *Ew, too salty!* The little fish swam around the black olives and onions, making me want to gag. I set the piece down on my plate.

Meanwhile, Tom told me his sad news. "I just broke up with my steady girlfriend."

So I'm a rebound date, after all.

Tom, intent on telling me his breakup story, didn't even notice me when I slipped the pizza slice into my napkin. Likewise, as I sipped on my beer, he never noticed that I didn't like anchovies.

Finally, he asked, "You wanna play a game of darts before we leave?"

"Do you wanna lose to a girl?"

I was a master at darts from playing with my older brother. On the way to the dartboard, I tossed my napkin with the disgusting pizza into the garbage can. Despite feeling tipsy from drinking beer on an empty stomach, I beat Tom with a final bullseye.

It was time to leave, and I insisted, over his objection, that he take the remainder of that awful pizza home. On the drive back to my apartment, I told Tom I was dating Bill, who was in the military. But because of the fishy taste still on my breath, not to mention the onions, I avoided giving him a good night kiss.

"Are you sure you don't want the rest of this pizza for your roommates?" Tom offered me the box as I got out of the vehicle.

"Thanks but no thanks," I said, closing the car door. I unlocked the door to my apartment and made a beeline for the kitchen.

Rather than be discouraged, Tom asked for a second date and suggested a drive. This time I did most of the talking on the way up to Scray's Hill, which overlooked the city lights of Green Bay. Bill and I had driven up there once before on the motorcycle, but it was daylight then. A full moon lit up the desolate countryside. In my mind, it soon became Scary Hill because there were no other cars on the steep winding road, and then there was still my vampire theory.

Tom finally pulled off at the twin TV towers, parked, and offered me a breath mint. When he smiled at me, I noticed his pointed canine teeth.

He slid his arm around me and asked, "You wanna make out?"

I didn't answer but leaned in with my eyes closed, waiting for a romantic kiss. Pulling me in close to him, Tom placed his warm lips on mine. But soon, his tongue was in my mouth.

Ew, Ew. This isn't how Bill and I kissed.

Breaking away from his embrace, I asked, "What are you doing? Trying to suck the life right out of me?"

"You've never been French kissed before?"

I shook my head no.

"Wanna give it another try?"

I shook my head, yes, and then pretended Tom was Bill. Feeling the tip of Tom's tantalizing tongue upon mine strangely aroused me, and I reciprocated. That amazing kiss took my breath away, and I pulled back from him.

"I, I don't like it." I lied because I really did like it. But I sensed that kiss was far too intimate, making me feel more uncomfortable and sweaty.

Will Tom try to rape me in the backseat and then say I wanted it? Or get angry if I don't cooperate, leave me here along the roadside, and make me walk home in the dark where a bad man might get me?

Tom looked at me disapprovingly. "What's wrong with you, Carole?"

"What's wrong with *me*? I'm a rebound date. That's what's wrong. You're still in love with your old girlfriend, aren't you?"

He sheepishly nodded his head.

"Tom, I don't like being used as a substitute. Please take me home."

On the drive home, Tom kept his hands to himself. Finally, I suggested he call his ex-girlfriend and make up with her because I never wanted to see him again.

Later, I heard from a mutual friend that Tom struggled with depression. That was the darkness I sensed in him. We wouldn't have been a good fit because sometimes I suffered from depression, too.

After that, I didn't want to date anyone but Bill. I felt trepidation around other guys I didn't know if I could trust. So when Bill wrote me this love letter, it touched my heart:

"I love you, Carole, more than there is sand on the shores of Lake Michigan and in more ways than there are stars in the sky. Like a Big Brother, I love you like a Father, sometimes like a Worshipper, and always like a Lover.

Before I enlisted, the Father's side sometimes would say, 'You dope. What if you get killed? How would that affect Carole, considering the close relationship you're having? It would probably kill her, too. If you cared for her, you'd break off this relationship. Anyway, you know it makes her feel guilty.'

Then the Lover replied, 'No, I'd only hurt her twice if I broke off and then got killed on top of it. At least she would know I died loving her. I don't think she feels guilty anymore about our romance because she realizes I truly love her.'

Big Brother says, 'You'd better not hurt her. If you do, I'll make you suffer ten times over for it, and be careful you don't knock her up and embarrass her permanently with her peers.'

Then the Lover replies, 'I won't. I won't. I'll be careful, but I need her. I love her. I'll risk anything rather than give her up.'

The struggle within me goes on and on. I adore you and even the silly replies you give. I don't even think I'll try to date anyone else anymore. It just makes me sad because it's not you."

Eventually, we both came to the same conclusion that dating others wasn't satisfying. We discussed in our letters what most young couples talked about in person, things like religion, marriage, and even having children.

Sometimes I wanted to marry Bill, but I was confused when in one letter, he confessed he'd almost asked me to marry him when he was home way back in December of 1967. However, due to a silly argument about me not wanting to shorten the hemline of my dress to please him, he decided not to ask. Yet, in a follow-up letter on January 10, 1968, he wrote: "I think you're wonderful, the most modest girl I know, and aside from worrying about your own happiness (as most girls do), you're really something sweet."

As it turned out, the competition for the military band was tough, and Bill didn't get picked. But being good at science, he was assigned to the Gas Generating Program at Fort Belvoir, Virginia, on April 4, 1968.

On April 28, he wrote,

Out of the one to two million people in the whole Army, there are only one to two hundred trained personnel in my field of work. There are only four mobile factories (all on wheels, in the back of semi-truck trailers), one here and three in Vietnam. So, without a doubt, you know where I am going.

Bill quickly learned how to make bottled oxygen for field hospitals and the highly flammable acetylene gas for welding. On July 17, 1968, he passed the program with flying colors and was promoted to Specialist 4. Then he received his orders to go to Vietnam for one year and was allowed to come home for his last leave.

Fort Belvoir, Va.
12 August, 1968

Dear Bunny,

> Save your money.
> Homecoming is your Honey
> Cause soon off your shelf,
> I'll take you for myself.

My orders were re-cut for August 20. So I leave here and report for Vietnam on September 13. You should have guessed the Army would mess it up, so I'm sorry. I probably won't make it home until the 22. I'll call you when I get to Green Bay.

Love,

Bill

Because our time alone was going to be brief, we planned a secret rendezvous on Bill's first night back. Around nine p.m. on August 20, Bill called me at my apartment and said he was in Green Bay.

"Hi, Sweetie. Did you make our room reservation?"

"Yes, at that nice motel on the East Side where we stayed last time you were home."

"What did you tell your parents?"

"I told them we're staying at your parent's house for the night, and we'd drive down to see them tomorrow."

"Good. I wrote my parents that we'd be staying with your parents. They'll never catch on."

"I have Mom's Oldsmobile. I'll be at the airport in fifteen minutes."

"Can't wait to see you."

Bill looked handsome in his dress uniform when I picked him up, making my heart pitter-patter. I drove, and we chit-chatted on the way to the motel. I stayed in the parking lot hiding behind the wheel of the "Olds" while Bill signed us in as "Mr. and Mrs. William Wagener." He soon walked out of the lobby victorious, holding up a room key for me to see.

Once in the room, Bill showered, and I jumped into our comfy bed. Bill came out of the bathroom wrapped only in a white towel. Seeing his muscular body was an aphrodisiac for me, with his dog tags still dripping wet onto his well-developed pecs, I pulled back the sheets, wanting to cuddle, but Bill was ready for action. Unfortunately, we were both novices regarding sex, and I couldn't relax enough to enjoy it.

In the morning, with the sunlight streaming in through the drapes and still entwined in each other's arms, Bill kissed me and was easily aroused for a second time. Knowing this could be our last time of intimacy, I treasured this moment together.

Bill got up and beat me to the bathroom. When he came out, he shook his head, dangling in his hand the used condom. "Look, my condom's got a big hole in it!"

"What? How could that be?"

"It must have got brittle in my wallet for so long."

"Ew. Now what?"

Bill threw the condom in the garbage can and washed his hands. I expected him to return to bed, but he knelt on the floor on one knee and took my hand.

"Carole, will you marry me before I leave?"

His other hand was empty. *What? No engagement ring?*

I said, "Maybe."

"I didn't buy a ring because I knew an engagement ring wouldn't keep you. Besides, I don't want to get a 'Dear John' letter while in 'Nam. So, what do you say, will you marry me?"

"I need time to think."

"You have three weeks to make your decision."

"Three weeks? That's hardly enough time to make a lifelong decision."

CHAPTER 3 - RUNNING OUT OF TIME

Three weeks had almost passed, and I still couldn't convince myself to marry Bill. He wouldn't budge either on my proposal to get engaged. Meanwhile, every day I hoped and prayed my period would arrive, but it didn't.

I'm late.

"Bill, my period should have come by now. What if I'm pregnant?"

Bill knew just what to do. He telephoned and made an appointment for us to visit his brother. The following day, we drove to Sturgeon Bay, and he accompanied me to Dr. Rod's office, where the three of us sat down and talked.

"Carole's worried she might be pregnant," Bill said.

"Aw, that shouldn't have happened," Dr. Rod said, looking me straight in the eye. "Carole, you should've asked me for the pill."

"Do you wanna get arrested for giving an unmarried woman birth control pills?"[4]

"I could have documented that you were getting married in three months, and then it wouldn't have been illegal."

Bill sat there, not saying a word. *What had I gotten myself into?*

"But I wasn't planning on getting married," I said. "Can't you give me a pregnancy test? See if the rabbit dies or something?"[5]

"There isn't time for that, with Bill leaving so soon."

"What are our other options?" Bill asked.

"In Wisconsin, it takes three days to get a marriage license. I can do the blood tests and arrange for my judge friend to marry you, or you can wait it out and see if Carole's period comes. If it doesn't, Carole, you can get married by proxy while Bill's in Vietnam, and I'll stand in for him."

"Marriage by proxy? That's ridiculous, and I can't have a baby out of wedlock, either. Let's get married now," I insisted.

Bill smiled. That's what he wanted all along. So we picked Wednesday as our wedding day. Rod called the judge while we went straight to the courthouse, applied for the marriage license, and then went back to his office for the blood tests to ensure we didn't have syphilis. The following day was a whirlwind of phone calls to my family and purchasing matching wedding bands, a turquoise wedding dress, flowers, and a cake.

Like his mother predicted, Bill was fifteen minutes late for our wedding because he lingered in his bedroom. I was nervous. Was Bill getting cold feet? But, finally, he came out of his room, and on September 11, 1968, at 2:15 p.m., in Bill's parents' living room with our immediate family present, we spoke our wedding vows in front of Judge Stevens.

In a rush, the judge forgot to have us sign our marriage certificate and drove back to the house with it just as we were cutting into our delicious wedding cake from Knoppen's bakery. After opening our gifts, we went to an early dinner with our parents, Bill's brother, and his family. At the Nightingale Supper Club, located just outside Sturgeon Bay, we had mixed drinks and enjoyed the new concept of a salad bar. Bill's dad and brother toasted us as we waited for our entrees.

"How do you know when it's time to get married, Bill?" Rod joked. "When you can't live with her, and you can't live without her!"

Everyone chuckled. Then Bill's dad, Captain Nick Wagener, went next.

"Carole, what's the hardest year of marriage?" he asked. I shrugged my shoulders at my new father-in-law. "They all are!"

My parents then proposed a toast wishing us many happy years together. While Bill's mother sang "Billy Boy," we all clapped and sang along, asking if she could bake a cherry pie. It turned out Charming Billy's wife was just like me, too young to leave her mother. That song put us all in a festive mood. At the song's conclusion, Bill's teenage nieces and nephew hit their butter knives on their drinking glasses. The clicking sound continued until Bill and I finally kissed.

We finally caught our breath when the celebration ended. I already had Bill's duffel and my overnight bag in the car. So while Bill drove the forty miles to Green Bay, I rested. Then, using some of our $200 wedding gift money, we treated ourselves as Mr. and Mrs. Wagener to a lovely honeymoon suite at a brand-new hotel with an indoor pool. That bitter-sweet night, I wore the pink negligee I'd received as a wedding gift.

That evening our final waking hours together ticked away. After a night of lovemaking, Bill was still asleep in the morning, and as if I wasn't in enough emotional pain, I awoke to painful abdominal cramps

Am I getting my period now, right before Bill leaves?

I didn't mention my hunch to Bill because he already had a lot on his mind. I didn't want him to get depressed if it turned out that I wasn't pregnant. Despite the shimmering silver and gold wedding band on my finger, our rushed marriage suddenly felt fake, like an empty Hollywood movie set. I turned towards Bill, admiring the sight of his chest rising and falling, and wished he didn't have to leave. Then my concern turned inward.

What will I do if Bill gets hurt over there?

The only way I could get through this year was to convince myself that Bill's Boy Scout survival training and my prayers would somehow save him.

I knew of only one person who'd been to Vietnam, a stranger I'd met during the summer of 1966. While Mom tended to customers inside the store, Dad decided to try something new and turned our Texaco station into "self-service." My job was to collect the gas money after customers filled their tanks without my help.

One day, a long-haired biker pulled up to the gas pump on a loud, black-as-sin motorcycle. I walked up in front of him, so he wouldn't drive off without paying.

"It's self-serve. Where you headed?"

He removed the cap from his gas tank and growled, "North, up to Door County."

Naively, I studied the colorful, embroidered map on the backside of his black leather jacket. "Is that a map of Vietnam?"

"Yup, I was a Marine. I had it specially made for me overseas and shipped home."

I thought the man was in his late twenties, but he looked like he'd seen too much in Vietnam with his weathered face, grizzly hair, and shaggy beard.

"What was it like over there?"

"Like going to hell and back."

He glared at me as if I was stupid, put the gas cap back on, handed me a dollar bill, and then jumped back on the bike.

"Now, all I want to do is get on this bike and ride all over this damn country that I defended with my life."

I wondered if all guys did that after they returned from Vietnam.

What if Bill gets on his bike and rides cross-country after he comes home?

I couldn't bear the thought of him leaving me again. I glanced at the portable alarm clock next to the bed on the nightstand—only two hours and thirty minutes left before we needed to go to the airport.

I turned away from Bill and sobbed into my pillow, praying silently for his safety and my sanity. I thought about how difficult it must have been for Mom when Dad was drafted into the Army during World War II. He left in 1944 when my brother, David, was only six months old and my sister, Jeannie, was five. In 1945, Dad was on a ship headed to Japan when the Japanese surrendered on August 14, but he remained overseas for an additional year.

Mom told me she hated being a single mother while living on the Obry family farm. She resented doing all the cooking for the farmhands while at the same time caring for a baby. In addition, she disliked my grandmother spoiling my oldest sister. It was tough for them, but my parents survived, and I resolved that Bill and I would survive, too.

Despite arriving at the airport early, we were down to our final ten minutes. As a military wife, I was allowed to accompany Bill onto the tarmac to the waiting plane. We both had tears in our eyes during our final embrace and a goodbye kiss.

Bill hated to see girls cry, so I held back the tears. Finally, he climbed the stairs to the small aircraft, turned, and waved a final goodbye before ducking his head to enter the plane.

The aircraft taxied to the runway. I stood there waving, hoping Bill could see me through the small plane's window. But my heart sank as the aircraft became airborne and rumbled out of sight, and I began sobbing. I ran into the airport bathroom to cry and pee. That's when I discovered I was spotting.

What's happening? Am I having a miscarriage? Can I still be pregnant if I have a period? Unfortunately, I didn't know the answers to my questions. My only sexual education consisted of a book Mom gave me to read during puberty about having my first period, not about being pregnant. So how did I allow myself to end up in this situation?

I ran to my car, sobbing like Alice in Wonderland, drowning in my tears. I could barely drive the thirty miles home as my world began shrinking, and I heard a voice inside me asking all sorts of troubling questions.

What if Bill comes back in a body bag like the other soldiers killed over there? Will he come back to me all in one piece, as an amputee, or worse yet, paralyzed? What if he's captured, listed as missing in action, and never returns? And the last question gnawing at the back of my brain was, *What if I'm not pregnant and didn't have to get married?*

I was down a rabbit hole and couldn't get out. Why couldn't I wake up like Alice and discover these past two days had all been a dream?

CHAPTER 4 - BECOMING A PHYSICAL THERAPIST

I cried the entire first week after Bill left for Vietnam. Then I dried my tears and packed my bags, firmly determined to finish my education in Madison. Even though my parents financially supported me, I was almost twenty, looking forward to being more independent, living on a Big Ten campus, and making my own decisions.

But my junior year was bound to be a tough one. I had two challenging science classes, already missed Bill, and knew I'd be homesick. Fortunately, Janet was moving and living in the same dorm as me. Luckily for her, she was now engaged to Bear. He enlisted in the U.S. Army National Guard, thereby avoiding the draft. Bear told Janet he would never go to Vietnam, but I told her not to be too sure about that.

I decided to become a physical therapist during my senior year of high school. Fortunately, in 1966 Kewaunee High hired its first guidance counselor. So, I made an appointment with Mr. Gerard to ask him what it would take to become a PT.

Mr. Gerard said physical therapy was a rigorous program, but he was confident I would make it through. Next, he asked what my parents did for a living as he wanted to determine if I qualified for financial aid. When I told him that Dad sold insurance and Mom was "just a housewife," he was offended that I used that term. So I added, "And she's a businesswoman."

Back then, I could count a woman's career choices on the one hand. I already decided I didn't want to become a teacher, secretary, nurse, factory worker, or my worst nightmare—a hairdresser trying to please fussy clients. But, on the other hand, I liked helping people and was glad I found PT. Or maybe physical therapy found me.

Growing up, I'd watched Jerry Lewis's Muscular Dystrophy Association fundraising telethons, where I saw physical therapists teaching disabled children how to walk. PT appealed to me because despite being partially vaccinated, I contracted polio during the summer of 1956 when I was seven. As a result, I became ill with a high fever, headache, and a stiff neck.

"Ouch! Stop it! That hurts," I screamed at Dr. Pollack, trying to examine me in my bed, moving my head down to my chest.

"Carole, you have bulbar poliomyelitis. If you want to get well, you have to stay in bed and rest," the doctor said.

Tears welled up in my eyes. "Does that mean I can't go to school?"

"Not for a long time."

Mom had a worried look on her face. "Carole's been vomiting a lot. Can't you put her in the hospital?"

"She'll do better at home. Besides, other children sicker than your daughter need hospitalization."

I was relieved. I didn't want to go to the hospital like my best friend, Sherry. She ended up wearing a leg brace and couldn't run anymore.

So, Mom isolated me in her bedroom for weeks with the shades drawn because the bright sunlight hurt my eyes. My days included napping, studying the colorful patches on Grandma's homemade quilt, and petting my cat, Tigger. Mom brought in all my meals, and I ate them lying on my side because if I tried to sit up, my head felt like lead.

Every night I prayed to God. "I'm too young to die. I'll do anything you want of me but don't ask me to be a missionary in Africa."

Eventually, I became frail and almost fell while walking to the bathroom, so I crawled instead. If Mom was available, she helped me to walk by holding onto my arm. Eventually, I learned to balance myself with one hand on the wall and could walk alone.

The doctor continued to show up at my house once a week, took my temperature, and then put his hand down my pants and felt my groin.

"Mama, what's he doing?"

"He's feeling your lymph nodes to see if you're getting better."

"So, it's okay for him to touch me down there?"

"Yes, honey. Dr. Pollack won't hurt you."

Finally, at the end of one of his many visits, the doctor wrote my long-awaited note for the teacher and said, "Carole, you can return to school, but you must sit out during recess."

Oh shucks, recess was my favorite part of the day. I snatched the note from him, happy to finally see my teacher and all my friends.

I returned to school for half days that semester, walked the one block home for lunch, and then took a nap. What a joyous day it was that following spring when I was no longer restricted and ran over to the swing set at school and jumped on a swing with my newfound freedom. With my feet pumping the air, I realized God spared my life, had a special purpose for me, and wouldn't send me off to Africa after all.

To become a PT, I needed to procure a Bachelor of Science degree, which took four years of schooling. After I obtained that degree, I was required to complete a three-month internship to receive a Certificate in Physical Therapy. Then, I'd take the state board exams, and if I passed all three sections, I would obtain my license to practice physical therapy in Wisconsin.

When I signed up for PT, it hadn't quite sunk in that part of my training required working with the deceased. Applied Human Anatomy was a five-credit course in the first semester and three credits in the second semester. It involved working in a lab on real cadavers. Had I realized this sooner, I might not have become a therapist.

The cold lab held two rows of metal tanks in which full-bodied or two partial bodies of corpses were stored in liquid formaldehyde. Inside the tank, the bodies lay on a metal table rolled up on chains using a hand crank.

The first time I saw a corpse, I shivered. Clear liquid formaldehyde dripped off as the body rose out of the tank. The sound of the dripping liquid grossed me out, and oh, the nasty smell. That odor was even worse than when Mom boiled vinegar to make her homemade dill pickles.

The formaldehyde caused my eyes to tear up and my throat to itch. Janet wasn't doing too well either when her face turned white, and she quickly sat down on a nearby stool. I swallowed hard, told myself to be brave, and then edged closer to the tank for a better view.

I saw a thin man lying there, stripped of his skin, exposing all the muscles I needed to memorize that semester. Yet, looking down at his shriveled body, I saw his male genitals were still intact. After getting over the shock of seeing the pickled man, I wondered what kind of life he'd lived. Had he been a Skid Row alcoholic or a working-class member of society? I decided it was best not to know.

Meanwhile, it was comforting to know that my classmates shared the misery. We looked around at each other, forty-seven girls and three guys, when our professor predicted that only forty of us would pass anatomy and the other ten would have to repeat it the next year or drop the program.

Surprisingly, after a few days in the anatomy lab, looking at dead bodies didn't bother me anymore. But the terrible smell of the formaldehyde overpowered me every time I walked in and made me want to vomit.

On September 19, I stepped out of the anatomy lab, wrinkled my nose, and took a deep, cleansing breath of the crisp autumn air to clear my sinuses. The raunchy odor of the formaldehyde followed me like a ghost. Although I scrubbed my hands well before leaving, the stench lingered, permeating my hair, nose, and clothing, even chasing away my appetite.

Janet and I headed back to the dorm for lunch. Since starting anatomy, even the sight of roast beef or turkey meat, anything that resembled muscle tissue, made me gag. But, always thinking about Bill, I mostly picked at my food anyway.

The fall leaves crunched under our feet as Janet and I hiked the six blocks back to our dorm, slowed down by our Gray's Anatomy books, weighing five pounds each. I scuffed my foot, kicking a stone out of the way.

"I wonder if I'll get a letter today." I sighed. I hadn't heard from Bill since last week when he called me before flying to Vietnam.

"You gotta be patient," Janet said, putting a strand of her hair back in place. "It took a long time before I got my first letter from Bear in boot camp."

"But no one's heard from him, not even his parents." I felt helpless. The closest I could get to my hubby was watching the nightly news and hoping Walter Cronkite would do a segment on Vietnam.

Janet and I walked through the small lobby of our dorm and stopped at a wall full of small mailboxes. Janet opened her box, peered inside, and then shut the door with a loud *bang*.

"No letter. Darn you, Bear! You're not going to be my fiancé for much longer."

In anticipation, I held my breath and turned the key to mailbox #206. It opened easily. Inside, I spied my first red, white, and blue envelope with the word 'FREE' written on the right-hand corner where a stamp and a postmark typically would be. I reached in and grabbed it.

"Janet, I got my first letter." A smile covered my entire face as I held the welcome letter to my chest.

The envelope felt thick and promising. Bill's penmanship was not the best, but I felt elated when I saw my married name written in his handwriting for the first time. That letter in my possession meant that a piece of Bill was back in my world.

I pulled Janet to the lobby. "Come sit by me."

My hands shook as I tore open the envelope. Then, finally, I regained my composure and read aloud to Janet as she leaned in close enough to see my first letter as Mrs. W.

CHAPTER 5 - SEPTEMBER 1968: IS SHE OR ISN'T SHE?

*O*ff *the coast of Siberia, USSR, over the Pacific Ocean, north of Japan,*

8:00 p.m. Wisconsin time
16 Sept. 1968

Dearest Carole,

Keep faith with me, my young and lonely wife. I know how hard this day and a half of married life was for you, my darling. Yet, you were very brave all the way to my departure. I hope you face the next year[6] with me with the same resolution and fortitude.

I must confess I cried a bit after boarding and have been gazing at my wedding band. I am so proud of it and the sacred relationship it represents. Although we will be apart the first year of our marriage, in person, in spirit, and thought, "I'll be with you always, even to the end of the world," as it says in the Bible. I truly love you and rest in my heart, knowing your fidelity to me.

Remember in spirit and thought, I'll be with you every night and walk up Bascom Hill with you every day. Remember, there's not a sidewalk on the UW-Madison campus[7] that I haven't trudged over. I love you and will treasure every moment we've had together, from the first time I walked you home from the UWGB campus through the long evenings in my apartment, and the cold Honda rides back to yours in the wee hours of the morning to our wedding day, and our last night.

I'm looking forward to continuing our honeymoon in Hawaii, another year in school together, and many happy days ahead. With a bit of luck and love, we will have a dozen or so boys to fill the world with happy Wageners.

At that point, my stomach growled, and Janet offered to make us sandwiches.

"Do you want ham or cheese?" she asked.

"Grilled cheese, please."

While Janet fixed sandwiches in the kitchenette, I sat on a nearby stool and finished reading Bill's letter aloud:

It's been nine and a half hours since our 707 left Ft. Lewis, Washington, yet I'm not lonely because I've got you in my heart and your ring on my hand. Yet, I wish we were still together. We should land in thirty minutes in Japan for fueling and then be at Cam Ranh Bay, Vietnam, in six more hours.[8] We passed our closest point to Siberia an hour ago. We could see the peaks of the mountains peeking through the dense layers of fog.

I'm glad to be out of Ft. Lewis, as it rained constantly. Some GIs got hooked for KP [kitchen police or kitchen patrol] for fourteen hours on Saturday. I just skipped all the formations but the last one. Smarty me, I never did any work there!

The payphone jammed as I put the last few nickels in when I called you. I hope Mary McGuire Hall didn't get hooked for the last forty cents of the call. So save my letters and this year's subscription to my *Playboy* magazine. I hope you have ordered it by now. We'll read them together when I get home, okay?

I will try to mail this when we land in Japan; otherwise, I'll send it free from Vietnam. The guy sitting next to me who works at Nha Trang Headquarters said the North Vietnam Regulars (composed of forty percent Chinese) nearly overran Da Nang last month. There's been much action around Long Binh too, so I hope I can stay in Cam Ranh Bay!

One-hundred-sixty-five GIs are on board this Airlift Boeing 707, ranging from lifers to two-year draftees and PFCs [private first class] to captains and Green Berets. The turbulence is slight, increasing as we near Japan now, but the first hours were smooth as silk. The airline hostesses are pretty, but they're not you.

Study hard, Honey, and let me know if I will be a daddy by chance. I'll send you some money as soon as possible. I've only got one dollar and seventy-eight cents left, but I have back pay coming from August.

Love always,
Bill

P.S. If there's censorship, and I want to tell you something, I'll use numbers: 1 for A, 2-E, 3-I, 4-O, 5-U, 6-Y = the vowels, and one letter after the letter for all the letters in the alphabet. For example, Carole will be written as D1S4M2.

Janet looked longingly at the letter on the table and reached to touch it. "Aw, I wish Bear would write love letters like that to me."

I grabbed the letter, placed it inside the envelope, and touched her hand. "Janet, please don't be jealous."

Despite Bill pouring out his heart and professing his love for me, I still harbored doubts about our rushed marriage. By now, I was pretty sure I wasn't pregnant, but there was no way to inform Bill until I received his new address.

My eyes filled with tears from a flood of emotions ranging from relief that Bill was okay to feelings of frustration and angst. I'd read Dr. Tom Dooley's books in high school and understood why our troops were fighting in Vietnam,[9] but I now hated this war. My happy-go-lucky husband's life was on the line, and I had second thoughts about marrying so young.

I hastily finished my lunch, thanked Janet, and ran upstairs to my room to reread Bill's letter. But, unfortunately, my sixth sense told me Janet was already jealous. So I decided not to share my future letters because they were all I had left of my relationship with Bill.

---

22 Replacement Station
Cam Ranh Bay, Vietnam
18 Sept. 1968

Dear Honey Bun,

I've just completed my second day and am still alive and healthy. I plan to stay that way for another 363 days till I get back to you. You're asleep now in your cozy bed on the other side of the world.

They say the base I'm going to is 100 percent secure because there were only five homemade mortars lobbed in last year, and there was zero damage. But last night, I saw flares in the overlooking mountains; seven Huey-Cobra gunships were up there giving hell. This morning, they said it was a VC [Viet Cong] sniper on a reconnaissance patrol.

It went down to a cool 80 degrees last night but warmed to 110 degrees today. I'm glad it's not the hot season. I'm already getting a good suntan, or "sunburn," as I spent the day filling sandbags. They're building bomb bunkers here like they're expecting a heavy rocket attack.

This morning six of my buddies were sent to the 518th here in Cam Ranh Bay. I'll be lucky to go to Long Binh Detachment. Otherwise, I'll probably go into the infantry. I hope to get into my MOS [military occupational specialty], not the infantry.

Love your hubby,
Bill

The following letter is my first reply to Bill, in response to his September 16 letter. I had difficulty studying, eating, and sleeping because I constantly worried about him. But I knew it was in his best interest to make my letter sound cheerful and not address the horridness of the war that surrounded him.

Madison, Wisconsin
September 19, 1968

My Dearest Bill,

You don't know how happy your letter made me today. You always know what to say to make me feel better. I've been so lonely for you. I've never missed you as much as I do now, and I never thought I'd miss anyone as much as I do you.

It makes me feel better knowing you are with me in spirit. Yesterday it dawned on me that you were thinking of me, too, and wondering how I felt. Know that my heart is in Vietnam with you, and I think about you constantly. I pray for you each night, realizing that when I'm asleep, you're awake, and when I'm awake, you're sleeping. I send you a kiss on my wedding ring many times a day and always at night and morning. Somehow, it makes me feel much better.

I was a courageous wife the first few days I was still at my parent's house, but when I came to Madison and started school, I was lonely—lonely for you and lonely for home. I hadn't felt happy until today when I hit the jackpot—I got your letter, my sister, Jean, sent pictures of our wedding, and Mom sent me the newspaper announcement in the Algoma Record-Herald with our wedding photo.

Next year, I look forward to getting to know you better by living together. I think I'll enjoy going to school with you, but it will be like starting over again, like when we first met.

I do hope Cam Ranh Bay will be the safest place for you. Please write to me about your job and what you do when you're not working. I want to hear about everything my husband does, thinks, and dreams.

I hate to disappoint you, but it looks as if your paternal status is null, so no Daddy yet.

I understand the code. It may come in handy someday. For example, Bill is C3MM.

My thoughts are with you. My Lord is with you, but do take care, Lover Boy.

Your girl,
Carole

160th HEM [heavy equipment maintenance] Company
Cha Rang Valley, Vietnam
22 Sept. 1968

Dear Love of my Life,

Wie geht es Ihnen? I've got the morning off, slept in, and missed chapel, so I went swimming instead. Would you believe they have a pool here and a photo lab?[10] I was amazed as I didn't expect this. This afternoon, we had a drenching downpour that cooled it down from 115 to 100 degrees.

My address is on the envelope, and I expect to hear from you soon. Unfortunately, my mail might stop for a week or two due to hostile action, but don't worry because I'm safe.

Currently, I'm working at the 160th HEM Headquarters. This base is isolated, fifteen miles inland from Qui Nhon, two hundred miles north of

Cam Ranh Bay. I'm in the Cha Rang River Valley near a tiny village called Cu Lau. They have my MOS here in gas generating, but I will probably work in the Company Headquarters due to my typing ability. It appears I'll replace the training NCO [non-commissioned officer], Sgt. D., who goes home in October.

Hey, we had a guy go AWOL because his wife got pregnant, and he hadn't seen her in eleven months! I know that wouldn't happen with you, but don't even flirt for male attention—*Verstehen* [understand]. I've got a lot of trust in you. You'd better know I love you selfishly, and you belong to me now.

After I enlisted until I came home on August 21, I told you to feel free, and you were free. Now that's in the past, and I said only a wedding ring (not an engagement ring) would tide you over the next nine to twelve months. But if you change your mind while I'm gone, tell me because you married a military man on the five-day waiting limit waiver. I've checked civilian and Army regulations since working in this office. I'd rather this than hear through the grapevine that you were untrue and tried to fool me.

I'm working on a way for us to be together during my seven days of R&R [rest and relaxation] leave. I'll try to get us to Hawaii after I'm here for one hundred days.

God bless you, my True Love.

LUV your jealous and selfish husband,
Bill

My response to Bill's letter dated September 19, 1968.

Madison, Wisconsin
September 23, 1968

Dearest husband of mine,

Bill, you have been outstanding in your letter writing. I received three letters and two postcards. I know the reason—free postage—but I also know you love me, and I'm happy. I have a map of Vietnam here, so I've been following you around. Just so long as you stay near a big city, I'll be able to find you!

When you left, I didn't cry while your plane was on the ground, but I cried like a baby as soon as it hit the air. I felt like my world was leaving me, and I realized it would be a long before I'd see you again.

I was pretty upset even to read you might go into the infantry. The Army had better not do that, or I'll write to my Congressman, Senator, President Johnson, and even his dog if that would help.

Glad to hear you're not too horny or that those Vietnamese girls aren't bothering you. Behave yourself.

My sister and I went home Friday night to shop for her wedding dress. Cheryl found a beautiful one at Prange's in Green Bay with a long white veil down to the floor. I will wear a bridesmaid's dress with a royal blue velvet top, a long light-blue crepe skirt, and a blue veil. I'll send you a picture of her wedding in December.

I'm taking fifteen credits this semester. I'm taking my English class on a Pass-Fail system, so I don't have to worry about a grade, but I will automatically get the three credits. I must get back to my books to get a year of college in while you're gone.

Love and thousands of kisses to my soldier boy,
Carole

Vietnam
24 Sept. 1968

Dear Honey,

It now appears that I'll be the new training NCO [non-commissioned officer], which means I have a good chance of being promoted to Sergeant E-5. Besides being stationed in a command post, that means sixty-five dollars more per month. I'll have an office room (5'x7') and more responsibility. I'll be the number two man next to the first Sgt.

Yesterday, after Sgt. D. told me how safe it is here, the guard on the storage depot post reported activity in the hills. So, along with twenty others, I had to search for VC or any trace of them.

Boy, you can't imagine how heavy an M-14 rifle (fifteen pounds), a shrap metal vest, five ammo magazines, a canteen, and a gas mask are in 125-degree weather through briars, vines, and thickets up over our heads and down stone-entangled vines. Most of the time, we couldn't see eight feet in any direction.

Good thing there weren't any VC around, or they could have easily wiped out half of us.

Sgt. R. and I found something. I discovered a VC bunker under a mound by a dirt road. The captain didn't believe me until he came over, and it caved in under him. He then asked me if I wanted to be a tunnel rat. I declined, so he picked on someone smaller than me.

I'm learning a little Vietnamese. My company hires eighty Vietnamese to work on the base. I don't like not knowing what these house girls and other Vietnamese are saying. They could be VC sympathizers, and we'd never know.

I haven't heard from you yet, but I expect a letter by Friday.

Love,
Bill

My response to Bill's letter dated September 22, 1968.

Madison
September 25, 1968

Hi there, Lover Bill,

I was glad to receive your address and get my side of the ball rolling. It takes your letters about three to five days to arrive. I'm so happy to read you're safe and sound and maybe even have an office job. Just keep up your typing ability so that you can stay put!

It would be absolutely, positively GREAT if we could get together for your R&R in Hawaii. Then you could have an R R & I—Rest, Relaxation, and Intercourse—like the GIs say. It would be neat if we could swing it! Like, WOW! I've heard married guys have the first choice of going to Honolulu.

Have peace of mind, Bill. As soon as your letters came, I brightened up. So, yes, I am concerned about you, but I'm not too worried.

I was not too fond of lying, but I knew Bill would feel bad if he knew how worried I was about his safety. So when Bill wrote about filling sandbags and building bunkers in anticipation of a rocket attack, I felt he wasn't truthful regarding the potential danger. And how could his base be one hundred percent secure with the VC dug into nearby underground tunnels or maybe even working on base? But concentrating on my studies was my highest priority. Failing the PT program was not an option, even if the time studying meant I had less time for letter writing.

September 26, 1968

Bill, did you know I've slept on your pillow every night since you left? Thank you for leaving it with me. It's a comfort.

School and studying have become harder for me, with much more homework than I ever had in Green Bay. My assignments pile up like dirty laundry! The book Lord Jim and I haven't been getting along lately. Joseph Conrad puts me to sleep at night instead of keeping me awake, and I have nearly two hundred pages to read this weekend.

Do you want to hear something sick? Today, we worked on cadavers (dead bodies in your language). It wasn't too bad because they didn't look real to me with their skin removed and their faces covered up. However, tomorrow we get to kill frogs in the physiology lab—in the name of science, we'll cut off their heads. Yup, that's what we do. Don't I sound cruel? I would rather look at cadavers than cut off a frog's head, but now I get to do both. And you're the one supposed to fight a war, not me.

It must be torturous waiting for these first letters, but there is no way I can speed them up. This week, I received a letter from the Wisconsin State Historical Society thanking us for donating your family genealogy book. They said, "The Society wishes to express its appreciation to you and your husband, currently in Vietnam, for the genealogy gift, From Wagner 1768 to Wagener 1968. Generosity such as yours has played a large part in the growth and enrichment of our library. Please accept our thanks."[11]

If you replace the training NCO (whatever that is), does that mean you'll become a sergeant, too? Please keep your cool to keep your job. Don't end up in a fight and get ousted to the battlefield. I don't know if I could forgive you if you mess up this good job, so please try hard to keep it, okay? I couldn't stand the worry if I knew you were running around in the jungles or on the battlefields.

So, they have a swimming pool on base? That's going in style. Next, you'll tell me you have a feather bed and four Vietnamese girls to wait on you—just kidding! Here I thought you'd nearly sleep on the ground every night.

But, Bill, I can't even flirt for your attention? I'm glad I belong to you now because you're mine, too, and I know you won't be messing around. I also vowed to forsake all others, and that's what I am doing.

So, love, don't worry about me. You know I'd never run around on you while you're gone. I love and respect you too much ever to do anything that low. You have a faithful and true-blue wife on this end.

I sure wish you were here so we could walk hand-in-hand around campus. I would enjoy that on such a lovely fall day like today. Here's a kiss for you on my wedding band. It will travel to yours and be ready for you when you hold it to your cheek.

I'm sending two more sexy pictures. One I call "V for Victory," and the other one, "The Look of Love."

Love and kisses,
Carole

A letter from Bill's father, Captain Nicholas Wagener.

Sturgeon Bay, Wis.
September 28, 1968

Dear Bill,

Mom wrote you two days ago, and I don't know what she told you in her letter, so if I repeat, it's not because we're getting old.

Last night, I went to the high school football game, and Sturgeon Bay won 14-12 against West De Pere. It was a good game and pretty evenly matched. J.R. is Sturgeon Bay's iron man in the backfield. He carried the ball seventy-five percent of the time. Guess the training you gave him at the empty lot at the old house is paying off.

This morning is a beautiful sunny day, so I think I'll ride your Honda motorcycle. I got a helmet yesterday and my motorcycle endorsement on my driver's license, so I'm all set. I had it out riding last weekend and had a ball.

We found Qui Nhon on the map we got from National Geographic. You're kind of a long way from home.

We've had several letters from Carole. She is a fine girl, Bill, and I know you will give her all the love and respect that makes for a happy marriage. She sure is in love with you.

Your old girlfriend, Misty, stopped by to pick up her picture, but I didn't get to talk with her. I think she's already gone back to college.

Have you any place to play a tape recording if we send you one?

Keep safe and well.

Love,
Dad

Vietnam
28 Sept. 1968

Dearest Carrot,

I'll drop you a word since I goofed up everything I attempted today. I've just done everything wrong all day.

Gee, it's Saturday again. All days seem alike because we work every day, 7 a.m. to 7 p.m., and do guard duty, too. There isn't much to do to break up the tedious monotony. All I look forward to is securing this job within a month, making an E-5, and hearing from you.

I still haven't heard from you because the first letter takes a long time to set up a recognized route. I'm looking forward to seeing you in Hawaii. The Army will get you there from the West Coast and back for $165. You'll have to pay for your round-trip ticket to the West Coast. When your military allotments start coming in, save as much as you can because that's what will pay your way. I need our sealed marriage certificate before requesting my R&R.

By the way, how are your grades? Of course, knowing I'm pretty safe, I'll expect you to 'Ace' everything. You've got security now because you're married and have a husband.

I'll call you at Sturgeon Bay by MARS [Military Auxiliary Radio System] and 'phone patch' for five minutes around your birthday. Can you be back home around October 12 or 13?

If you've heard about a recent battle, don't sweat it. The battle was ten miles away.

Love your hubby,
Bill

A letter from Carole's mother, Viola Obry.

Alaska, Wisconsin
September 29, 1968

Dear Bill,

I got your address from Carole. I am glad to hear you are in an office. I thought about you so much, worrying about where you would go. I hope the time passes quickly so you can be home with Carole. The first week of college was rough on her, and I put in a hard week feeling sorry for both of you.

How was your trip? I suppose you see a very different country there. Are there mountains or all lowlands?

Our weather is still as beautiful as the week you got married. It's the best September we've had in a long time. I hope December 28 (Cheryl's wedding) is a good day too!! I think how you and Carole did it was better—nothing to worry about for very long. Ha!

Write when you can.
Mom

Vietnam
30 Sept. 1968

Darling Carole,

I was so happy to get your three letters. I was reading them in my office, and the captain came in and said something about typing over some Article 15 punishment papers. I told him to "Go away. Check with me later, not now. I'm busy." I didn't fully realize what I was saying to my commanding officer, and ONE JUST DOESN'T TELL YOUR CO [commanding officer] TO GO AWAY. But he went away, shocked, and didn't say anything, so I guess I got away with it. Besides, I have a new 1st CO (Carole Obry).

Even though I haven't slept in sixty-four hours, I was so pleased to get your letters today that I feel one hundred percent better. I had guard duty last night and reactionary guard (a standby guard), but I'm wide awake now. I can't wait to hear from you tomorrow.

No, I haven't forgotten your birthday. How could I forget it, Silly? The only problem is that I'm seventeen miles as the crow flies and twenty-five miles by road from the Qui Nhon PX. So I don't get much of a chance to go there.

Did you get your $50 yet? I'll send another $60 money order next time I get to Qui Nhon. I was paid $235 today in the military script.

Please send me five fly swatters, Rice Krispie bars, twenty cents of Luden's red cough drops, and my pair of loose shorts with the hole in them as someone stole my swim trunks. Try to keep packages under five pounds so they get here faster by airmail.

By God, you know something, Carrot—I love you.

Hey, I just thought about how your sister bought a big white dress for her upcoming wedding. I'll bet that's what you wanted, too. But is there such a thing as a church wedding duplicating a civil one? Thinking back, I know now I cheated you and my folks. They would have liked to plan a big wedding for their last marriageable son. It makes my heart ache! I'm so sorry. I hope there's a way to make it up to all of you.

Love and thoughts for you,
Bill

P.S. I put the newspaper clipping from our wedding under the glass desktop with the photos of you in your swimsuit and wearing your tight sweater with me by the Christmas tree.

P.P.S. Qui Nhon and other villages are off-limits, so don't worry about me. Guys go down anyway, but I won't because I've noticed in my company that 45U 4G UX4 I5OES2E 1OE O3O2U6 N2O UX4 I5OES2E G3GU6 I1W2 WE [out of two hundred and ninety men, two hundred fifty have VD].

The first year of our marriage would be the hardest, a year of doubt and uncertainty. Our biggest battle would be carrying on a long-distance relationship in the mail while questioning our commitment and fidelity to each other.

Bill had a girlfriend, Misty, before I met him. They had a close relationship, but both were very religious, so I believed Bill was still a virgin when I met him. As for myself, I was a virgin when he met me. After having just gone through what I thought was a possible pregnancy, I had no intention of, as Bill would say, "screwing around."

But a year was a long time to wait. Plans to meet in a jewel-like place, Hawaii, for a romantic holiday gave our longing hearts hope that we would soon be together again

CHAPTER 6 -
PETE, POT, PANTHERS, AND PIGS

Seeds of discontent were scattered throughout the 60s by the antiwar protestors, civil rights activists, outspoken musicians, and actors, as well as members of the Students for a Democratic Society and its Underground Weathermen, the Black Panthers, and athletes from the Black Power movement. Feminist women burned their bras in the Freedom Trash Can outside the Miss American pageant in Atlantic City, while young men burned their draft cards and the US flag out on the streets. Like Johnny Appleseed, they sowed their truths to my generation in an attempt to change the direction of our nation.

In March of 1967, my second semester at UWGB, Pete Seeger visited the campus. My best friend, Dixie, insisted we see the famous singer-songwriter together. She didn't want me to miss out on the fun-filled concert, which meant I had to ditch a class.

By then, I'd made a few more friends on campus but usually hung out with Dixie. She came from Green Bay while I'd grown up in a small rural community. Dixie was a fun-loving, liberal-leaning, free spirit, while I was a conservative worrywart who played by the rules. I'd never heard of this socially conscious songwriter and didn't want to miss my chemistry lab.

Dixie laid out her argument in a logical manner. "Ms. Edwards probably wants to go to the concert, too, but she doesn't want to cancel chemistry lab. So if you show up for class tomorrow, she and you could be the only ones there. Then you'll both miss the concert."

My chemistry lab instructor, Ms. Edwards, was an unusual character. She didn't strike me as someone who would want to attend a folk-music concert, but perhaps she wouldn't mind if I went and would allow me to make up the lab later.

"Dixie, I don't even know who this Seeger guy is," I argued.

"Of course you do. Remember the song 'If I Had a Hammer'?" Dixie stomped her foot to make her point. "Carole, I'm not taking 'no' for an answer. I'll get there early and save you a place."

"But I've never skipped a class, so it'll be your fault if I get in trouble."

"Don't worry about it. It's all gonna turn out groovy."

The next day after speech class, I rushed to the cafeteria and arrived just as the concert began. The janitors removed all the tables and chairs to make space for about three hundred students and faculty members. Students sat on the floor while faculty and latecomers, including Bill, stood against the back wall. I glanced around the room and was relieved not to see Ms. Edwards. Instead, I spied Dixie waving frantically and hurried down the middle aisle to join her.

"Geez, it's crowded. Thanks for saving me a spot. Why did you have to pick the front row?" I sat on the floor, tucking my brown tweed dress underneath me. I squeezed in close to Dixie, but my bottom stuck out halfway into the aisle. "You know, you didn't leave me much room."

"Stop your silly complaining and enjoy the free concert."

"Did I miss anything?"

"Just Pete tuning up his banjo."

I stared up at Pete, who was unaccompanied and didn't even have a microphone. He stood three feet in front of me, strumming his banjo. Pete was tall and thin, like a bean pole, and his casual dress and work boots made him look like he'd just come in from the garden. Because of his receding hairline, I thought he was around my father's age.

Every eye in the room was on Mr. Seeger when he finally stopped strumming and held up his banjo for all to see. He pointed to the hand-written motto on its front and called his banjo a political machine for social change.

"This banjo surrounds hate and forces it to surrender," Pete explained. "Folk songs are part of America's heritage, full of people searching for their roots. Many of my songs ask hard questions about war, hate, and injustice. But go ahead and hum, sing along with the choruses, and feel free to ask questions."

Then Seeger talked about his life. At the age of seventeen, he joined the Young Communist League. Then, in 1942, he was drafted into the U.S. Army, started as an air mechanic, and later served in Special Forces, entertaining the South Pacific troops until 1945. After the interception of a wartime letter he'd written to his Japanese American fiancé denouncing the deportation of all Japanese Americans, Pete was on the military's radar for advocating his political opinion.

Seeger left the Communist Party U.S.A. in 1949, but his involvement led to him being questioned in 1955 by Senator Joseph McCarthy, who led the House Un-American Activities Committee. Instead of answering McCarthy's questions, Pete pled the First Amendment, freedom of speech, which almost landed him in jail!

I heard of people pleading the Fifth, but never the First Amendment. Looking up at Seeger, I already admired this man. It didn't seem fair to me that radio and television stations blacklisted him, and he couldn't get bookings at concert halls, so he took his message to college campuses.

Pete picked and strummed the banjo and talked about a song he'd written about the World War II era. A captain, who Pete labeled "the big fool," drowned while leading his platoon across a muddy river. President Johnson saw the lyrics in that song as a personal attack on his Vietnam policies. During the final verse, I could envision Pete sitting at his breakfast table, reading the morning headlines, and contemplating this new war in Vietnam.

In 1967, that song got him censored, this time from *The Smothers Brothers Comedy Hour*, a popular television variety show. Again, it had been all over the nightly news. The Smothers Brothers were quite outspoken against CBS for regulating freedom of speech. Finally, on February 25, one month before this concert, Pete won a court victory, and CBS aired him singing, strong and hard for all to hear, his controversial song, "Waist Deep in the Big Muddy."

As the troubadour spoke about his next song, he looked down at me with caring eyes and made eye contact. "The inspiration for this song comes from, *And Quiet Flows the Don*, a book I read while on an airplane. It describes the Cossack soldiers galloping off to join the Czar's army, singing as they go:

> *Where are all the flowers?*
> *The girls plucked them.*
> *Where are all the girls?*
> *They're all married.*
> *Where are the men?*
> *They're all in the army.*

"As I already had the melody for this song in my head, I wrote the lyrics in about twenty minutes."

Then Pete sang my favorite song, "Where Have All the Flowers Gone?" made famous by folksingers Peter, Paul, and Mary. While the audience swayed and sang along to the choruses, I daydreamed about a time when I broke what I considered an unfair law and started questioning my religious upbringing when I was nine.

Every spring, as far back as I remember, my aunts and cousins met at Grandma's house to celebrate Mother's Day. Grandma Anna lived in an old-fashioned, two-story house next door to the Casco cemetery and had nine granddaughters. The eldest three girls were grown but had passed on a tradition to us younger cousins of picking Grandmother a unique bouquet of wildflowers from a pristine, virgin, white birch forest that grew directly behind the cemetery.

Our baby-boomer pack leaders were my older sister, Cheryl, and my two cousins, Lynn and J.A. Their task was to make sure that we three younger cousins made it safely to the woods and back while complying with Grandma's strict order, "Do not pick the trilliums."

Our path led us through the stalwart Catholic cemetery to a back lot. Like the pokey little puppy in a popular children's book at the time, we scrambled up and over the fence and down the green grass, ignoring the "No Trespassing" signs as we embarked on a noble adventure. The grassy hillside led us down to a meadow, a small marsh, and a forest thickly carpeted with tiny purple violets, bright yellow buttercups, and unusual Jack-in-the-pulpits. But the most coveted of all the flowers was the trillium.

The trillium, or trinity flower, was endangered and protected by the State of Wisconsin. It had three white petals with a small yellow center that burst out from its brilliant green leaves. That spring day, I gave in to its allure and picked one. Its bloody rhizomatous root came up along with the flower and stained my hands bright red. Now that I had its blood on my hands, I reasoned there was no point in abandoning its beauty in the woods.

Our flower picking completed, one-by-one Cheryl and Lynn boosted us younger girls up and over the wooden fence while J.A. caught us on the other side. We'd been successful, as no one had gotten a scrape, muddy shoes, or a torn Sunday dress. But I had a small problem, the bloody trillium. As we walked back to Grandma's through the whisper-quiet cemetery, J.A. noticed my blood-stained hands and handed me her handkerchief to wrap around the flower's weeping stem.

As we passed by three small tombstones in the back forty corner of the cemetery, I asked, "Why are these graves so far away from the others?"

J.A., who attended Catholic school and was therefore considered an expert on Catholicism, piped up the answer. "Those are babies who died without being baptized and can't go to heaven. That's why they're buried back here."

Huh? Can't go to heaven? I instantly felt sorry for those babies and placed a tiny purple violet on each small headstone.

I pointed to a more prominent headstone. "But what about this one?"

"That one belongs to a nun. Mother said she committed suicide."

"Suicide? What does that mean?"

"It means she killed herself, dummy! It's a mortal sin."

My breath caught in my ribs. "Why'd she do it?"

"Because she had mental problems."

"Does that mean she'll go to hell?"

"No, she'll go to purgatory instead."

Cheryl whispered, "Carole, we Lutherans don't believe in purgatory. When people die, they either go to heaven or hell."

I laid my beautiful white trillium on the nun's grave, relieving myself of any guilt associated with breaking the law. Then, I carefully cleaned my bloody hands with the handkerchief and handed it back to J.A.

I contemplated what Cheryl had said. I didn't believe for one minute that babies ever went to hell or that nuns went to purgatory, but I kept my mouth shut. At an early age, I learned that it wasn't suitable for differing religious beliefs to divide families cruelly. So even though I disagreed, sometimes it was better not to argue to keep the peace.

Dixie poked me with her elbow, startling me out of my reminiscing. Finally, Pete finished singing and dispensed the audience one last piece of advice.

"Learn to question the status quo. Please don't play it safe or become complacent. The most dangerous thing to do is to play it safe."

Still deep in musing about playing it safe, I didn't realize Warren Gerds, a *Green Bay Press-Gazette* reporter, snapped a black-and-white photo of me demurely sitting at the folksinger's feet. The next day my picture landed on page eleven of the local newspaper. The caption read, "Folksinger Pete Seeger strums and sings while a student watches enthralled."

It wasn't safe to skip chemistry class and have my photo in the newspaper, but Ms. Edwards never said a word about it and allowed me to make up the lab. Dixie was triumphant. It all turned out groovy. Meanwhile, I contemplated the morality of this undeclared war in Vietnam dividing our nation.

Around the same time in my evolving life, I was exposed to new cultural concepts regarding student rights and the use of marijuana on the UW campus. Bill wrote in one of his letters that some American GIs in Vietnam smoked marijuana which caused them to fall asleep at night during guard duty. My husband expressed concern about his camp getting overrun by an enemy attack. Although it was illegal, Bill warned me that I'd probably come across someone smoking marijuana on campus.

In one of my letters, I asked him, 'How will I know if somebody's smoking pot?'

He answered a week later. "Oh, you'll know by the smell of it."

My liberal arts English class, held in a building high on top of picturesque Bascom Hill, was a short but steep walk from the medical campus. One day after anatomy class, Janet and I hiked there, carrying our books and off-white canvas bone bags. Climbing up Bascom Hill was no easy task, with arms aching from the weight of textbooks and leg muscles cramping from the hill's ten percent grade. The heat of Indian summer caused beads of sweat to roll down our foreheads while the dry human bones in our bags clicked in unison with every step we took.

"Janet, bringing our bone bags to English class is gross." I huffed as we shuffled past the seated Abraham Lincoln statue at the top of the hill.

Janet kept walking. "It's too hot to walk back to the dorm."

We arrived at class early. A pungent odor greeted us as we walked through the door of the old auditorium. I waved my hand in front of my nose.

"Ugh, did a skunk get in here?"

Janet pointed to a guy with long, shaggy, greasy hair smoking a joint.

"What? You never smelled marijuana before?"

I chose a row of empty seats next to an open window. The bones rattled and complained as I set them on the floor beside my chair.

"Oof. It stinks. I'm surprised the professor lets his students smoke pot in the classroom."

Janet giggled as she took the chair beside me. "Our professor probably smokes it, too!"

I took a long deep breath of fresh air from the opened window and looked behind me to see who else might be smoking. But instead, I saw a tall black man with a giant afro walk into the auditorium. I never saw a black person in our classroom before. Dressed oddly for such a warm day, he wore a black beret and a black leather jacket and confidently strolled to the front of the auditorium to speak to our professor.

"Could he be our new teacher's assistant?" I whispered to Janet, who shrugged her shoulders.

Our professor introduced the man as a member of the Black Panther Party from nearby Chicago. "Raise your hand if you'd like me to turn over my classroom so that you can find out about the Black Panther's just social causes."

During the vote, Janet and I kept our hands down. We were there for an English class, not a rally, but most students eagerly raised theirs.

I leaned in towards Janet. "What's a Black Panther?"

"Let's stay and find out," she whispered back.

The Black man stood behind the podium with a raised, fisted, black-gloved hand. I jumped in my seat when he shouted, "Power to the People! Down with the pigs! Malcolm X don't want any more of this subservient 'Negro' crap; just call us Blacks."

The man's booming voice scared the bejeebers out of me, like when I was a kid trying to nap through a long sermon at St. John's Lutheran Church. So when Pastor Weis hit the podium with his fist warning of my eternal damnation and shouting, "You're headed to hell if you don't know Jesus," he had my full attention.

The Black Panther explained that Blacks were attempting to form a new political party and stand up against police brutality. In addition, Blacks wanted to carry weapons openly, have better housing, and have equal rights for jobs and education. Although speaking primarily to a white audience, he appealed to us to join him as one of his "brothers."

By now, the auditorium was jam-packed with curious students. However, the raunchy smell from the burning pot and the speaker's words set off my claustrophobia. My stomach twisted as I thought about Dow Days which occurred a year earlier.

On October 18, 1967, UW students held a peaceful sit-in on Bascom Hill to block Dow Chemical Company from job recruiting on campus. Dow made napalm,[12] a flammable gel used in flame throwers and bombs for the U.S. military in Vietnam. Napalm was deadly and burned the skin off its victims.

Hundreds of students blocked the hallway of Commerce Hall, where Dow Chemical held job interviews looking for chemical engineers. The demonstrators' leaders spoke to the Dean and asked him to forbid Dow from recruiting on campus. The Dean refused their request and insisted that the students leave. There was a standoff, the students continued their sit-in, and the Dean called in the police.

A violent, bloody riot ensued. Police beat students with billy clubs to evict them from the hall. Finally, classes let out, and almost two thousand students gathered outside the building. Some locked arms and confronted the police. Others chanted, "*Sieg Heil*," gave the police the Nazi salute, or pelted them with rocks, pebbles, and sticks.

Then for the first time, police set off tear gas to break up the protest. Nearly seventy people, including police officers, were injured and sent to the hospital. In the end, the university suspended thirteen students. Other students were outraged and organized a two-day student strike with the help of select faculty.

Like a stone thrown into a pond, Dow Day, a pivotal event on campus, caused a ripple effect out to the city of Madison, the state of Wisconsin, and our nation as people began to talk about and openly question the morality of U.S. involvement in Vietnam's civil war and the draft. In addition, protests on other college campuses increased as young people thought they could change the world and end the war by bringing their message to the streets.

Coming back to the present, I heard the Black man call upon the crowd to riot. I gave Janet a hand signal. We grabbed our books and bone bags and snuck out the side door.

As soon as we were outdoors, I took a deep breath. "Wow, I needed some fresh air."

Janet squinted in the afternoon sun. "I was so relieved when you stood up to leave."

"I understand Blacks have grievances, but that man is far too militant for me. And calling the cops 'pigs' is asking for trouble. It scares me when I see PIGS scrawled on the campus walls. My sister, Cheryl, warned me not to get involved with these outside agitators. She's afraid I might get beat up or expelled."

Janet wiped the sweat from her forehead with a flimsy tissue. "My parents would disown me if I ever got arrested!"

We resumed our long walk back down Bascom Hill to the rhythm of our bone bags. I finally broke our silence.

"Let's study our bones this afternoon. I have to memorize the bony landmarks of the femur, tibia, and fibula."

"Ha! I have the foot and the ankle. Together we have a leg to stand on!!"

We both laughed, feeling giddy, the rest of the way home. Later that afternoon, Janet and I studied together, prepping for a quiz in anatomy, hoping to each earn an A.

Despite what Pete Seeger had said, I planned to play it safe on campus, focus on my coursework, and earn my degree. I wholeheartedly agreed with Dr. Martin Luther King's non-violent civil rights movement, but the Black Panther's proposals were far too radical for me.[13]

Mom and Dad would have withdrawn their financial support if I hadn't played by their conservative values and rules. Besides, how could I support the anti-war movement with my precious husband actively fighting in Vietnam, especially after receiving the following letter?

DEPARTMENT OF THE ARMY
160th Heavy Equipment Maintenance Company
APO U.S. Forces 96492

AVCA QN-86-160
30 September 1968
SUBJECT: Sustaining the High Morale of SP 4 William Jon R. Wagener
C.O. (MRS. WJRW)
1317 Spring St.
Madison, Wisconsin. 53715

It has come to our attention that SP 4 Wagener has been in high spirits because he received your letter. Since receiving the letter, he has performed his duties exceptionally well.

It is, therefore, in the interest of the 160th H.E.M. Co (GS) and the U.S. Army that you continue this action.

It is hereby, therefore, requested that you continue the moral support.

NEWBURY JONES
SP 5
Company Clerk

CHAPTER 7 -
OCTOBER 1968: HENRY VS HELEN

I felt unsure about my relationship with Bill, because now that we were married, he acted as if he owned me. Why did he try to control me from ten thousand miles away? Like an insecure child bride picking petals from an off-white daisy, I repeated to myself, "He loves me. He loves me not." And referring to me as "dum, dum" in his letters sure didn't help my ego.

Vietnam
1 Oct. 1968

Hi Dum, Dum,

How's my happy little girl? It appears that the monsoon is coming. It rains a bit every day, and it's been chilly here lately, between seventy-five to ninety-five degrees.

Okay, you asked about my job. I haven't touched a gas cylinder since I left training in Fort Belvoir. But, because of my typing and personnel file, acknowledging I wrote a book about my Wagener genealogy, they figured a guy like me has to have some smarts! I'm training to replace the sergeant as NCO for our company, re-enlist NCOs, and be second in command under the CO and his Executive Officer.

I'm also responsible for the daily history report and a dozen odds and ends. Every fourth or fifth night, I still pull guard duty or reactionary guard duty. I only sleep in my bed eighteen nights out of thirty a month.

They're having a small battle between here and Qui Nhon, so this letter may take a day or two longer to get to you. So don't worry about me.

Bill

Madison
October 1, 1968

Hi Bill,

I thought I'd write a short note and let you know I'm thinking about you. I hope you like the stick of cinnamon gum I've been sending in every letter.

There was a drug raid here in Madison last night—thirty-three people arrested and thousands of dollars of drugs confiscated.

Today Janet and I dressed in white uniform dresses, white nursing shoes, and pantyhose for our Orientation to Physical Therapy Lab. We'll go to the UW Hospital to observe for the next few weeks.

My dreams are getting worse and worse. Last night I dreamed you didn't have a nose when you came home, but they did a pretty good job of mending you up. Instead of your nose sticking out, it stuck in!

October 2, 1968

I didn't know you were on guard duty. Maybe by the time you receive this, you'll just be working in the office.

There is supposed to be a Hong Kong flu this winter. But unfortunately, it's a brand new flu, and there is no shot yet. So Janet and I have been drinking tons of orange juice and eating fresh fruits to build up our immune systems.

Whatever you want to send me from your next paycheck is fine. Twenty-five dollars will easily cover my monthly expenses. But of course, if you send more, I'll put any extra money in our savings account.

I am overwhelmed with lovesickness, but reading your letters makes me feel well again.

Happy third-week anniversary! Take care, my lonely soldier.

Carole

Vietnam
2 Oct. 1968

Dear Carole,

I didn't get your letter yesterday because of a battle five miles down the road. But, boy, I loved the scent of your first and second letters and all four photos of you, especially "V for Victory" and "Look of Love." Please make an 8" x 10" color enlargement of "Look of Love" for me. PLEASE, Dearest!

You better believe I won't be messing around with these Vietnamese girls. I went on sick call today, and almost everybody else was there for VD.

It looks pretty sure that I'm the new NCO in charge of training enlisted men—all 278 of them. I'm also in charge of all company publications, orders, regulations, and legal advisors. The 1st Sgt. said they'd probably make me an acting NCO since I haven't been in the Army as an E-4 long enough to make E-5 rank.

If you haven't ordered *Playboy* yet, make it a three-year subscription. Make it my birthday present if you want, but don't send them here as they usually get stolen out of the mail.

Love,
Bill

Madison
October 4, 1968

Dearest Bill,

I received two letters from you today. I laughed and laughed; you're such a nut. I had to chuckle about you wanting me to send a loose pair of shorts with the patch in the rear to replace your stolen swimsuit!

I spent so much time tonight preparing and wrapping your first Care Package that I almost didn't have time to write. More than once, I was tempted to steal some of your Rice Krispie bars.

I don't mention my sister's wedding much in my letters because I know it makes you sad. Yes, I was jealous when I saw Cheryl in her beautiful long wedding gown, but if I had answered 'yes' the first time you asked me to marry you, I would have had time to buy a white dress, too. So, don't blame yourself. I was so happy to be married to you on our wedding day that all the frills didn't matter.

Dearest One, I'm looking forward to sleeping with you every night. You're so warm and cuddly. I enjoy having you in my bed. Your warm body touching me on these cold nights and seeing you sleeping peacefully at my side would mean the world to me.

All my love and kisses forever,
Carole

Vietnam
5 Oct. 1968

Hi Carole,

I got a letter from your folks today. They were afraid you'd quit school the first week after I left. I'm glad you stuck to your guns. Keep working, Honey. It's to both of our advantage that you finish. Besides, I can't stand to see you working for $1 an hour as a waitress, especially since you're my wife now.

How are your grades? You haven't mentioned any yet. I hope you do well on that 'killer' anatomy test.

The Doc here suggested I read *Playboys*, so your photos wouldn't be so shocking. Also, he said to spend my entire R&R in bed to help me recover from the last few months. I think that can be arranged, don't you?

Sgt. D. had photos of girls under his desk glass and on the wall. So I took them all down and then put them back up because they won't make me love you any less.

Hey, where are my flyswatters and red licorice?

6 Oct. 1968

Today, I took a ride down the road from our compound to the 666th Sig Bn., about one mile away. Some ass shot a hole through the front window of my jeep. Boy, that pissed me off! I couldn't even tell from where it came. He didn't have the guts to take another shot, or he'd give his position away. That's what I hate about the VC. They hit and run. They're afraid to fight unless they outnumber us six to one.

Have you been horny at all? Don't go NITU5SC1U3OH with anything. *Das ist ein* order!

Promise me that you'll never get fat. I'd consider it grounds for divorce except for when you're pregnant. You should be doing your leg lifts and 'sexercises' about now. You're thin enough and fine-looking, but there's a little (though very little) room for improvement. When you go to the Student Health Center, why don't you ask if certain foods or exercises will enlarge your boobs? Oops, I mean Baba and Boo Boo.

Much work to do, I must go.
Bill

Bill's last letter left hurtful notches in my quickly diminishing self-esteem. If he loved me, why was he so worried about me getting fat and the size of my breasts? At 5'6", I barely weighed 118 pounds. And why wasn't he satisfied with my B-cup-sized breasts?

Maybe he compared me to those voluptuous women he gazed at in his magazines. He kept badgering me to order his *Playboys*. He regarded his girly magazines as art appreciation, but in my mind, Hugh Hefner was a curse to all women.

I viewed *Playboy* bunnies—who thought it was a great honor to be photographed stark-naked as centerfolds—as whores who had no shame. Maybe they did it for money or fame, but I wasn't even comfortable posing nude for my husband.

But the idea of Kaiser Wilhelm ordering me not to be N1TU5SC1U3OH (masturbating) with anything ticked me off. Who was he to tell me what I could or couldn't do with my body? What business was it of his as long as I remained faithful to our wedding vows? According to my husband, I was supposed to practice my Kegel 'sexercises' regularly. Was that all he thought about, having tight sex with me?

Now that we were married, Bill didn't seem to appreciate me for who I was—a young, intelligent woman who believed she loved him despite all his faults, like how he called me "Dum, Dum" in his letters. Yes, I was naïve when he first met me, but I'd grown up. Maybe writing "dum, dum" was his way of putting me down or keeping me in my place. On the other hand, perhaps he meant no harm, and it was part of a melody from a popular song. Should I stand up for myself and confront him?

I never tore up any of Bill's letters, but sometimes at night, I wrote very negative letters, blasted him, and then tore the letter up into tiny pieces. It was my way of coping with my anger. By the following day, I buried my anger, started fresh, and wrote a cheerful letter. Of course, bottling up anger wasn't healthy, but we'd only been married for one month, and I didn't want to have a knock-down, drag-out marathon fight in the mail.

Madison
October 11, 1968

Hi Hon,

I got your letter today and the money order for $25. So now I can order your *Playboys* and the enlarged picture you requested. If you were here, all it would take is a snap of your fingers, and you'd see the "Look of Love" as often as you wanted, and you wouldn't need your magazines.

How's my hard-working soldier today? It sounds like they make you work from 6:30 a.m. to midnight. That's a long day. But you'll be thrilled to know the flyswatters are on the way and will soon be there to help you in your plight.

Wisconsin has another football game here on Saturday. I'm so glad I bought season tickets, as the games give Janet and me a break from studying. Unfortunately, this game will probably be another one down the drain. I'd be happy if the team could get one touchdown or even a crummy field goal.

Did you know my birthday is turning out better than planned? Janet bought me a chocolate cake with cherries on top, and a group of girls got together for cake and coffee in the dorm kitchen.

Twenty years ago, as a wee babe, I came into the world—an innocent child—I still feel like a child but not so innocent.

Love always,
Carole

I made the best of my twentieth birthday despite the disappointment of not receiving a gift in the mail from Bill. Then, around 10:00 p.m., Janet pounded on my door.

"Come quick; it's a collect phone call. It must be Bill."

Janet and I shared the expense of the telephone in her room. We ran down the hallway in our pajamas, whooping and hollering at the top of our lungs. Once in Janet's room, I grabbed the phone receiver.

"Hi, this is Carole."

An operator with a nasal-toned voice spoke. "I have a collect call from Ashland, Wisconsin, for a Mrs. William Wagener.[14] Will you accept the charges?"

"That's me. Please reverse the charges."

Then a male voice came on the line. "This is your ham radio operator, WN9SSD. My handle is Silly Sad Dog. Before connecting you to your husband, let me explain how this works. First, you will talk and then say 'over,' and I'll hit a switch, so your husband can talk. Then, when he says 'over,' it's your turn to talk again. Copy that?"

Nodding and sharing the receiver so Janet could listen in, I replied, "Yes, I understand."

"Go ahead."

"Hello, Bill. Can you hear me?" I almost forgot to say—"over."

"Roger, I can hear you fine. Happy Birthday, Carrot. What did you do for your birthday?—over."

"I had a cake and shared it with my friends—over."

"I'd have loved some. Next year I'll be there to celebrate your twenty-first birthday. How are you doing, Honey—over?"

"I'm lonely, but it's so good to hear your voice, Billy. Do you miss me—over?"

"I miss you, and Henry misses you, too—over."

"Other people can hear us talking," I said in a low voice, blushing. " Take care of yourself, Bill. I love you—over."

"I love you, too—over and out."

The connection cut off, so I thanked Silly Sad Dog and hung up. In addition to the two ham operators, Janet heard every word of our conversation.

"That was so exciting, but who's this guy named Henry?" she asked in a near whisper because of the paper-thin walls.

My face was beet red. "That's a pet name for Bill's private part," I whispered back.

Janet giggled. "What's yours called?"

"Helen."

"We call ours Peter and Penny."

"Oh, that's hilarious, Janet."

We yucked it up and didn't stop laughing until rolling around on the floor in tears. Then, Janet and I hugged and finally said good night. It was one birthday I'd never forget.

Vietnam
12 Oct. 1968

Dearest Carole,

>Your hair, like scarlet-brown leaves in color,
>Your face, like the innocence of youth,
>Eyes of sadness make pools of thought.
>Teeth white and clean,
>Neck slender and lean,
>Shoulders firm and strong,
>For shelter sought.
>Nay, the term is long,
>And your man's arms are gone,
>But fear not, nor mind fret,
>For someday,
>I shall return.

I wrote this just now, gazing at your photo under the glass plate of my desk. The memory of your tears at the airport especially inspired me.

Happy Birthday and have a happy one-month anniversary. I do hope you do something fun to celebrate.

Love,
Bill

Madison
October 13, 1968

Dearest Bill,

I am so happy that your phone call made it for my birthday. It was so sweet of you to call to say I love you.

> How do I love thee, Bill?
> You're the king of my castle.
> You have the key to my heart.
> You're the lion of my jungle,
> The man in my bedroom,
> And the guy in my shower.
> In other words,
> You're the guy for me.

I've tried to accept that I can't have you yet, that Uncle Sam wants you first. I am lonely but not crying every night like the first week after you left. Now, getting a letter from you is my best vitamin.

After the tenth time I've heard, "Where're my flyswatters?" it's my turn. Be prepared to be bombarded. Where's my birthday present? Like Ann Landers would say, take thirty lashes with a wet noodle, you cad!

I bought you a Playtex toothbrush today—the living toothbrush. Tomorrow, I'm going back to buy myself one. Gosh! Matching toothbrushes! What a privilege!

Love,
Carole

Land of the Tropical Breezes and Monsoons
15 October 1968

Hi Little Angel,

No goodies, no flyswatters, no photos, no letters, no nothing. My Sunshine has let me down. Boohoo. It doesn't matter because I know you're behaving and you love me!

Well, I hope you did alright on that anatomy test. You didn't sound too confident. If you do your best, I'm sure you'll do fine. You're one of the brightest girls I've ever known regarding school. I'm the reverse, plain stupid.

Holy shit! Hell just broke loose down the road (Hwy 19). We're going on red alert. I got to go.

16 Oct. 1968

Boy, last night it was bad for a while. I best not give any details, but I didn't get a scratch. Wow, when those Korean Tigers got in there, I didn't think there would be any of the enemy left. They cleaned things up. It only took the South Korean Tiger Division two hours, and they got an estimated ninety percent of the VC, and it was all over. I doubt they'll hit this area again for a LONG time.

We helped with support fire from behind our perimeter and flares and spotlights. The attack wasn't on us (they know better), but it's closer than it's been since 1965. I told everyone that sooner or later, it would get close.

They'll probably take us off of alert if it stays quiet, and we can get back to the regular hum-drum monotonous routine. It's been an exciting day. I've been up forty-one hours now and am awfully tired.

They air-dropped our mail and top-priority supplies today. I received two letters from you. Our mail won't go out until the red alert is over. Only combat vehicles are moving on or off the post.

Rain, rain, rain. The monsoons are here.

17 Oct. 1968

They're air-dropping mail again. Today I got your letter dated October 10. Hey, great going on that test. I knew you'd do it. Keep up the excellent work.

Don't worry about me, Honey. I believe the worst is over, and everything happens for the best. I guess it's all part of God's plan. I'm safe while I'm inside our barbed-wire wall.

I can't say this sort of married life does anything for me. I feel almost like I'm still single. Yes, having no qualms about stupid societal taboos will be nice. But, I think if I can hold out here, and I will, I deserve any damn thing that I want. And you'd better be ready, able, and willing to give it. So, keep doing your 'sexercises.' Suppose you don't know how then find out ASAP.

You don't run the show. I'm the director, and you're the assistant. *Verstehen?*

I still love you very much.
Bill

Previously, I received a letter from Bill telling me he had already applied for his R&R to Hawaii in December, as he would qualify once he'd been in Vietnam for one hundred days.

Madison
October 17, 1968

Dear Bill,

R&R in December. Already? Yikes! No money and no new mini-skirt. That puts me in a frazzle! Hawaii? Really? Tell me again. I don't believe it! Let me know when you find out your chances of it going through.

I suppose you're hard at work in your little office in the sweltering heat with swarms of flies while I'm sitting here in my pajamas, slowly sipping a Coke. I never considered this small cubicle of a room a luxury until I think of you.

I thought I detected a note of dissatisfaction in your previous letter. The night of our honeymoon, when you called me "little girl," I felt like running around the bedroom, playing with you, and having fun. Instead, I held myself back because my tummy hurt, and you were leaving the next day. Now, I feel like I have about as much sex appeal as a limp washcloth or a dried-up carrot, but a little brown-eyed boy named Billy once told me, "There's more to marriage than just sex."

Yes, sex is essential, especially in the early years of marriage. Sorry, I'm slow at catching on. Can I help it? Give me lots of time and practice, and maybe I'll be alright. But don't expect miracles in Hawaii.

I admit that I don't know much about sex, but I've been reading the book you gave me. I need one with better details, though. And I didn't find out until last year in my psychology class that some little girls masturbated!

I often think of that day at the airport, right before you left. You held me so tightly in your arms and held me and held me. Then, when you let go, I saw tears on your cheeks. In times like those, I like to see you cry because then I know you feel as I do inside. If only time could have stopped, you could always be holding me in your arms.

Love,
Carole

I wasn't prepared for the news that Bill and I would soon meet in Hawaii. For sure, Honolulu was a popular honeymoon destination. I eagerly looked forward to traveling there, yet I needed time to plan. First, I had to find a travel agent to set up my flights. Second, I had to obtain the proper travel forms and my military ID from Truax Air Force Base near Madison. Third, would my professors be willing to give me the time off and their permission if I needed to miss a week of classes?

I needed to save the money from my allotment checks (this was before credit cards), buy a sexy outfit, and start the birth control pill. And yikes, what could I expect from my husband? Would he want sex daily, twice a day, or all day? My mind whirled in trepidation and part elation as I grabbed a fresh notepad of paper to start my new to-do list.

Madison
October 18, 1968

Dear Bill,

I received a letter from you about marriage today. Sometimes I know that you're not going to be easy to live with, but once you get used to me and I get used to you, it will all work out. At least we are both willing to try and budge more than halfway, so I think we will be okay.

Don't worry. I won't be like your mother. No matter how busy I am, meals will be on the table, dishes done, the house cleaned, and beds made. I guarantee I won't be overly clean and fussy as I like a home to look lived in.[15]

Funny, I don't even know what foods you like, so you'll have to eat whatever I put on the table. You'll be happy to know I've graduated from making hot dogs and hamburgers. Janet's teaching me how to cook pork chops and squash tonight.

I think it is a blessing in disguise that we are apart. It gives me time to learn more about life, cooking, and household responsibilities. But, most of all, I don't want to forget about you when I'm so busy with school next year. We must not become so bogged down with homework that we forget about each other and our happiness—that's where I am most afraid of falling short.

Love,
Carole

Vietnam
21 Oct. 1968

Dear Honey Bun,

I was happy to get two letters from you yesterday. I've been too busy here to write. Today they are changing all the military pay certificates for a new series, and the old ones are no good. They do it so all the prostitutes along the road in town and all over will lose out. The old stuff the GIs paid them is now worthless.

I've seen so many guys go off the deep end here. It makes me feel great to know you won't disgrace our vows. The formal marriage vow means little to me. What matters is my promise that I won't screw any of these Vietnamese girls no matter how horny I get and your vow that you'd be faithful and not get screwed by anyone but me. I'll keep my promise.

Love,
Bill

Madison
October 22, 1968

Dear Bill,

What's this? I hear and read about the possibility of a halt in the bombing of North Vietnam.

It sounds like that battle was pretty close to your camp. Glad to hear the Korean Tigers were there to clean them up. I'm happy to hear you didn't get hurt. Your mom told me you were ambushed but not injured. She said you wouldn't leave the compound again without your rifle and that you were beginning to feel unsafe. Why didn't you tell me that yourself?

Returning to our marriage discussion, the more we talk about sex, the more we go around in circles. I don't want to argue about it. I don't want to hurt your feelings, and I don't want you to hurt mine. But it makes me so mad to read that you deserve 'any damn thing' you want. If that's the case, I had better take Judo lessons.

Don't think it's easy for me, being in Madison alone. This campus is rated number one for sexual permissiveness by *Playboy* magazine. Don't believe you are the only one who has it rough because you're in Vietnam. I know it's more difficult for you than I can imagine, but it's not so much fun here either. We are both in this together, so let's not complain about it or think it's easier for either one of us to keep our fidelity when we are so far away from one another.

Tomorrow, you will have one year left in the Army. Hooray, then it's my turn to be your CO. How can I be your CO if you want to be the boss? It looks like we have a long way to go. But we can get along if we try, can't we? We can be happy, can't we?

Love,
Carole

My anger began seeping into my letters like a slow-brewing cup of tea. I was furious with the strategic way the war in Vietnam was being conducted and about Bill being ambushed and not telling me. But instead, he confided in his mother, who then informed me.

I had much to contemplate as I walked along paths between classes. Bill, insisting on being the boss in our marriage, had me fuming because I firmly believed married life was supposed to be a 50/50 arrangement. I was living day by day on a campus surrounded by eligible handsome young men but already had my MRS. degree.

Immaturity was our playground. Bill's loving letters, followed by his controlling ones, had me scaling heights and plummeting like being on a teeter-totter. The endless merry-go-round discussions about sex and marriage went nowhere and kept my head spinning. I was on a continual emotional roller coaster ride, ending with a distinct thud.

What happened to the wistful playfulness and the joyful romance we once had in our relationship? Would it ever return, or would it always be this emotional?

Vietnam
22 Oct. 1968

Dear Carole,

You can't imagine how much I miss you. I want to see you and hold you. I'd be satisfied to hear your meaningless expression, "uh-huh," acknowledging that you hear me say something or even hold your hand. I've almost forgotten what your touch is like or how soft your hair is. Dammit, I think I'd almost go AWOL if I knew I could make it home.

You're the only one I can depend on for a letter. The beautiful scents of your perfumed notes cheer me up and bring back memories. Each different fragrance reminds me of a date we went on.

There are so many guys here having wife problems. They're eating their hearts out and going mad out of their minds. Spec. 4 D., the new guy, has been here three weeks and got one package from his wife and no letter. He's grouchy! I'm so lucky to have a wife like you who is trustworthy and loyal. Don't worry. No matter how horny I get, I won't go to a clap shack, not even a clean one.

> As the sun shines,
> So, my love shines for you.
> And times will change
> But naught, my love.
> For your love has taught me
> The wonders of your sublime nature,
> And I shall love you for all time.

I'm glad you got the *Playboy* subscription. Guard them with your life, and don't give any away. You got a three-year subscription, right?

Love,
Willy J.

24 Oct. 1968

How's my baby girl? Okay, no more talk about sex. We'll work it out (or in) later. I promise not to mention sex anymore because I realize you're pretty bored talking about it.

I'm sorry if I sounded like I was criticizing. I'd better not hear you saying my wife has as much sex appeal as a wet washcloth. Nobody talks about my wife that way, not even my wife! If you must know, I think you will be sexually sufficient for me when you learn to enjoy sex.

Love,
Bill

Madison
October 25, 1968

Dear Hubby,

I got your letter today. It took a week to get here. You don't have to worry about a 'Dear John' break-up letter from me. I'm a good little girl. Yes, Sir, I am.

Goodness, I've been writing almost every day for the last few weeks, but it doesn't sound like my letters are coming through very well. On October 28, it will be three weeks since I sent the first box off, so if you haven't received it yet, who knows where it is? I heard the drinking water is terrible in Vietnam, so I sent presweetened Kool-Aid—Jolly Olly and Goofy Grape.

Thank you for the sheet of cartoons. I thought they were funny, especially the one of the doctor and the girl where the doctor says, "You're going to have a baby, dear…provided nobody interrupts us!"

Oh, the disappointment! I didn't do well on my six weeks physiology test. I had a seventy-four percent, and I thought I knew the stuff.

Tonight, I'm taking the bus to go grocery shopping. Janet and I never seem to have enough food on hand to eat. Maybe it's better that way, as we have nothing to steal but ice cubes. Several girls have had cookies, potato chips, and quantities of meat stolen, which is a real shame.

Janet's fiancé, Bear, is coming home from his National Guard training next month shortly after Thanksgiving. He's only been gone since June. Good for him, as now he'll have six years to serve in the reserves. Janet is confident that he will never have to go to Vietnam, but I tell her not to be too sure about that.

Sob, sob. No birthday present from you. You don't know how much I'd appreciate seeing a package from you on the mail table downstairs. Soon the *Playboys* will be here every month, but no boxes for me.

Your loving wife,
Carole

My dad wrote to Bill, too.

Alaska, Wisconsin
October 30, 1968

Dear Son-in-Law,

We received your letter today, dated October 23, so it took just a week to get here. Unfortunately, it seems the Paris peace talks aren't progressing well. North Vietnam wants us to stop bombing altogether.

I know how you feel about being away from home and Carole. I was overseas in Japan for over twelve months. It seems like a long way from home, and it is, but when it is all over, it won't seem so long.

Carole told me about the windshield deal and that someone had taken a shot at you. So you'd better stay in the office. At least if you fall off a chair, you can always get up again.

Your R&R will be hard to get by Christmas because you haven't been in the service long enough. However, Cheryl's wedding will be on December 28, so maybe you can get a Christmas leave. Also, tell the boss you have a special invitation to come to the States.

Write again soon.

Love,
Harlan

Not having an ideal honeymoon or time to talk things out in person made for a challenging first year of marriage. Sometimes I thought ours was a marriage of convenience for both of us.

The first time I said "maybe" to marrying Bill, I felt guilty because if anything happened to him, he wouldn't have the opportunity to square things up with me, himself, or God. But, believing I might be pregnant, I couldn't bear the shame of possibly having a child out of wedlock, so I opted to marry. And being married to me assured Bill he had someone who cared enough to write him and return to when he came home.

In one of his letters, Bill asked what I would have done if I hadn't married him. Indeed, I would have dated other guys in Madison because I felt I had a right. But Bill always told me I gave guys the cold shoulder and scared them off. I believed him because, in high school, I'd heard through the grapevine that guys thought I was arrogant even though I was timid.

Would I have continued to write Bill while he was in Vietnam? Yes, certainly. I wouldn't have abandoned him because I already loved him and saw his potential to succeed.

When we decided to marry, I took our wedding vows seriously. When the judge said, "Forsaking all others," something hit my head like a gong. I felt the iron strength behind those spoken words of commitment, "for better or worse." Perhaps if we stopped picking on each other in our letters, things could smooth out for calmer sailing, but I still had my doubts.

In his letter dated October 13, Bill wrote me this warning.

"I'm hard to live with. I demand perfection and get angry if I don't get it. My dad is the same way, and when you get to know my folks better, you'll see what a miracle their marriage lasted. With us, it's me, I'm afraid, who will be the biggest pain in the butt.

"So I'm going to try extra hard to be understanding and patient. I don't have a choice. It's make it or break it. If you know me as well as I do, you know I couldn't take leaving or giving up on someone I loved and cared about. It would mar, if not destroy, me for the rest of my life. So you see why I'm going to try so hard.

"In a way, it's a blessing in disguise that we are apart because perhaps the missing you, and the wanting you, and not getting you for a year will make me more willing to curb myself to keep you. And lastly and most dear to my heart, perhaps it's a blessing we didn't have a child yet."

After our upcoming honeymoon in Hawaii, I wondered, would our relationship be better or worse? Although the church frowned upon divorce, would one of us want to call it quits?

CHAPTER 8 - NOVEMBER 1968: ISLAND FEVER

Madison
November 1, 1968

Dear Bill,

Aren't you hopping mad about President Johnson stopping the bombing? I suppose you guys heard it was coming long before we did. On the radio, I heard Hanoi had said nothing about the bombing halt, but they'd keep fighting until every American was out of Vietnam.

Curses upon you, Hanoi! Blast Hanoi off the map! I'm so angry, and if I weren't a lady, I'd swear! It's just what you said those dirty so-and-sos would do. I hope the U.S. bombers go in and give them hell if they start anything. I wouldn't mind if something good came from this, like you were to return home sooner, but I'm sure the fighting will go on. You will only be in more danger. If there are peaceful negotiations, I believe it will be on North Vietnam's terms, and South Vietnam and the United States will get the raw end of the deal.

Oh, Bill, I'm so disappointed. It's been four days since I got a letter from you. I hope everything is well and that I haven't heard from you because you're busy getting ready for the big inspection.

After class today, Janet and I went to a football pep rally called "Yell like Hell." I want to take my camera to the game tomorrow and take pictures of the UW Marching Band in formation. After the game, Janet and I will go to the Simon and Garfunkel concert. I wish you were here to join me

---

That Saturday, Janet and I sang the team's fight song, "On Wisconsin," as we carried our rolls of toilet paper (stolen from the dorm) on our short walk to the UW football game held at Camp Randall Stadium. The leaves on the deciduous trees had turned all shades of yellow, orange, and red, and it was shorts weather, a beautiful day for a homecoming game.

Woefully, the Badgers lost again, but Janet and I had fun celebrating each time our team scored by throwing a roll of TP down the bleachers. The toilet paper formed a long, white flowing streamer that fluttered in the warm breeze. After the game, Janet and I rushed home and primped and dolled ourselves up for the Simon and Garfunkel concert.

The concert was a rare treat. Janet's older sister bought the tickets and offered to drive us. Before leaving, I put on my Apache tear necklace, a treasured gift from Bill. The summer before he'd enlisted in the Army, he had traveled to the western states to visit the national parks. Upon returning, he gifted me with a small box containing the necklace and explained the legend behind the Apache tear.

"Legend has it that in the 1870s, the U.S. Calvary launched a surprise attack on an Apache tribe near a cliff overlooking Superior, Arizona. They killed fifty Apaches. The remaining twenty-five warriors rode their horses off the cliff and plunged to their deaths. The mourning Apache women shed tears which landed on the rocks below them, and The Great Father turned their tears into black stones."

Bill dangled the tear-shaped black obsidian necklace in front of me, held it up to the light, and showed me that it was translucent.

"I can see the light coming through it," I cried, mesmerized by its unique beauty.

"Think of me when you wear it. It's supposed to bring good luck."

It was my first material gift from Bill. After he put it around my neck, I threw my arms around him and kissed him with all my might.

"I promise I will."

Madison
November 3, 1968

Dearest Bill,

I MISS YOU, HON. I'm on a lonely streak. I wish you could've been at the Coliseum last night. When Simon and Garfunkel played and sang songs from *The Graduate*, I remembered how you laughed when we saw that movie together last April. My heart ached, and my eyes stung when they sang "April Come She Will," "The Sound of Silence," and "I Am a Rock." I held onto the Apache tear you gave me until its cold black stone became warm, and I snuck you a kiss on my wedding band. As I sat there, I thought, I don't want it to be like this. I don't want us to be separated anymore.

When I got home, I went right to bed. I woke up during the night and remembered what it felt like to have you at my side before you left. I'd kiss you, wake you up, and make love. Knowing how little time we had left together, I didn't want to sleep it all away. If only those nights hadn't come to an end so quickly.

I still haven't gotten a letter from you. That's another reason I feel so lonely. When I get letters, it feels like I'm talking to you. If only I could see you today and be in your arms again, I'd be so happy that I'd be crying my eyes out.

November 4, 1968

I finally got a letter from you today, and the two pictures came of you in the jungle surroundings that you developed yourself. I was glad to see you are wearing your wedding ring.

I'm not bored with sex or tired of talking about it. On the contrary, I'm very interested in you, but I'm not particularly eager to dwell on the subject. I know I need improvement. I'm sure you, Mr. Sexpot, will be able to give more lessons when we get together again. I can't wait for my next class.

Your loving wife,
Carole

Another letter to Bill from my mom.

Alaska, Wisconsin
November 4, 1968

Dear Bill,

Carole has so many plans for you when you get back. She is doing good in school, and I am glad she is getting her P.T. degree. It'll help you both to enjoy a good life by her earning extra money.

Bill, you seem to feel that I don't like you. I do think very much of you and always did. I didn't want Carole to get married as I was afraid she wouldn't finish college. But, believe me, I'm happy you did get married. If Carole weren't married, she would go to bars, and who knows what kind of guys she would meet. I know she is very happy now except that she misses you.

There isn't much news here at all about what's going on in Vietnam. I read every bit of the *Press Gazette* but can't understand much about all the towns with different names. When I memorize a few towns and find out where they are, there are new ones!

I pray the war is over soon, and you can come home. I don't know how it could be, though, when there seems to be no agreement on peace talks.

I hope you received the red licorice strings and the flyswatters I sent so that you can kill some of those insects. Ask me what you would like and what you know will keep during the long trip.

Take care of yourself so you can fulfill your plans. Write soon.

Love,
Viola

Vietnam
5 Nov. 1968

Hi again, sweet Carole,

You're damn right. You can trust me not to go to a clap shack. I know I can trust you, too.

I'm not pushing re-enlistment and am trying to keep people from it. I stopped one GI from re-enlisting—the Bn. NCO told him that the only way to get home was to re-up for four years when he only had four months left. He had wife problems and was so desperate that he'd do anything. I set him straight and saved him from re-enlisting.

My earlier injury was just a stab wound from a VC who attacked us in broad daylight on our way to Qui Nhon. It was nothing serious. It's about healed, and the bandages are off. Sometime I'll explain why I didn't get a purple heart.

On the Armed Forces Vietnam Radio, I heard Vice President Humphrey say that the bombing halt helped. Fuck Humphrey! Someone send his fat ass over here, and he'll change his mind fast. Sorry if that sounds horrible, but he's a royal pain in the ass.

Love and miss you always,
Bill

Being stabbed did sound serious, but Bill acted as if it was no big deal. Maybe it was time to start worrying about him, but how could I worry and still focus on my studies? But then, I remembered a scripture I'd learned as a child that said not to worry about anything but pray about it instead. So I resolved to say an extra "Our Father" for Bill's protection.

Madison
November 6, 1968

Dear Bill,

U-rah-rah, Nixon! I was very relieved to hear Nixon won the election. It was close. When I went to bed last night, Humphrey was ahead with forty-one percent of the vote and Nixon with thirty-nine percent. They were neck and neck when I got up, with Humphrey having the edge, but Nixon came through later. What a huge relief!

Would you believe it's snowing already? Unfortunately, the snow melts as soon as it hits the ground, but I'm dreaming of a white Christmas.

Love,
Carole

Vietnam
9 Nov. 1968

Good morning, Vietnam!

That's the greeting I hear every morning from somebody's radio from the Armed Forces Radio and Television Network. Last week this guy came on and said, "Hello out there in the boonies. I'm returning to the States, so this is the last time I'll say Goood Mornnning, Vietnam."[16] That meanie. Now, a civilian girl wakes us up and plays the morning music on our only radio station.

Wow, what a sexy voice she has, so soft and friendly in tone, giving everyone a big hard-on.

Sorry if you didn't get my letter for almost a week. Sometimes a mail truck gets hit, and a few mailbags get lost.

I miss you, Babe.

Love,
Bill

Madison
November 9, 1968

Honey,

It's Friday night. What will we do—two lonely people on opposite sides of the earth wanting to be together but always apart? Of the two years we've known each other, we've been apart more than we've been together. You can call me Mrs. Lonely.

Every day I wait for a letter and then for a week or a month to pass. Awe, heck. Why can't we be together right now?

Carole

We'd only been apart for two months, but a deep loneliness filled me and followed me around like Pig Pen's (Charlie Brown's friend) imaginary dust cloud. Sometimes I felt like walking up to a male stranger and saying, "Love me." Not sexually, of course, but I imagined having a solid muscular arm around my waist, sitting close to a guy, and having a little blissful attention. Instead, Bill wrote, I know you need attention and an arm around you, so hug yourself! Seriously, we'll be together soon, so hang loose.

Knowing Bill was lonely, too, would he venture out to the clap shacks with the other lust-filled GIs? Could I count on my virile husband to be true to me for ten more months?

I prayed to God to give us the strength to get through this time of separation. We vowed to be faithful to one another at our wedding, but how could we both endure this heart-breaking loneliness which even invaded our dreams?

Vietnam
10 Nov. 1968

Hi Angel,

I've been getting a little restless lately. No, I didn't go to the clap shacks!!! But Henry is missing Helen, something fierce, almost as much as I miss you.

Last night I dreamed about the night we slept together when I was home on leave before Fort Belvoir. I woke up hugging my pillow and realized I was ten thousand miles away. I got this awful pain in my chest. I couldn't breathe for some time. I lay there in the darkness with tears coming out like they were the source of the Amazon and Congo Rivers. Finally, I cried myself back to sleep.

Auf Wiedersehen,
Bill

Madison
November 11, 1968

Dearest Bill,

I wish we could be together, enjoying ourselves, without worries or cares. It would feel like heaven. After supper, I went to my room, sat on my bed, and grabbed my guitar. Looking out the window, I saw one little star, sang a song about it, and came up with this poem for you. Bill, just the mention of your name perks me up. You are my happiness.

OUR LITTLE STAR

Somewhere in the sky, I see,
One sweet star for you and me.
Though I am here, and you are far,
We still have our little star.
But now you're gone, and it's the dawn,
And my little star is where you are.
And when it returns to me,
On its beams, a kiss I'll see.
And when it's gone, in the dawn,
It will bring a kiss to thee.
For stars will shine through all the night,
Though the moon is out of sight.

So, our love shall glow untold,
As this ancient star of old.

Hey, why didn't you tell me you were wounded when it happened? Why did I have to find out by seeing it in your photograph? There was a lot of bandaging on your hand, and you said it was "nothing serious." So out with it, let's hear the whole story. Why didn't you get a purple heart?

I hope your camp won't be affected by the bombing halt. I read the Red troops are massing near Cambodia's border. I try not to worry about you as long as your letters keep coming.

Tell me about your work. I'd like to know what my hubby does morning, noon, and night. Please write about the average or un-average day of Sp. 4 Wagener. I'm dying to know. I like the pictures in your office because they help me visualize where you work.

I was so happy to deposit eighty dollars into our savings account today. Once I have the money saved for my plane ticket, our honeymoon is closer to becoming a reality, and I'll see you there in "Blue Hawaii," where dreams come true.

Love,
Carole

Vietnam
11 Nov. 1968

Dear Carole,

I didn't receive a purple heart because the guy with me was "technically" AWOL and was court-martialed for half a dozen things. He blunted one of the attackers and got cut up worse than I did, so he deserves a purple heart. But the hard-ass Lieutenant Colonel wouldn't recommend him for it, so I said, "If he can't get it, then I don't want it either." I'd be dead if that guy weren't there to take care of the attacker on the passenger side of the jeep. I would have been stabbed in the back while fighting the VC on my side.

12 Nov. 1968

WOW, GUESS WHAT? I got my R&R. It's for December 11–18, not December 30 to January 6, as I asked. I'm shocked! Today, I went up to the Bn. office to take and pick up distribution (military correspondence and business), and there was the R&R roster for Hawaii. On the last page of two-hundred people, the sixth name from the bottom was mine.

START THE PILL.

I'm too overjoyed to think straight. I can already feel my arms around you. I can't wait to hear you whisper in my ear silly things and serious things, to be able to swim with you and see you, all of you. It'll be so sweet, and Hawaii will be fabulous.

That was deliriously wonderful of you to send a *Playboy* calendar for my birthday. I was surprised and thrilled to get it, especially from you. When we get to Hawaii, I will love you as you've never been loved before. I will try to make you happy because you made me so happy. We won't have to be lonely much longer.

> Roses are red,
> Violets are blue,
> And right now,
> I want to screw you.

Okay. It doesn't sound pretty, but at least it rhymes.

Love,
Silly Billy

Madison
November 16, 1968

Sweetheart,

I got your SURPRISE letter today, and I was so shocked I didn't know what to do, do, do! So, I called my anatomy professor, and she thought I could make up the three labs I'll miss when I return. I have an anatomy test on the morning of December 11, and then I'll catch the first flight to Hawaii. Missing school isn't as much of a problem as I thought.

Northwest Orient offers a flight out of Seattle for service members' wives for $165. On excursion rates, it will cost me an additional $156 to fly to the West Coast. So that's a total of $310, but I only have $245 in savings. I'll call Mom and Dad tonight to see if they can loan me the money, check with the Dames Club, which offers married students loans, or steal it!

Next week, I'll start my birth control pills. But, unfortunately, they may not be working by the time I see you, so we'll have to use another form of contraceptive. But, if all fails, you'd like to be a daddy, wouldn't you?

I may be seeing you in only three weeks from the day you receive this letter. I won't believe it until I'm in Hawaii and you're there too. Oh, I love you!

November 17, 1968

Happy 23rd Birthday, Bill. You may get this card a little early, but better to be too early than late. Too bad we can't be together to celebrate. If we were, I'd plan an evening like this.

First, I'd dress up in something pretty. Then, when you came home, I'd kiss you hello, sit you down in your most comfortable chair, and bring you a newspaper and a Tom Collins to drink. After that, we would splurge on a tenderloin steak. Then, I'd bring out a beautiful homemade birthday cake after supper.

Then I'd slip into a sheer black bikini nightie and sit beside you on the sofa. We could watch television or do other things together. You know what I mean! Maybe by next year, we can complete this story and make it even better than it sounds. How about it, partner?

Love always,
Carole

P.S. It just occurred to me that I don't even own a black nightie!

Vietnam
17 Nov. 1968

Hello, Angel of the Morning,

I can't wait to hear from you about whether or not we'll meet in Honolulu.

Tomorrow is a pre-Inspector General inspection. I wish we'd have an all-out attack during one of these inspections. They are making us lock up our rifles in the rifle racks now. It would be bad if we ever got hit, and there would be no one to explain what happened. The guards on the towers might be able to slow it up enough to give us time, but it's questionable.

Chin up, Darling. I probably won't call you unless something unexpected happens, and I can't go to Hawaii, which is very unlikely.

18 Nov. 1968

You must have heard the Bishop's statement on leaving birth control up to the Catholic couple's conscience. I'm worried about the long-term health effects of the pill on you.

Gee, today, Sunday, was so groovy. I worked straight through to 13:00, getting ready for the inspection, and then took the afternoon off. It was eighty degrees with a nice breeze and no humidity. I put on civilian clothes. It was great to wear something other than Army greens. I went swimming in our pool and then fell asleep in the sun.

Did you hear about Da Nang catching hell? The Korean Tigers in Rock Valley got hit hard, too, the same night. So, we're just waiting.

Auf Wiedersehen,
Bill

Madison
November 18, 1968

Dear Bill,

My parents were so sweet about lending me the money for the trip. They said, "You're going to Hawaii, and that's all there's to it. Of course, you've got to go." Your parents were happy for us, too. Since your dad asked me how you were, I had to tell him someone stabbed you, but it wasn't serious. You know me; I can't tell a lie.

November 20, 1968

Last night before I fell asleep, I could hardly believe that I was leaving for Hawaii in three weeks. I finally convinced myself that this trip was real, I was real, and you were real. It would only be a matter of time. Being by your side and having your arms around me again will be neat. Remember, I love you, and I'm saving every speck of my love for you.

November 21, 1968

It gives me the shivers to think about how close you came to being stabbed in the back. Now I know why you didn't want to tell me. When did all this happen? Was it on the day you went to Qui Nhon to phone home? I'm glad that fellow was with you, even if he was technically AWOL.

The VC better leave your camp alone, at least until you go on R&R. I know you would hate to miss the action, but it would be okay with me if you did.

November 22, 1968

Today I bought my mini-skirt for Hawaii. You don't know how hard it was to find one with only winter clothes available. It's red velveteen and sexy. I also bought a white V-necked cotton blouse with a ruffle on the neckline to go with the skirt. Oh, I do hope you'll like it!

Number one wife, 34-24-34, requests special permission to be allowed one last leave to Birchwood Gardens on November 30, 1968, from 22:00 to 24:00. Please, Sp. 4 Wagener?

After my sister's bridal shower, a group of girls will go to the beer bar, and I'd like to go along. All the kids will be home from college. I promise to behave and not talk to my old guy friends from high school. If anyone asks me to dance, I'll politely refuse and explain that I'm married. I'll only dance with my high school girlfriend, Eleanor. Okay, Honey, can I go?

I can't wait to get home for Thanksgiving. I hope you have turkey to eat; I know how much you love turkey. We have a lot to be thankful for this year.

God bless and keep you.
Carole

Just before Thanksgiving break, my stress level was hitting the roof. I needed a break from my studies and ran down to Kitchen #2 to grab a Coke and get some ice. Janet was there, too, getting a snack.

"Hey, did you use up all the ice cubes and forget to refill the tray?" I asked, slamming the freezer door shut.

Janet shook her head. "It must be those darn graduate students helping themselves again. Look at this mess they left behind. I'm sick of it."

On the countertop were dirty plates, half-filled mugs of stale coffee, and a left-over, bloody wrapper from raw ground beef. Because Janet and I were undergraduates, we cleaned up these abysmal messes of the two obnoxious graduate students who shared our kitchen. Janet reached under the sink for a gallon of vinegar to clean the counter. I snatched the jug from her.

"Wait. I got an idea."

I filled the ice cube trays with vinegar and popped them into the freezer. Then, we carefully placed their dirty plates and cups full of cold coffee back into their side of the shared cupboard. Next, we opened salt and pepper packets and liberally sprinkled them into their silverware drawer.

I grabbed my Coke. "Let's get out of here before anyone sees us."

We ran up the back stairwell to our rooms, giggling.

Madison
November 23, 1968

Dear Mr. Wagener,

Eighteen days from today, we can enjoy our continued honeymoon just like we said we'd do on our first honeymoon. I get a pitter-patter in my heart when I think of seeing you. But I realize it will be much better than I imagine when we are together. Free sex and no taboos! The parents are out from under our feet. There's no worrying about getting caught or making excuses. It will be great fun, just you and me.

Seven consecutive nights will be the longest time we've been together in one stretch. We are beginners, aren't we? It is a good chance for us to get started on married life!

I hope you have that happy smile that you smiled the first time we slept together when you came back from Fort Belvoir. Such a happy smile, you couldn't hold it in. I thought you would start giggling from sheer joy.

I have a vision. I'm looking out the plane window and can see you standing there, frantically waiting. Then, when I step off the planc in my red mini-skirt, your eyes pop, and you jump up and down like an excited little boy!

Imagine one-hundred-forty-nine other wives on the plane; each will expect to be the first one off the plane. So you'll be standing on the runway with one-hundred-forty-nine other GIs wanting to be the first ones to their wives. It will be utter chaos!

Can you imagine all the women on the plane coming over with one thing on their minds—sex—but everyone making petty conversation with their neighbor sitting next to them on the flight? Likewise, all the men will be pacing at the airport like expectant fathers with one thing on their minds, too. Imagine when those two forces combine after being deprived of one another for three months to a year.

Planes are landing in Hawaii every day. This same thing is happening all the time, except this time, it's happening to us!

Honey, will you meet me at the airport if you get to Honolulu before me? Once I'm on Hawaiian soil, I don't think I could stand to wait a moment longer. I'm waiting patiently for time to pass, for my airline reservations to come through, and to see you, my love.

There will be only one thing wrong with this R&R; it'll be too short.

Your girl,
Carole

Vietnam
24 Nov. 1968

Hi Honey,

I've just made reservations at Ft. DeRussy on Waikiki Beach for December 11–18. Meet me at the arrival point because the changes and chances make it hard to meet at the airport. Don't worry if I'm a day or two late. Remember, there's a war going on here, and flights can't always run on schedule.

Let me know what flight you'll be on if I get there before you so I can pick you up. For God's sake, stay healthy and don't catch a cold or get sick. Wear or bring your micro-skirt.

25 Nov. 1968

You once asked me what I do. First, I order, check off, and distribute publications from Stateside to the sections. Second, I make weekly training schedules and file Army Regulations, US Army Republic of Vietnam Regs, First Logistics Regs, and Supply Command Regs. Finally, I type up re-occurring monthly and weekly reports. Some are marked "Confidential," and some are marked "Secret" and cannot have a single error or even a smudge mark.

November has been hell for me because of the inspection, but it will be over in twelve days. I still can't believe we have a review here with an ongoing war.

28 Nov. 1968

Our mail comes through in bunches now, every four or five days. Less than two weeks from now (one week for you), we'll love and love. We'll have day after day to wake up together.

Yes, I had a good Thanksgiving. I had the morning off and worked in the afternoon. I'm mailing you a card with our Thanksgiving menu and the Chaplain's message for us to read:

Far from the Thanksgiving of our childhood, we find ourselves this day not at the family table enjoying the turkey, companionship, and thoughts of yesteryear, but at a new table with other friends and different thoughts. The more mature Thanksgiving that this year has brought us has found us in a place we had not expected, facing an exacting challenge. We have found ourselves in a world that does not measure up to our childhood standards, a world in which a basic ideological conflict requires us many sacrifices and strenuous endeavors. Can we not find, however, in this situation the real meaning of Thanksgiving, the reality of a hard-won and hard-kept peace for ourselves, our families, and our nation? Can we not thank God for this day with a true realization of the value of our several blessings? Have we not learned to be truly thankful?

Honestly, I will never forget the price of freedom. God bless you always, Carole.

Bill

It was a miracle the military approved Bill's R&R, as he'd barely been in Vietnam for the one-hundred-day qualification period. I was looking forward to the trip, but being on an airplane was a new experience for me, including flying over the ocean.

The girls in my P.T. class were extremely jealous that I was allowed to cut class and miss a quiz (probably more so knowing that I'd be on my honeymoon), and the fellows embarrassed me by saying, "Did you know Carole's going to Hawaii to get a lei?"

CHAPTER 9 - DECEMBER 1968: A FULL MOON, EMPTY ARMS

Vietnam

2 Dec. 1968

Hi Angel,

Boy, the work here is tremendous. I'll be so glad when the Inspector General's inspection is over.

I should be arriving in Hawaii at noon on December 11. Then I'll have to wait nine hours for you. Ugh! Too bad you couldn't get there sooner. When you get this letter, we'll be only two days apart.

Love you, Babe,
Bill

Madison

December 2, 1968

Hi there, Sugar,

My plans are complete for my Hawaiian trip. I'm perfectly healthy, with no colds or flu, and I'll be through with my period. My government check arrived today so I can buy that special surprise for you. This time you won't be yelling, "Take it off!"

You know what? I love you to pieces.

I was surprised to hear about the ambush on the tank you were riding in—your life threatened for the third time. Things would be fine if you would stay in your office and not be hitchhiking around to go sightseeing. God must be protecting you because if he weren't, you'd be an angel in heaven by now. Do be careful, Honey.

Only a few days are left when you get this letter, and we'll be together. I try not to think about it as I get too excited and can't study. But we're going to have to make every day count. So, I declare a cease-fire for one week, which means no arguments.

You know what else? I have a one-track mind. It reads HAWAII. Nine days to wait before I can see my great, wonderful husband. It's a short time, but it feels like an eternity.

Your impatient wife,
Carole

The beginning of our second honeymoon in Hawaii wasn't as I'd imagined in my fertile mind. Instead of a flight full of military wives going to see their horny husbands, it was a quiet flight onboard United Airlines out of Los Angeles with only one other solitary military wife on board. As there weren't many passengers, I moved to the plane's rear and sprawled out over three empty seats. That morning, I'd taken a killer anatomy test, finished packing, and boarded a flight from Madison to Chicago, transferring to Los Angeles and Honolulu. Despite my excitement, it was a long day. The time change topped it off. Finally, tired, I lay down, and the plane's vibrations lulled me to sleep.

An hour before the flight landed, I padded in my stocking feet to the restroom and changed out of my bulky winter sweater and wool pants into my white cotton blouse with the ruffled collar and the red velveteen mini-skirt. As I disembarked the plane, the stewardess commented, "What a transformation. You look great! Won't your husband be surprised to see you?"

I anxiously walked down the tarmac, awaiting my husband's first romantic hug and earth-shattering kiss, but Bill wasn't there. Perplexed, I maintained my cool, gathered my luggage, and caught an airport limousine to Fort DeRussy, an old U.S. military base in Honolulu, where we planned to stay. As I checked in, Bill snuck up behind me, and suddenly I was in his arms.

"Aloha. How's my girl?"

"Bill!" I melted like hot butter into my Bill, wearing a bright Hawaiian shirt to show off his suntanned muscular arms. My eyes welled up with joy as his almost star-struck, sparkling brown eyes looked down at me.

"Carole, I'm sorry I wasn't at the airport to meet you. Some guys invited me to go to that new outer-space movie, *2001: A Space Odyssey*."

I pulled away, annoyed. "Why didn't you wait for me? We could have gone to the movie together."

"I expected your flight to be late. I thought I could still get to the airport on time, but the movie was three hours long." He sheepishly took my hand. "Let's get settled in. I bought some snacks for you."

Bill grabbed my suitcase and held my hand as we walked down the hall to our room. He unlocked the door and pulled on the light bulb chain from the ceiling. A small drab room with dingy brown walls appeared, sparsely furnished with a double bed, a nightstand, and a dresser. It had a musty odor and no air conditioning. The warmth from Bill's hand instantly disappeared.

So, this is it?

I set my bags on the bed, checked the dresser drawers for cockroaches, and decided not to unpack. I could no longer hide my disappointment. First, Bill stood me up at the airport, and now this poorly substituted rendition of a motel room—a converted World War II officer's barracks.

"Bill, this is our honeymoon! We can't stay here."

"Now, don't be upset, Honey. This afternoon I checked out a brand new hotel with a beautiful rainbow tile mosaic on its side. It's just down the street and right on the Waikiki " Bill hugged me and assured me that he would use his military discount so it won't be too expensive.

"This is just for one night."

Feeling deflated, I shuffled to the bathroom, changed into my everyday pajamas, and climbed into bed. The mattress springs poked me in the ribs, creaking every time I moved. Bill curled up next to me and put his arm around me. Soon I felt Henry poking me too. But I was exhausted and immediately fell into a deep sleep with a disturbing nightmare

> *My cocoon-wrapped body feels as cold as the white snow banks outside the window as I hear muffled footsteps and heavy breathing and feel a presence beside my bed. Is someone touching me? Down there?"Stop it! Go away!" I cry out, waking up just as the softness of my downy quilt is pulled up and tucked in under my chin. My eyes pop open. It's old Hank, our hired man. What's he doing in my room? His*

beady eyes peer down at me. "Shh! Don't say a word," he whispers before sneaking away, leaving behind the pungent odor of his beer breath, which lingers in my mind until the next time…

I awoke, covered in sweat, heart hammering through my chest. Moonlight, streaming in through the window, illuminated Bill's form sprawled out on the bed beside me, reorienting me back to Hawaii. I took my husband's hand and held it in mine, wishing I could tell him about my family secret.

Hunch-backed old Hank lived with us and helped to pump gas and tend the store. When I was eight years old, Hank asked me to sit on his lap. I accommodated him until I grew older, and he became bolder, trying to fondle my sprouting breasts.

How many times had a "drunken" Hank "accidentally" wandered in and out of my bedroom, which was previously his room? Sometimes, I awoke and told my mom about him in the morning. But, of course, Hank denied it, and soon, I despised him.

Dad finally stopped Hank's shenanigans when he caught him standing beside my bed, pulling up the covers. So, had I been sexually abused or just harassed? Remembering my frequent yeast infections, the abuse most likely occurred while I slept. And after Hank's unwelcomed visits ceased, my genital irritations miraculously disappeared.

But Hank was long gone, so why did I experience this reoccurring nightmare? When could I tell my husband that I was afraid of a man's touch because of Hank? Now was not the time, with Bill resting so peacefully. I curled up next to him, still holding his hand, and fell asleep.

The following morning, Bill and I dragged our luggage down the path alongside a white sands beach to the Hilton Hawaiian Village Rainbow Tower. When we entered the lobby, I noticed the hotel had a restaurant, a beauty shop, and a camera/gift store. What little treasures would I find there? While Bill checked in, I browsed through a rack of muumuus, slipped on a flashy ankle-length floral dress with a pink ribbon at the empire waist, and purchased it for a future special event.

Happily, our honeymoon suite was brightly decorated in a Hawaiian theme and featured a queen-sized bed, a color TV, a table with two green chairs, and a private balcony with glass doors that allowed the morning light to stream in. We stepped onto the balcony to drink in the view of Waikiki Beach and

Diamond Head, and my attitude instantly changed to radiant anticipation. I pinched myself. Yes, I was in paradise with my husband and felt utterly content for the first time in months.

Sadly, my contentment was short-lived. Having just come from the cold climate of Wisconsin, the weather was miserably hot. The humidity caused my neck to sweat from my long hair, and I wanted to cut it short. Maybe it was a sign of my growing independence, but, on the other hand, could I have unconsciously wanted to discourage Bill's sexual advances by making myself less attractive?

I called and made an appointment at the hotel beauty shop. Bill tried to talk me out of it, but I insisted on cutting my hair. While he sat and watched with furrowed brow and slitted eyes, I held my finger up to my earlobe and told the operator I wanted a short bob. It was hard to miss Bill's unhappy face when he saw the finished product—my new pixie hairdo. Nevertheless, I relished the feeling of being able to deal with the elements and having some control of my life.

When we went for brunch, Bill insisted on sitting in the chair facing the front door at the restaurant. "Since Vietnam, I can't sit with my back to the door in case someone tries to attack me from behind," he explained.

It seemed overdramatic, but later, as I learned more, I realized how those few months of war had changed my soldier-husband. Realizing we both needed to unwind, I suggested a relaxing evening.

"Can we sign up for the steak dinner cruise I saw advertised at Fort DeRussy?"

"I'd love a steak. The base only serves SOS—shit on a shingle."

In our room, Bill took off his shirt and lay quietly on the bed, watching TV while I unpacked our belongings. Maybe this would be a good time to tell him about my nightmare. But then, in the gleaming sunlight, I noticed small white lines glistening on his lower back. I sat on the bed next to him and touched the well-healed scars. Why hadn't I noticed them before?

"These scars on your back aren't from Vietnam, are they?" I asked.

"They're from the belt buckle Mother used to whip me."

"She beat you? Why didn't you tell your father?"

"Nine months of the year, Dad was sailing on the Great Lakes and wasn't around very much. But one summer, when I was big enough, I grabbed the belt away from Mother and threatened to beat her back. So that ended the whippings, but I still hear her telling me every morning, 'Billy, you're no damn good, just like your father.' I can't get her words out of my head."

"I'm so sorry. That must have hurt." I stroked his back.

In that moment of vulnerability, I understood that Bill had his own childhood demons to overcome. Unfortunately, sharing my problem would have to wait for another time.

With my housekeeping chores completed, we took a long walk on Waikiki Beach and eventually sat on the sand, watching the waves lap the shoreline. I sat in silence as Bill boyishly knelt and made drip sandcastles. We hardly talked as the sound of the ocean waves quieted the outward annoyances between us. Finally, on returning to our room, I asked Bill if he was angry with me for cutting my hair.

"That's partially it. But after three months in Vietnam, I'm having a hard time adjusting to being back in the States."

The truth was that after three months apart, I had difficulty adjusting to being together as husband and wife. But I just nodded and murmured that I understood.

At sunset, we walked back to Waikiki and embarked upon a catamaran cruise with a small group of other tourists. With its two parallel hulls and sails, the catamaran skimmed along the calm water like a stone skipping across a pond. A tropical breeze guided us while millions of white shimmering diamonds glistened from the setting sun upon the clear blue water.

An elderly Hawaiian man strummed his ukulele and serenaded me. While he sang "Pearly Shells," I sipped on a Mai Tai, pampered like the last queen of Hawaii, Queen Liliuokalani. After a delicious ribeye steak dinner, the catamaran returned us to shore with the moon silhouetting the Diamond Head volcanic cone in the distance.

No wonder so many newlyweds came to Hawaii for their honeymoons. The word romantic felt like an understatement in describing the island's ambiance as it embraced Bill and me. The heavenly sights and smells of orchids, plumeria, and hibiscus flowers, so exotic, filled every inch of air around me.

As we strolled hand-in-hand back to our hotel, it felt like dé já vu, as if Bill was walking me back home to my apartment in Green Bay. I couldn't help but fall in love again—with Bill and then with the islands. In my heart, I forgave him for not meeting me at the airport and his earlier insensitivity to me cutting my hair.

That night, I slipped into a light-blue babydoll nightie, my surprise gift for Bill. He asked me to pose for pictures. Later that moonlit night, we made passionate love using extra contraceptive protection in our beautiful island getaway.

Over the following couple of days, we enjoyed typical tourist activities. We took a bus tour and visited Pearl Harbor, where we enjoyed a boat ride to the *USS Arizona* Memorial. We shopped at a famous Hawaiian clothing factory. Bill bought Christmas presents for his family, Hawaiian shirts for the men, and a carved wooden jewelry box for his mom. He'd also bought duty-free bottles (purchased cheaply in Guam) of vodka, Champagne, and Red Herring, which I had to hand-carry back to the States as gifts for the remainder of the family.

Another young couple we'd met on the sunset cruise invited us to hike at Sacred Falls in Koolauloa. They picked us up in a rented car and explained that it would be a beautiful two-mile hike to the falls along a lush green tropical forest. At the end of the walk, we could swim in a pool at the foot of the falls.

As we entered the river gorge with its 1,400-foot steep sides, our friends encouraged us to lay a leaf on the ground and place a stone on it to show respect to the Hawaiian god of this valley and ask for his protection. *Say what?*

As we began the hike down, I noticed the warning signs for flash floods and rock avalanches, but it was too late to turn back. Bill, a seasoned hiker in the Boy Scouts, made me feel confident we could make it there and back in one piece. The jungle-like trail ran alongside a stream with slippery rocks. Bill took my arm and helped me cross.

"I'm not going to twist an ankle," I said, holding onto my walking stick and confidently picking my way along the rocks. A country girl, I was sure-footed and accustomed to rough terrain.

Still, it was a treacherous slippery hike. Around every bend, we hoped to hear the laughing sounds of the waterfall. But, when we finally arrived at Sacred Falls, we found a disappointing trickle of water coming out from an eighty-foot rock embankment dripping into a small pool beneath it.

I dipped my toe into the water and swiftly pulled my foot back. "Burr. We risked our lives for this?"

Bill laughed. "Be grateful we made it. Now you know why it's so sacred!"[17]

On day four, Bill and I took private surf lessons in Fort DeRussy Beach's shallow waters. When our instructor said, "Stand up," I did and felt proud to out surf my husband until I fell off my board. I only knew how to dog paddle and struggled to swim back to shore.

Then, in a near panic, I yelled to Bill, "Help me."

Floating on his surfboard, Bill shouted, "Stand up, Carole." So, I stood and embarrassingly found myself in only four feet of water.

On our fifth day, Bill and I attended a Hawaiian luau and ate poi, fermented taro root, which tasted like wallpaper paste. However, the fresh, juicy pineapple made up for the poi we renamed "phooey." Afterward, we walked to the International Market Place at the edge of town and purchased a souvenir that would fit in my suitcase: a beautiful, black velvet painting of Diamond Head with a full moon above it. We planned to hang it in our first apartment in Madison. When we were apart, Bill and I had this saying, "A full moon and empty arms," but our arms were full of heady, perfumed dreams this particular night.

On our final day in Hawaii, we rented a car and drove the Kamehameha Highway to Oahu's scenic North Shore. We stopped to watch the incredible twenty-foot waves at the Banzai Pipeline surfers' beach. We also toured the Polynesian Cultural Center and learned about the cultures and traditions of six Pacific Island nations, including Tonga, Tahiti, Fiji, Aotearoa, Samoa, and Hawaii.

On our drive back to Honolulu, we rounded a curve on the country road to discover a small herd of dairy cattle, a scene that wouldn't have been unusual in Wisconsin, but this was Hawaii. We stopped to take photos for the folks back home. When a bull mounted one of the cows, Bill grabbed his movie camera out of the car.

"This will make a great home movie for the folks." Bill laughed.

I walked away in lady-like disgust. *And what am I supposed to say when the folks see these two cows humping?*

That last night back in Honolulu, Bill insisted we check out a particular bar. I wore my new muumuu, and Bill wore his Class "A" uniform. We entered the bar, sat at a table, and ordered our favorite Mai Tais. As we sipped pineapple juice mixed with rum, I looked at the entertainment on the small stage.

"I can't believe it's our last night together, and we end up here at a topless bar."

Bill had a coy smile on his face. "Some of the guys told me not to miss this."

The belly dancer must have noticed how handsome Bill looked in his dress uniform and tried to entice him onstage with her gyrating hips. She finally gave up and laughed while nodding at me.

"This one won't let go of her husband's arm."

She was right. I was terrified of losing my beloved GI.

As the full moon shone over Diamond Head, we walked back to the Hilton, linked arm-in-arm. I knew that come tomorrow night, it would be a full moon and empty arms again. So before I lost my nerve, I suggested something I'd been thinking over all week.

"There's something I've been meaning to ask. Will you fly back to Wisconsin with me? From there, we could run away to Canada and seek asylum."

Bill abruptly halted in his steps, turned, and glared at me.

"Sonofabitch, Carole. Do you mean to become a deserter? Are you crazy? I will not spend the rest of my life in prison at Fort Leavenworth. I'd rather die honorably in Vietnam."

Heartbroken, I knew there was nothing more I could say or do to convince Bill to go AWOL. Bill turned away and walked down to the ocean while I ran back to the hotel, crying.

Numb, I accompanied Bill to the airport the following day to await his flight. When it came time to part, I hugged him and laid my head on his warm shoulder, sobbing uncontrollably.

Will I ever see you alive again?

When other passengers began looking our way, Bill took me by the shoulders and said sternly, "Stop crying, Carole."

Bill's harsh words stung and caused another torrent of black tears filled with my mascara. By our final embrace, Bill boarded the Pan American[18] flight back to Vietnam, swiping at his tears.

As soon as Bill was out of sight, I found a bathroom and ran into a stall, continuing to weep. I hiccupped, occasionally coming up for air, and cried until no tears were left. Then, finally, the cleaning lady in the bathroom called out to me.

"Missy, are you okay?"

I came out and explained that my husband had just left for Vietnam. Then, glancing in the mirror, I saw a sad-faced clown with red eyes and long black streaks running down her cheeks looking back at me.

I ran some water to rinse off the mascara, then gathered up my heavy liquor bag and, in a daze, walked back to the gate to wait for my flight to Los Angeles. There I would spend Christmas with my brother—but without my husband.

On December 27, I flew back home from Los Angeles via Chicago to Manitowoc, a small town about forty miles southeast of Green Bay. We landed to let passengers off, and I remained in my seat, looking out the plane's window.

I couldn't believe my eyes. It was snowing heavily, and our copilot climbed onto our tiny plane's wing using a tall ladder. Then, he swept the deicer onto it using a bucket and a broom.

Oh my, should I get off now? But I couldn't get off. My parents were waiting for me in Green Bay.

The pilot finally announced, "We're cleared for takeoff."

I tightened my seatbelt and continued looking out the window. Then, miraculously, our little prop jet flew right through the snowstorm, above the clouds, to where the dark star-studded night sky was amazingly clear. We had a smooth flight and landed safely in a snowy Green Bay.

At Austin Straubel Airport,[19] I found Mom and Dad waiting at the gate, expressing relief that I had made it back for Cheryl's wedding. Dad grabbed my suitcase, brought up the car, and then skillfully drove us home to Alaska through the drifting snow.

Snuggled up in a woolen blanket in the back seat, I talked nonstop about our wonderful time in Hawaii, leaving out the embarrassing part about the mating cows. That could wait until homemovie night.

The following morning, I awoke to the sound of someone sobbing. I slipped on my bathrobe, wandered out to the kitchen, and found Cheryl sitting at the kitchen table, eyes red from crying. Mom was on the phone.

"What's all the commotion about?" I asked as I poured myself a cup of coffee.

My sister grabbed a tissue and blew her nose. "I can't get married."

"What the hell? You changed your mind?"

She pointed toward the window. Huge snowdrifts covered the entire porch and backyard.

I choked on my coffee. "Goodness! We're snowed in."

"I wish we'd eloped instead of planning this big wedding! Mom's talking to the minister to see if he can marry us tomorrow, and then I have to phone all the guests." She put her head down on the kitchen table, her body shaking as she sobbed.

Maybe she should have listened to Mom and Dad's warning not to have a winter wedding.

The snow postponed the marriage by one day. However, I wasn't too upset because I had an extra day to rest, read Bill's awaiting letters, and write back. I hoped he received the Christmas card I'd mailed from Los Angeles.

Vietnam
19 Dec. 1968

Hi Angel,

I'm writing from Cam Ranh Bay. I hope you get this by Christmas. We have some good memories to help hold us through these last months. I enjoyed being with you in Hawaii. I was pretty proud of your surfing triumph. That surfing is out of sight.

Although I didn't say much about Vietnam, you were very understanding that day at the beach when you didn't say anything and watched me build sandcastles. I appreciated that. Nobody knows better than I how it hurts to fear something [like getting killed in Vietnam] and try to have someone else understand.

God bless you, lighten your heart, and bring Christmas joy to you, Darling. I hope you and your family enjoy yourselves the entire season.

Everything is quiet here, so don't worry. I'm taking an early flight back to Qui Nhon tomorrow.

Bill's Christmas card message to Carole.

It may seem sad now since we will be apart for eight and a half months, but Darling, remember, the next time I come home, I won't be leaving anymore. That's my consolation knowing that the Army is over and past the next time I leave Vietnam. God bless you and keep you safe, snug, and secure until this coming fall when I get back home.

Bill

Los Angeles, California
December 21, 1968

Dearest Bill,

Indeed, I wish you a Merry Christmas this year. Even though we are both far from home and each other, perhaps we can still have a happy Christmas.

On this day, let us not forget the true meaning of Christmas, for this is when Christ, our Savior, was born. Perhaps by keeping the true meaning of Christmas in our hearts, we can have a joyous holiday without all the frills.

All my love to you on this Christmas Day,
Carole

Back home, after just being in the tropics and now in the freezing snow, the harsh weather made it feel more like being in the state of Alaska than Wisconsin. Sixteen inches of consistent snow had fallen in just two days. All day Saturday, I helped Dad shovel snow. Then, finally, at long last, the snowplow made it through at 4 p.m. to open up the roads.

Despite the freezing arctic temperature, I was determined to have a blast and had hoped to dance my heart out at my sister's wedding on Sunday, but fate intervened again. The night before I left Hawaii, I stubbed my little toe on a chair leg and broke it. I'd be lucky to make it down the aisle in heels.

While Cheryl and I dressed in the bedroom we'd shared as children at my parent's home, she warned me about the groomsman, Charles. He was her fiancé's best friend from the Navy, and although we'd never met, he was to be my escort for the day.

"Watch your step with that one," Cheryl said. "Charles is a big flirt and drinks way too much."

"Thanks for the warning, but he knows I'm married, right?"

I studied my reflection in the dresser mirror. Even with my short pixie hairdo, I looked like a princess in the empire-waist, floor-length gown which hugged my slender body. Its scooped neck and dark-blue velveteen bodice accentuated my small breasts, and when I took a step, the light blue crepe skirt audibly swished. Putting on my pearl earrings and cross necklace, I felt like Cinderella.

Being married, I didn't expect to be caught off guard by a groomsman who happened to be single. However, when we met at the church, I found Charles friendly, witty, sophisticated, and captivating. Good-looking like a young Paul Newman in a black tuxedo and a white shirt, he moved quickly among the bridal party. When the ceremony began, I couldn't help but smile as Charles walked me arm-in-arm down the white-carpeted aisle.

Cheryl's bouquet of red roses shook in her hand as she and Dad followed us to the altar. Once there, I straightened her long white veil so it flowed gracefully down the steps, and she handed me her bouquet.

I snickered when Pastor Weis, our elderly minister, asked her fiancé, "Do you take Carole to be your lawfully wedded wife?" Cheryl quickly corrected him. Fortunately, the remainder of the wedding service went off without a hitch, and then we headed to Hillside Gardens for the reception.

After the sit-down dinner and cake cutting, my toe throbbed. While everyone else danced to the live band, Charles and I sat alone at the Bride and Groom's table. I removed my right shoe and elevated my sore foot on an empty chair. When Charles asked what was wrong with my foot, I chatted about my recent trip, wanting to make sure Charles understood I was married.

"Two days ago, I flew back from seeing my husband in Hawaii on his R&R. I loved the beach, the sun, and the feeling of the tropical breeze on my skin. But on my last night there, I broke my little toe and had to wear flip-flops in California."

I paused to take a breath. "Have you ever been to Hawaii?"

"No, I was stationed on the *USS Compass Island*, a navigational research ship on the East Coast." An awkward silence followed before he asked, "So, you visited California, too?"

I explained my brother settled in California after his stint with the Navy, and I stayed with him at Christmas. That broke the ice as Charles told me one hilarious story about his life in the Navy.

"You know, we sailors cuss a lot. I forgot that when I came home for Thanksgiving. Our entire family always says grace before a meal, passing the food around the table. You should've seen Mom's face when I asked her to 'please pass the fucking mashed potatoes.' She passed them so hard it was like catching a fucking football."

He made me laugh as I relaxed. Cheryl was right about Charles being captivating, but she was also right about his flirting. He repeatedly reached over, stroking the top of my foot, and his forwardness made me distinctly uncomfortable. I was too timid to tell him to stop touching me, so I sent him to the bar to get me a drink each time he did. Unfortunately, they didn't serve

Mai Tais in Wisconsin, and the screwdriver was the only other mixed drink I knew.

"Charles, would you get me a screwdriver?" Using my most sophisticated voice, I added, "Have him put it on the rocks."

I was twenty years old and legally only allowed to drink beer, but the groom's parents had paid for a free bar, and the bartenders didn't bother checking IDs. As a result, Charles made frequent trips back and forth to the bar, refilling my glass. I lost count of how many orange juice and vodkas I drank.

When the wedding party was invited to the dance floor for The Bride's Dance, I kicked off my other shoe to dance in my stocking feet. My toe stopped throbbing, but my head was spinning to the tune of the screwdrivers.

"I'm dizzy," I said when I stood up. I asked Charles to take my hand as I walked sophisticatedly onto the dance floor, trying not to zigzag.

The alcohol and the music transported me to a fantasy world where I became Cinderella at the ball. Prince Charming steadied my balance and held me in a tight embrace. I closed my eyes and placed my head on his chest, listening to his quickening heartbeat as he guided my drunken feet across the slick, wooden dance floor. Tingles ran up and down my spine when Charles pressed his cheek against mine, breathing into my ear and effortlessly waltzing me around and around. At the end of the dance, a long deep dip left me breathless. Then, when I came up for air, I felt his kiss glaze my cheek.

Oh, oh! Now I'm in trouble.

When I opened my eyes, they locked onto my best friend from high school, Eleanor, sitting alone on the sidelines. She hadn't brought a date to the wedding and so danced only with her sisters. *Maybe I could pawn Charles off on her?*

I separated myself from Charles and motioned to Eleanor. "Ellie, come over here and join us for the *Schottische*."

Charles glanced from Ellie to me. "The shotish? What the hell's that?"

I explained to Charles that the *Schottische* was a fun Bohemian folk dance I'd learned as a child. It was a bit like the polka but more like a line dance.

"The night is young," I said, linking onto Charles's right arm. "Come on, El."

Eleanor skipped over to us, demonstrating the one-two-kick dance, and linked onto Charles's other arm.

I patted his arm. "See how easy it is?"

After that dance, Eleanor joined us at our table, so I felt safe, and before I knew it, midnight arrived, and the guests began to disperse. Charles told me he'd had a wonderful time and asked if I needed a ride home. That's when my fairy godmother, Mom, showed up out of nowhere.

"Carole, you're drunk! Get your shoes and coat. Dad and I are taking you home."

The following day, I awoke to a splitting headache, a sore toe, and the painful memory of my shameless behavior the night before. I downed tomato juice, but it took a whole day to recover from the hangover and a day and a half to recover from my sudden infatuation with Charles, my fantasy prince.

Thank God I never heard from Prince Charming again, but I did hear from my aunt, who phoned the next day to criticize my drunken behavior while dancing with Charles. Auntie reprimanded me.

"Carole, you'd better start acting like a married woman."

Auntie was right. There was no turning back the clock. So instead of celebrating with my friends, I spent New Year's Eve at home with my parents, resolving not to get drunk in 1969.

Vietnam
30 Dec. 1968

Dear Carole,

I saw the Bob Hope Show or the first part where Ann-Margaret came on, but then they said we had to leave because it was getting dark. I also attended a Lutheran-Vietnamese church service that morning and helped the Chaplain deliver food packages to the local people.

The show was at Phu Cat Airbase. I had a good seat next to the stage on top of the roof of a small building. Too bad I couldn't afford a movie film, but I was down to my last dollar. I did get some close-up pictures in black-and-white still film.

We have a new commanding officer. I had to pull guard duty the other night because some guys complained about getting it every third night or every other night, and then reactionary duty on top of that.

We have begun our second major step towards interplanetary travel [Apollo 8]. Isn't that something?

Hey, I miss you something fierce. Rest up and enjoy the snow. I wish I could go skiing in the worst way. God keep you safe. See you in eight months.

Love,
Bill

Alaska
December 31, 1968

Dear Bill,

My last letter of 1968. Tomorrow we will be in the year when your time in the service will be up. Hooray!

We have been snowbound, so our mail wasn't picked up or delivered yesterday. I was disappointed as I was hoping to hear from you, not that your letters have done that much to let me know you love me like the steamy ones you used to write during your basic training. Those letters were long and loving, but I know you're busy. So, please keep them coming. If they must be short, then let them be more often.

Remember I told you I'd be standing up with my future brother-in-law's friend from the Navy? Well, his name was Charles. Anyway, I danced and drank too much at the wedding. The following day despite my hangover, I still felt captivated by all the attention Charles had given me, but I think I'm over him now. So, if you hear about it from someone else, don't worry, okay?

I don't think Hawaii truly reflected married life for us. It all started on the wrong foot, so to speak—the first night and the last morning. It wasn't the way I pictured married life to be. It was all a rush, and you seemed preoccupied with sex. I didn't want to deny you because I knew you deserved every morsel I could give you for being true to me and not going to the clap shacks. But I feel so bad because it seems like I failed to satisfy you.

Oh, Babe. I wish you were in my little bed to keep me warm tonight and hold me tight because it's minus twenty-three degrees outside. So, I'll imagine you're here and snuggle up close to my pillow to stay warm.

Loving you, missing you, and kissing you in my dreams,
Carole

PICTURES

1 - Bill Wagener

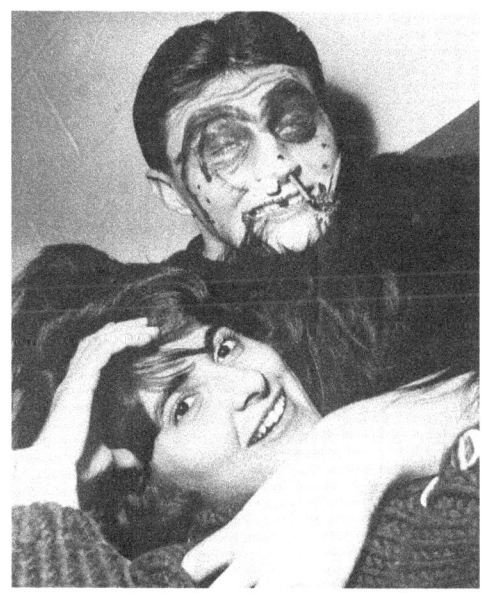

2 - Ugly Man Bill With Victim, UWGB (October, 1966)

3 - Carole Wagener P.T. Student, UW-Madison

4 - Bill And Carole's Wedding Day, Sturgeon Bay, Wis. (September 11, 1968)

5 - Bill at the 160th H.E.M. Co. Army Base, Cha Rang, S.V.N. (September 1968)

6 - Bill in full army gear

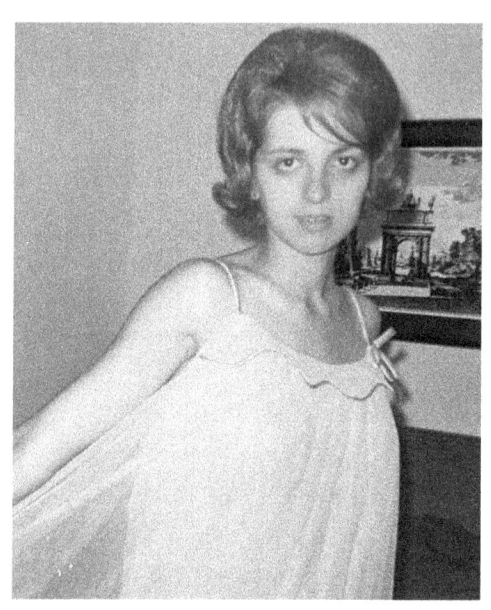

7 - Carole's Look of Love

8 - Thanksgiving Day S.V.N. (November 28, 1968)

9 - Bill and Carole at Hilton Hawaiian Village, Honolulu (December 12, 1968)

10 - Cheryl L., Matron of Honor, Bridesmaid Carole (December 29, 1968)

11 - South Korean Tiger, (left) with Wagener

12 - Bill in Office With Stack Of Military Regulations

13 - Bill at the 865th Gas Generating Plant, S.V.N.

14 - S.V.N. Family, Son L., Father, Mother

15 - 1969, Middle Class Family, Boa Binh, Binh Dinh Providence, S.V.N.

16 - Water Buffalo In Rice Paddy

17 - Qui Nhon Pagoda. S.V.N.

18 - Office Buddies, Arnold L., Bailey, Wagener (in Hawaiian shirt), Thorm (seated)

19 - Caldwell L., Greene, Wagener

20 - Cam Ranh Bay Buddies, Wagener In Foreground

21 - Bill In Helicopter Pilot Seat

22 - A.F. Cargo Plane, Phu Cat Air Base

23 - Unhappy Bill Leaves R&R In Thailand (August 1969)

24 - GIs Leave Bangkok On Pan American Flight

25 - Diesel Truck Explosion (August 1969)

26 - Welfare Mothers Demonstration at Wisconsin's Capitol (September 1969)

27 - Bill Taunts National Guardsmen, Madison (September 1969)

28 - Carole L., Twins Rebecca and Rachael, Visit Apartment House In Madison (2005)

29 - Carole and Bill Behind the Alaska General Store, Alaska, Wisconsin

30 - *The Wall that Heals* - March 29, 2018 (Credit: Malinda Lodge Photography).

PART II

CHAPTER 10 - JANUARY 1969: UNHAPPY NEW YEAR

After Christmas break, I returned to UW-Madison. With finals hanging over my head and not getting enough sleep from worrying, I awoke with a stomachache and ran to the dorm's shared bathroom. I had just finished washing my hands when Janet arrived.

"Did you sleep any better last night?" Janet asked as she busied herself, washing her face.

I opened my bag and started applying my makeup. "I couldn't fall asleep—just lay there thinking for a long time."

"Ooh, look at those dark circles under your eyes. Here, use my concealer."

"I forgave Bill for enlisting because I knew he was afraid of being drafted."

I put the concealer onto my lower eyelids and patted it in. When I handed it to Janet, she pushed my hand back. "You need a second coat."

Janet was right. I resembled a raccoon.

"But I can't forgive him for volunteering to go to Vietnam when he could have stayed safe at Fort Belvoir. If only he'd taken that teaching position they offered him, I'd have married him on the spot."

Janet's eyebrows shot up. "So why in the world didn't he take that promotion?" I guessed she questioned Bill's sanity as much as I did.

"One night, out of the blue, Bill called and said he'd thought about it some more and wanted to serve in Vietnam. I couldn't talk him out of it, as he'd already signed the papers. I was so mad I could've strangled him with the phone cord."

"I would've killed my fiancé if he did that to me. So why do you think Bill wanted to go?"

"Maybe he wanted adventure, or he watched too many damn John Wayne movies," I said, brushing my teeth.

Janet smiled, back-combing her hair. "You mean he wanted to become a hero?"

"Maybe he needed to prove himself—to become a man."

"Or fight communism?"

"That's a strong possibility. But, on the other hand, maybe the Army brainwashed him, and Bill thought fighting communism on a foreign shore was better. Anyway, I had no say in his decision."

"Maybe he wanted to see the world?"

"Hilarious, Janet. Who'd want to go to that bug-infested country and get shot at?" I gave Janet the stink eye. I always blushed when I got angry, and now my face was red.

"Well, why didn't you ask him?"

"I did, but I couldn't believe his answer. He told me he wanted to get as far away from his abusive mother as possible."

"That's just crazy. So, why'd you marry him?"

"Maybe 'cause I'm the crazy one," I shouted, grabbed my toiletries, and ran out of the bathroom door in tears.

With the honeymoon over, I dealt with the uncertainty of not knowing whether Bill would come home alive, injured, or in a body bag. I resented that he'd chosen to go to Vietnam over his love for me. If he'd stayed at Fort Belvoir, I'd have happily married him, moved to Virginia, and finished college on the East Coast. But I was never given that choice.

Since Bill joined the Army, it was a series of comings and goings. But, like in the popular long-distance love song, "Leaving on a Jet Plane," my heart broke a little more every time he left me behind.

Vietnam
3 Jan. 1969

Dear Carole,

Hooray! I'll get out of the Army this year. I got your Christmas card on December 23. I forgot about your sore toe. Xin loi! (Sorry about that!)

Henry has been dead since the last time you saw him lively. He hadn't bothered me much except when those girls came on stage at the Bob Hope Show. Henry showed only a twitch of interest, but Bob Hope sure has it made!

The former clerk here, Sp. 5 Jillian, came back from the States from his thirty-day leave. He extended for six months and transferred to a different unit. In five days, he's going to the Mekong Delta to the 1st Calvary. I went drinking with him and some other buddies last night—beer, bourbon, whiskey, and 90-proof gin—I thought it was water. Of course, I shouldn't have gone overboard, but what the hell? It's probably the last time I'll see Jillian again.

I was so drunk that I thought this bus was backing up at me, so I attacked it. That explains why my left hand is swollen, bruised, and sprained this morning. It hurts! At some point, I passed out. When ammonia salts didn't arouse me, the guys carried me to my bed. When I became conscious, it was 08:00, and I'd missed reveille.

15 Jan. 1969

You sound like you want me to be jealous of Charles. First, you mention he was just an escort. Then, you say it was a momentarily close and innocent friendship in your following letter. Finally, in the third letter, you tell me you were infatuated for one and a half days.

Well, that's okay, as he's probably a more likable guy than I am, and besides, I trust your character completely. You couldn't be unfaithful in the least, even if you wanted to be. You wouldn't know how to start, and you'd be afraid. Your inner glowing coldness towards men scares them off. Even if someone told me you tried to rape Charles, I wouldn't believe them. So, you can stop making explanations for whatever happened.

I've got to admit I love you in a way I can't turn off, but I think I represent security to you. If I'm dead, you get $10,000 in life insurance money. If I'm alive at the end of this war, you get a lifetime of being a Missus. Oh, I think you love me, too, in a more or less unselfish way, but a large part is to hang onto security.

It may sound cold, but I'm honest about how I think you feel about me. The sad part is that I'll love you to a certain degree, not because I want to, but because I can't help myself.

Bill

Madison
January 16, 1969

Hi Honey,

Guess what I watched on TV tonight? *The Bob Hope Christmas Special.*[20] I saw the part filmed at Phu Cat Airbase and some small buildings off the stage with men standing on top. They didn't take any close-ups of those fellows, so I couldn't tell if you were one of them. Then, they showed the part where four girls in miniskirts sang a song about how I want to make you happy.

I was thrilled to think I probably did see you and enjoyed the show, as it made me feel we were sharing it. Seeing how you didn't watch the ending, I'll tell you how it ended. Linda Bennett sang the first stanza of "Silent Night," and everyone joined in for the second stanza.

It was sad to see all those GIs so far from home, but they looked delighted to see the show and fussed over all the girls. Someone in the audience held a sign that read, "Where There's Girls, There's Hope."

January 18, 1969

To: William Jon Wagener

I do believe there is a conspiracy around here to make me unhappy. Monday will be a week since I've heard a word from you. You'd better have a good excuse. What's wrong? I hope everything is fine and that nothing is seriously wrong. I shall begin to worry if I don't hear from you by Monday. Take good care of yourself. Don't work so hard for the Army, but please put in a little overtime on me.

Be good.
Carole

P.S. Clap shacks are still a No-No

I'd gone days without even a postcard from Bill, and his January 15 letter pissed me off when he insinuated that I couldn't even attract a guy or be unfaithful if I wanted to be. How dare he tell me how I felt? He made me sound unappealing to men. So why the hell did he marry me if he thought that?

Friday night, after my last final exam, a group of my old friends from UWGB invited me to a going-away party for our friend, Michelle. We met at the Amber Grid in Madison. I arrived fifteen minutes early and walked into the smoke-filled room with "I Heard it Through the Grapevine" playing overhead. I didn't see my friends but did notice a two-guys-to-every-girl ratio.

A tall blonde gentleman, around thirtyish, wearing black horn-rimmed glasses, walked over, greeted me, and offered me a beer that he pronounced *bier*. I surprised him by saying, "*Ja. Danke.*" [Yes. Thanks.]

"*Sprechen Sie Deutsch?*" [Do you speak German?]

"*Ein bisschen.*" [A little]

We spoke in German, and he told me his name was Daniel Mueller. He was from Switzerland and was working on his Ph.D. When he finally asked my name, I couldn't lie.

"*Frau* [Mrs.] Carolyn Wagener."

With a perplexed look on his face, he said in English. "You look so young. How old are you?"

"I just turned twenty."

"I would never have guessed you were married. How long has it been?"

"Four months."

"So, tell me now, do you enjoy being married?"

Such a personal question felt like an invitation. "Ah, that's difficult to answer as my husband's stationed in Vietnam."

Luckily, my friends arrived, and I waved to them from across the room. "*Entschuldigung, bitte* [Excuse me, please], Daniel."

We four girls found an empty table with two chairs and begged for two more chairs from the guys sitting next to us, and they asked to join us. One sat by Michelle and Susie, and the other by Molly and me.

After conversing about where we were from and what we were doing in Madison, the fellow talking to me asked, "Are you going steady with anyone?"

I held up my left hand, wiggling my ring finger. "Sorry, but I'm married."

Well-endowed Molly laughingly played along, showing off her fake engagement ring that she wore to discourage potential suitors. "And I'm engaged!"

"You won't believe this," the poor guy said. "But this is the second time I started talking to a girl this week, and she was married."

That conversation ended abruptly as he and his friend moved on. Then three more guys approached us, and a cute brunette guy sat down next to me. In no time at all, he found out that I was married but decided to stay and talk anyway. But, as my husband would say, the dark-haired fellow talking to Molly had "Roman hands and Russian fingers."

"Anyone gotta pee beside me?" Molly asked.

"I do." I gulped down the remainder of my fourth beer.

"Whoops," Molly said as she stood up quickly from her chair, knocking a full glass of beer into roaming hands and rushing fingers' lap.

Molly and I made a beeline to the restroom. "What the hell, Molly? That guy seemed to have the hots for you."

"He was drunk. Did you see him trying to touch my boobies?"

We passed the bar area, where I noticed Daniel still had his eye on me. Other fellows were wolf-whistling and catcalling from the sidelines.

"Hey, Toots!"

"Hi, Beautiful. Say, are you from Illinois?"

"What the heck, Molly?"

"Ignore them, Carole. They won't bother us when they find out you're married and I'm unofficially engaged."

We went to the bathroom without being detained, but the alcohol suddenly hit me, and I could no longer walk a straight line back to our table. Finally, Molly offered me her arm and helped me sit. Then, Michelle suggested it was time to leave, and I objected.

"It's not even midnight! Why can't we stay longer?"

"I have to catch an early flight out to North Carolina tomorrow for my internship at a Black college," Michelle said.

As we approached the door, Daniel came to say goodbye.

"*Fraulein*, I can give you a ride home if you wish to stay longer."

"*Nein*. My friends will walk me home."

"Let me help you with your coat."

I slipped on my jacket and headed for the door. "*Auf Weidershen*, Daniel."

Molly held tightly onto my arm as we walked along the icy sidewalk of University Avenue back to my dorm. The frigid night air sobered me, but the alcohol hit again when I opened my door. As I dropped to my bed, the four bare walls spun around me like being on a Tilt-A-Whirl.

The following morning, I awoke with a pounding headache and found myself still in my street clothes. Had all the blood in my veins been replaced by alcohol?

As I recuperated from my second hangover, I reread Bill's letter telling me that he thought I needed a man in my life for security. If I need a man, at least now I know where to find one—the Amber Grid—because last night, I acquired a new self-confidence to replace "my inner coldness."

And how rude of Bill to insinuate I married him for his $10,000 life insurance policy! *How could he think that of me*? After reading a bit further, I realized all my talk about Charles had finally made an impact. *Haha! Bill's jealous*. I swallowed an aspirin with a glass of water, sat down, and wrote another letter.

BANG—I got you. You may think it's cruel of me to have been trying to make you jealous, but I knew if I could, then I'd know you loved me and make more of an attempt to show it to keep me.

Remember how I wanted you to say you loved me that night when you told me how you felt about your dad and grandpa—that you loved them more than me? All I wanted to hear was that you loved me. I wouldn't have cared if you'd lied, but I needed to hear those three words.

So please, tell me how you'd feel if Gramps or I died tomorrow, at whose funeral would you cry more? Sometimes, Bill. I think you're only trying to fool yourself.

Then I wrote a detailed account of my night out with the girls at the Amber Grid, walked down to the mailbox, and dropped the letter in. But the following day, I felt remorseful, so I wrote another letter to apologize.

Madison
January 22, 1969

Dear Bill,

I may have been rude to you, and that's why I'm writing again so soon. I realize now what I said in two pages yesterday, I could have stated in just one paragraph.

"We girls went out and met some guys. They left me alone when I told them I was married."

No, but what did I do? I gave you a play-by-play action of the entire evening in hopes of making you jealous.

So, if I succeeded in making you jealous and unhappy, I'm extremely sorry, because a week from now, I'll be sad when I get your letter in answer to mine and two weeks from now, you'll be unhappy when you get my response, and so it will go back and forth. So, please, Honey, don't be too unhappy about it.

I've been exhausted, depressed, and lonely for you. Life on campus with finals got so discouraging for me. When things got tough, I missed you ten times more.

I sure wish you were here now.
Carole

Then the following week, I received two more letters from Bill. Unfortunately, misunderstandings often occurred in our letters. Aware that my period was late again, Bill jumped to conclusions.

Vietnam

18 Jan. 1969

Dear Carole,

I hope I didn't hurt your feelings. That's the last thing I wanted to do, although I often do. You're a fine girl, wife, and young woman. You tried hard to please me in Hawaii, but I was so grumpy one morning that I put you down for this and that.

I'm sorry, Honey. God bless you, Darling. You're terrific.

Say, am I going to be a Papa or not? You haven't said anything lately in your letters.

23 January 1969

The 54th and 43rd Battalions, two miles down the road from us, got mortared and machine-gunned the night before last. The choppers were called in; one dropped flares from way up, and the other two shot fifty-caliber rounds and rockets at the enemy. Boy, the helicopters socked it to them. The sky lit up like the 4th of July. We didn't go on alert until it was all over, and that was just a practice alert. In the morning, they found several VC bodies, which was unusual since the enemy had all night to carry them away.

I'm fine, kid, so don't you worry.

Bill

Madison

January 24, 1969

Dear Bill,

I was so glad to hear from you yesterday. Mail must be getting held up somewhere. It's taken days for your letters to arrive.

I almost fell off my chair when you said, "I'm glad you're p.g." I had to do a double-take. I don't know how you came to that conclusion. Sorry to disillusion you, Honey, but I'm not pregnant.

Love,
Carole

Vietnam
25 January 1969

Dear Carole,

Being in Vietnam has depressed me. This duffer of a 1st Sgt. took a gander not to promote me to E-5. I'm pretty pissed off lately.

Maybe I love you as much as before, but I don't feel the same anymore. Perhaps it's Vietnam and all the misery here. I don't write fake letters about how deeply I love you. I don't feel bad because I don't want to lie. I hope I get over this lack of feeling.

One thing I'm sure about is that you'd have been better off if we had broken up and not married. I made you so unhappy in Hawaii. You were also miserable last Christmas, sitting and watching me work on my family tree book. Poor you! You got screwed in more than one way.

I know this letter won't get out any sooner because the bridge between Qui Nhon and us was blown up. No mail, no milk, no fresh foods. Those men who are DEROS-ing [date estimated for return overseas] must wait beyond their discharge dates. Our mail here is piling up, too. I don't care if it piles up as long as it gets out and doesn't get captured by the VC.

I hope you appreciate the beautiful snow in Madison. I'd give an entire month's pay to have seven inches of snow in one day.

Be good, and do well in school.

Bill

Madison
January 28, 1969

Dearest Bill,

I'm enclosing an article I read in *Reader's Digest* magazine,[21] "What Sex Means in a Happy Marriage." I underlined a few things that pertained to us as a couple.

I underlined the part about "the greater the pleasure we enjoy today, the greater the pain we suffer tomorrow if we lose the person who gives us pleasure." In a way, it's the only sex we have known—making love for one or two or three nights and then realizing we will be apart for four to five months again.

And on the last page of the article, "From earliest childhood, girls are taught, mostly through fear and guilt, to restrain their natural drives. Once the female body has been inhibited this way, it cannot be set free in one night, in one week, or one month—a young girl is fortunate if her complete liberation occurs in one year."

Know I was a virgin when I met you. It may take me longer to warm up to you as some inappropriate things happened to me in my childhood and may have warped my attitude about sex. So, please give me lots of time to adjust to married life.

Gee, I miss you.
Carole

Vietnam

31 Jan. 1969

Hi Dum, Dum,

I'll bet you think I'm a bum for not writing. Don't sweat it. I haven't been to a clap shack. So, you don't need to worry, okay?

I'm disappointed. I wish you hadn't made me think Billy Junior was on the way. Two weeks ago, I had his whole childhood planned, from varsity wrestling in his freshman year to Eagle Scout in his senior year of high school, and now nothing.

Since this is how it is, let's keep it this way until we have spent a summer grooving in Germany, Europe, and California to get the traveling bug out of us. Okay!

No one has shot at me in a long time. Today I went to Phu Tai scrounging for office supplies (stencils, mimeograph paper, etc.). Then I drove two warrant officers out to Rok (Rock) Valley. You know what? They went to helicopter flight school in Waco, Texas, one cycle before me. I crashed their pre-flight party and danced with the same girl they did. Groovy, huh?

Please check with the university and see if I must return on probation status. If I'm on probation, I won't be able to leave here early.

Love,
Bill

Alaska
January 31, 1969

Dearest Bill,

Hey, listen, you didn't make me that unhappy in Hawaii, and just think, we still have a lifetime and fifty years of marriage to make it up to one another. So, cheer up. It's you I love, and I'm glad we didn't ever break up.

I read the letter that you wrote my parents. Sadly, one fellow had to get killed needlessly because the CO wouldn't permit your camp to help. It might have saved his life; it's a terrible thing. I worry about your safety when I hear things like that. If Charlie tries anything, I hope you bomb the life out of him.

I listen to the news about the fighting in Vietnam, but outside of the action around Saigon, I hear very little. Today, I searched the *Press-Gazette* and only found one article about US planes bombing Laos. I hear the most news from you, but your letters are few and far between. I suppose the mail isn't going as it should with the bridge out.

I could tell by your letter to Mom and Dad that you missed me. But I'd appreciate a sweet, romantic letter that I could repeatedly read when I'm lonely for you. I'm starting to feel numb from missing you. There's nothing I can do about it but wait. I long to kiss you again, have you here to tease me, and hold me close.

I still find it difficult to believe we're married when we can't be together, see, or speak to each other. Now I merely exist and wait for you to come home and bring me life. I perk up at the mention of your name. I wonder what your homecoming will be like in seven and a half months, but waiting for you feels like an eternity.

It's hard for me, sitting back here in the safety of my home, to understand what life is like for you. I know it is dangerous, so take care and don't leave your typewriter unless Charlie comes in the front gate! Every day I hope and pray for your safety.

Forget about the E-5. I'll love you just as much as an E-4. But, honey, it doesn't matter what your rank is in life. It's how you played the game.

God bless you and watch over you tonight and always.

Carole

CHAPTER 11 - FEBRUARY 1969: ALL HELL BREAKS LOOSE

Madison, Wisconsin
February 8, 1969

Dear Bill,

Today there was a demonstration at the basketball game. Students stood at the main doors of the locked gym, yelling, "Reinstate the Oshkosh Blacks." All this business about the Oshkosh Blacks started at Thanksgiving when a hundred Black students at the University of Wisconsin-Oshkosh got arrested for breaking into school buildings and destroying equipment.

So, Janet and I found another open gym door. There was a small group of protestors outside that door, but the National Guardsmen wouldn't allow them to get close. One of the soldiers escorted us to the door by showing our tickets.

When we entered, police wearing helmets and carrying nightsticks filled the gym. It was scary, like something I'd read about in *The Daily Cardinal*. The gym was packed, and Janet and I had to climb to the top bleachers to find seats.

A group of Blacks walked single file around the basketball court, trying to disrupt the game. Soon the crowd booed. Finally, students stood on the bleachers at half-time and yelled, "Go home! Go home!" That's when the cops escorted the Blacks out of the gym.

This well-organized group even used walkie-talkies. Later, we heard of a few broken windows, four arrests, and the Governor's car tires slashed.

Yesterday some Black Power groups broke into six classrooms and tried to disrupt them by overturning wastebaskets. Because students wouldn't engage in a fight, nothing serious happened, so no one was arrested. It burns me up, though, that a few Blacks looking for trouble should make a bad name for the Black students here for an education and not an education in tearing down the campus in thirty minutes or less.

I hope some of the goodie boxes I sent have arrived. I must run now.

Love,
Carole

Vietnam
12 February 1969

Dear Carole,

Today, I got more of your goodies and two letters from you. I like your picture in that blue velveteen dress you wore for your sister's wedding. You looked so pretty. I love the photos of winter back there. I love you, love you, and love you (broken record—are you tired of it yet?).

Do you realize I'm almost at the halfway point from the time you get this letter? February is going fast for me because of my Russian History class and the preparation for the Tet Offensive.[22] Don't worry about me, though; everything is fine.

Love you,
Bill

Madison
February 12, 1969

Hi Babe,

I watched the news last night. I didn't hear much about Vietnam, but Madison made the national news on Walter Cronkite and the Huntley and Brinkley news shows. Governor Knowles called out the National Guard to assist Madison City and Dane County police due to the Black Student Strike. Unfortunately, the news media made it sound worse than I saw. Still, due to the anticipated strike, the Madison campus buses have closed [to prevent students from tipping them over].

There hasn't been much disruption, just kids trying to block traffic on campus. But Tuesday night, they tried to take over Bascom Hall, Van Hise Hall, and the Commerce and Social Service Buildings, and the police kept them out. So, there are now three hundred police officers and nine hundred

National Guardsmen on campus. They will be about equal to the one or two thousand students striking.

I just heard on the radio that Black leaders say groups like the left-winged Students for a Democratic Society and other revolutionary groups have taken advantage of the Black cause. That does sound like trouble, so I don't blame the police for being prepared. There are police officers here from twenty-two other cities and sixteen other counties. Tomorrow the police force will be from 1,200–1,400 men strong. Holy cats! It costs $1,200 per hour for all this protection.

Love,
Carole

Demonstrations on the UW-Madison campus became everyday occurrences, with the antiwar protesters, the Teaching Assistants Association (TAA),[23] and the Blacks Rights movement sometimes joining forces. Being on the medical side of campus sheltered me from most uprisings, but I read about them in the student newspaper, *The Daily Cardinal*.

On February 13, 1969, *The Daily Cardinal* reported that TAA resolved to support the Blacks by participating in a three-day sympathy strike as their demands allied closely with the TAA. The TAA's demands were more student-faculty control over education and the power to negotiate for themselves, i.e., form a union.

UW's Vice-Chancellor Young said his main disagreement with the demands concerning the control of the Black Studies Program was that it should not be autonomous and out of the university's control. He urged the readmission of the seventeen suspended Oshkosh Blacks, but the Chancellor overruled his decision.

Vietnam
13 Feb. 1969
Hi Angel,

How's my girl? I just heard about the riots and picketing on the Madison campus. I hope it didn't interfere with your studies.

Say, girl, be good to yourself as well as being good. Go out with your friends and enjoy yourself at the Amber Grid but don't let any guy get his "Russian hands and Roman fingers" on you. Dance if you like, but not slow ones.

I trust you, Honey, completely. Henry has lost interest in life, and so have I, bit by bit.

Take care, and get ready. I'm coming home in seven months or less.

Love,
Bill

Madison
February 15, 1969

Hi Babe,

I guess we have both been slack in writing lately. I've only gotten one postcard in four days.

Yesterday a girlfriend of mine's boyfriend returned home from Vietnam. Just thinking about it, I got all excited for her. They haven't seen each other for one year. Her boyfriend was stationed around Saigon and in a lot of fighting but came home without a scar. So see to it that you make it home safe, too, okay?

I imagine you'll be busy now with Tet going on. I've been watching the news, and it sounds like Charlie's going for an all-out offensive again this year. I hope you don't see much of it, and if you do, I hope your camp wipes out Charlie.

Love,
Carole

Hundreds of Army National Guardsmen dressed in full uniform now occupied Madison. On their first day on campus, the soldiers set up two machine guns at the top of Bascom Hil, which they later removed. Mom called me daily to tell me how worried she was and what she'd heard on the news. I assured her the medical side of campus was safe as most of the unrest occurred on Bascom Hill, where the liberal arts classes were.

I laughed when I saw a military truck in front of a laundromat one morning. But, of course, even the military needed clean underwear. When I walked home for lunch, I counted thirty police officers marching single file, headed to the Field House to eat. In the evening, it was common to see Army trucks parked on University Avenue, loading up Guardsmen. Even Bob Hope joked about the campus uprisings. "Did you hear about the National Guardsman on campus so long that he earned a degree?"

But whenever I saw the uniformed National Guardsmen, I thought of my husband. While students rioted on Madison's manicured streets and lawns, Bill lived under inhospitable conditions in the muddy Central Highlands of Vietnam.

The day was almost over, and I still hadn't found the hard contact lens I'd lost in my room that morning. The lens was expensive, and I wasn't giving up until I found it. I turned the radio on to keep myself company.

"You're listening to the late-night news on WLS-Chicago…"

Crawling around on all fours on the worn green carpet gave me a new appreciation for the American GIs dressed in camouflage uniforms in the Vietnamese jungles, searching for VC fighters. I combed the shag carpet with my hand, like doing a sweep in the tall elephant grass, looking.

Where is it?

"Today is February 22, the end of the week-long Tet Offensive…"

I grabbed my flashlight. Down on my tummy, I shone the light under my desk, in slow motion like a searchlight, until the lens appeared.

Got ya!

"Yesterday in Vietnam, seventy cities and bases were hit in a show of force by the North Vietnamese Army."

Oh no. Not Bill.

Madison
February 22, 1969

Dear Bill,

I wasn't going to write until I heard the eleven o'clock news. I feel like your base was hit, but I also have a feeling in my bones that you weren't hurt. I pray my woman's intuition is correct and that you're okay. I'll buy a newspaper in the morning and see what more they have to say.

Please don't let the war get you down. While listening to your audiotape recording, I detected something worrisome in your voice, like you were trying to make yourself sound happy when there's little to be happy about. It's too bad Vietnam has to be such a miserable place for you, day in and day out.

I'll try to make you happy by sending you lots of Rice Krispie bars, and if there's anything you desire, shoot. I'll do my best to send it ASAP.

Yesterday was one of my best days when I listened to your voice tape recording. It was like falling in love with you all over again and going through the same symptoms. I could hardly force myself to study today. I absolutely can't wait to have you home, my sweet, sensitive lover.

Love,
Your Angel

Vietnam
21 February 1969

Dear Carole,

Less than two hundred days left when you get this letter. I haven't written for the past three days as the mail wasn't going out anyway. Tet's officially over now, and I'm still in one piece. We got mortared, and three rockets hit, but the casualties were light. They hit a few barracks, the mess hall, and parked trucks. There wasn't any ground assault on our location, but a convoy down the road was pinned down. At the office, we received a radio call for help, but they wouldn't let us go out because of our weak perimeter defense.

I was with the CO's driver, Austin, at the time. I'm not sure who talked who into it, but we took off in an amour-plated three-quarter-ton truck with a fifty-caliber machine gun mounted on it. We appropriated two M-79 grenade launchers and all the grenades we could grab.

When we got down to the main gate, it was shut and locked. The security guards wouldn't let us through until we told them we were under the Bn. CO's orders to help the convoy. They only half-believed us but let us through. One security guard joined us while the other called the Bn. to check out our lie.

When we arrived, there were VC on the bridge. Austin drove straight at them. You should have seen those brave NVAs jump when we hit two of them. The convoy was half a mile farther down the road. Austin told me to open up with the fifty-caliber machine gun when we got there.

By then, the gooks were already stripping the convoy's first two trucks, the drivers' bodies, and their guards, so I shot right at the convoy. Unfortunately, the VC shot out our headlights, so I didn't know if I killed any gooks until we found their bodies later. Unfortunately, that string of ammo lasted only fifteen seconds, as in all of the excitement, we'd forgotten to bring extra ammo.

Then I opened up with our M-79 grenade launcher. Scary! It was rather cold and chilly, but I was sweating like Niagara Falls. Sweat kept pouring into my eyes. Austin was brilliant and drove right up to the convoy. By this time, they'd shot out our tires, too.

Most of the VC were on the west side of the road and too close to hit straight on with the grenade launcher as the grenades need to go at least thirty-eight yards before they explode. So I shot the grenades practically straight up to come down directly on the VC. Those grenades are bad news. In about three minutes, Charlie was hauling ass.

Then it was fun as I could shoot straight at them with the grenade launchers. I could see their silhouettes in the moonlight as they ran away, but a single sniper kept us there until morning. We were too afraid to move as he kept circling us, and we never knew from where he was shooting.

Then, finally, when daylight broke, we could see the sniper about three-quarters of a mile away, running through the rice paddy. A chopper went after him. Did you ever see a person running scared with a 'big bird' shooting at him?

In the morning light, we could see the half-stripped bodies of our GIs. Those VC bastards believe a person can't go to heaven if defiled, so they cut the ears off of our dead GIs. I think I shot one dead gook on the back of the second truck. There were six dead gooks, and five dead Americans. Most of the convoy was injured.

The senior NCO said the first half of the convoy (seven trucks) would have been taken by the VC and men killed, perhaps the whole convoy destroyed. No one else came to help them for a while because the choppers weren't there yet, and our compound was still being mortared.

I know you'll feel awful when you read this, but I feel much better now that I've told someone. My dad was so disappointed when I dropped out of the U.W. and then washed out of helicopter flight school that I can't tell him this. But you can tell him if I go to prison for disobeying orders. Worrying my Dad makes no sense because I might get off the hook. I strictly forbid you to say anything to my dad or your folks, as our parents tend to stick together.

I'm so tired, and my neck hurts. I'm too scared and too worried to sleep because I'm waiting for word on a trial. There's a meeting at the Bn. to decide if we three should be court-martialed for leaving the compound.

I don't think I've ever been so miserable in my whole life. All last night, I was crouched behind a half-inch steel plate, sweating and ducking down. And now I may go to prison for all that risk, trouble, and danger.

How can the world get turned upside down in one night? I thought if I did this, it might win me a promotion or a Commendation Medal. Funny how I was so worried about a minor upgrade to E-5. Now I couldn't care less. I want to erase the last twenty-four hours. It's been one long nightmare.

Late last night, Austin and I thought we'd be heroes; instead, we may be convicts. I can't blame anyone but myself because I suggested going out when I heard the negative reply for assistance on the radio. No one was around to stop us because everyone who wasn't at the guard post was ducking into ditches and bunkers.

My CO thinks the worst they'll do is bust me to Pvt E-1 and sentence me to six months in the Long Binh Jail. However, they'll probably suspend the six months in prison and restrict me to the compound as my CO needs me in the orderly room. At least, that's what he said when he left for the meeting.

If there's a trial, it'll be at least a month away. Sitting here and writing, I've recollected my cool. I'm not all nervous as I was before. Remember to keep this to yourself, and don't tell our parents unless the worse happens. If it bothers you as much as me, you can tell your confidante, but no one else. I don't want people to know I may be court-martialed.

I just thought of something else. If I get a suspended sentence, I won't get the GI bill for school. Oh shit. I'm so tired.

I'll let you know what happens. Right now, I'm restricted to the compound. I can't go down to photograph the convoy's wreckage, but I can photograph the destruction on the post, so I'm going to do that instead.

Keep your cool, and study hard.

Bill

I reread Bill's letter about the possible court-martial and paced my dorm room like an expectant father. I had to tell someone. Maybe I could tell Janet on the way to church. At the sound of her first knock, I yanked the door open. Before Janet could say hello, I grabbed my purse, jacket, and gloves.

Janet furrowed her eyebrows at me. "Ready for church? Do you wanna walk or take the bus?"

"Let's walk."

I locked my door, and we ran down the front stairwell together. The weather was cloudy but mild as we headed toward University Avenue. I put on my gloves and pulled the fur-lined hood of my jacket over my head.

"What's wrong, Sweetie? Are you sick?"

I shook my head.

"You don't look okay. What is it? Something's wrong with Bill?"

I sniffed, trying to hold back my tears. "I'm sworn to secrecy."

"Whatever in the world? It's that bad?"

"But if I have to, I can tell you, my confidante. Bill's being court-martialed."

Janet stopped dead in her tracks, placed her hands on her hips, and fixed her eyes on me. "You've got to be kidding me. After what he's put you through, and now this? Court-martialed for what?"

I threw up my hands. "Disobeying orders, stealing a machine gun, and a three-quarter-ton truck."

"What the hell? Was he making a run for it?"

I started walking again, faster, while Janet hurried to catch up.

"It was the last day of the Chinese New Year, and Bill's base was under attack. A radio distress call came in from a convoy pinned down by a bridge. Bill overheard that they were taking on casualties." I took a deep breath. "But his CO responded he couldn't send anyone to help."

"Oh, that's awful. Then what happened?"

"Bill did the dumbest thing. He talked the CO's jeep driver, Austin, into going out with him to rescue the convoy. Austin drove the truck."

"Slow down," Janet said, puffing. "I can't keep up with you."

I shortened my stride. "Austin lied to the guards, drove to the bridge, and Bill gave the VC hell."

"Sounds like a war movie."

"More like a horror movie." As I told Janet the rest of the story, tears rose.

"Oh, Carole. Was he hurt?"

"I don't think so."

"Sounds like he wanted to be a hero, though."

"Then he should've joined the Green Berets. He could have got a medal on his chest."

Janet stopped me, grabbed me by the shoulders, and spun me around to face her. "Bill's up against some pretty serious charges here—"

"I'm so worried that he might be in the Long Binh jail or on a plane headed to Fort Leavenworth."

"But in battle, sometimes lines get blurred."

Then Janet hugged me as I broke down and sobbed on her shoulder. By telling Janet, a weight lifted off of me. Finally, I pulled away and wiped the tears from my cheeks.

"I'm scared. Will I ever see Bill again?"

"You will," Janet assured me.

"Whew, I must look a wreck."

Janet sounded like John Wayne when she said, "Aw, you look fine, Missy, minus some eyeliner." She handed me a Kleenex from her purse.

I laughed through my tears and wiped the mascara off my face. "Janet, you're such a good friend. I'd better stop crying before my tears turn into icicles."

We resumed walking with only the sound of our boots sloshing through the melted snow. When we rounded the corner of Wisconsin Street, I saw the stone walls of the solid stone-built Norwegian Lutheran church. As we got closer, I read the placard out front.

God is our refuge and strength, an ever-present help in trouble. Psalms 46:1.

Janet looked at her watch. "We're early. Let's go inside, warm up, and take a few minutes to pray."

I put my pinky finger out to Janet. "Promise me. You'll never say a word of this to anyone?"

Janet entwined her little finger with mine. "Pinky promise. Mum's the word."

"Thanks, Janet. I knew I could trust you. I feel better now."

I lit a candle for Bill in the foyer and then went inside and sat down in a wooden pew. Looking up at the old wooden cross in the front of the sanctuary, I admired the colorful stained glass windows surrounding it and then knelt at the pew and prayed.

"Our Father, who art in heaven...."

Vietnam
22 February 1969

Dearest Carole,

I found out today I won't be getting a court-martial unless I demand one, so they can't try me later. I hope I didn't upset you too much. The important thing is you know that I'm off the hook. I still might get busted to E-3 or even E-1, but it would be an Article 15 for leaving the compound against orders and not a court-martial.

I'm going to sleep a lot better tonight. I don't think I'll lose more than one stripe, though, as I told the CO I would work in company headquarters for PFC pay or go down to the acetylene and oxygen plants to work. But they might need me up here at the office, so I may not lose any rank, but I'm not counting on it.

If I don't get home in time to start school, I thought I could work and keep saving money until you're finished with school. Then we could move to California, and I'd start fresh at a new school. That way, we'd be near my sister and your brother. We could go surfing, visit relatives, and eat at topless restaurants!

Remember the groovy, sunny day we took a rowboat ride on the lake? I guess memories are all I have to live for now.

Hey, Angel, I adore you. You're too good for the likes of me, but I'm being very good to make up for it. I send all my love.

24 February 1969

I got your big Valentine's card today. Thanks ever so much.

We were mortared last night at the 540th Bn. Depot, Location 42. Our Bn. didn't get hit, but the two are adjacent. I spent the night in a foxhole guarding part of the perimeter. The night before last was the same thing. Casualties were light. I'm okay and only got a few scratches on my right leg. Tonight will probably be the final attack if there's any at all.

No mail will be going out today, so I'll write to you tomorrow and tell you I'm fine. Have you mailed the Hawaiian films to me yet? Is that the surprise for me in the package? I hope so.

I wasn't too fond of the chocolate Rice Krispie bars you sent, so I gave them to my CO. He ate all of them and then said he's not giving me an Article 15 or a bust in rank because the incident's been forgotten as so much worse has happened since then. I'm off the hook!

I'll have more free time when we get off this alert—gray and yellow and red status—back on gray. Then I'll make and send you another audiotape.

Bill

Madison
February 25, 1969

Dear Bill,

This is the hardest letter I'll ever write you. I hope the meeting at the Bn. went in your favor. I hope your CO was correct when he said the worst thing that could happen would be to drop you to an E-1. By the time you receive this letter, you'll know what your future holds.

Honey, don't stop caring about yourself, your life, and the men around you. Bill, after I read your letter, I remembered that verse you sent me:

"Dear Lord, I may not understand

The way Thou leadest me.

Suffice to know that Thou, oh God,

The path ahead doth see."

And remember, Honey, whatever punishment they give you will be punishment enough for you, so don't keep punishing yourself.

Didn't you ever read that a hero doesn't ever plan on being one? It just happens, so don't try to be a hero again. A hero isn't looking out for himself and all the honor or promotion he can get. A hero is trying to save another person's life and doesn't care what glory it brings him. By the sound of your letter, I think you realize that now.

Carole

Vietnam
26 February 1969

Dear Carole,

I'm sorry that you received only one postcard in the past four days. I've been busy dodging mortars for the past two weeks. I'm still all in one piece, so whatever it's worth to you, I'll be coming home in one piece.

Please check with the UW-Madison administration, and see if I can start school there without probation. For example, if registration is on September 1, I'll get an early out and be home in the middle of August.

I read the articles you sent about the antiwar riots on campus. I'll keep my thought to myself until one of those bums gets in my way.

As of today, I'm off this permanent reactionary guard duty. I'm glad, too, after being in the perimeter and in and out of bunkers for four nights in a row. I've learned the meaning of bunker existence and saw a few guys earn their Purple Hearts (some posthumously). I only lost one friend, so I can't complain too much. I knew him, but not that well. Yesterday afternoon, I took movie pictures of the awarding of two Purple Hearts.

For now, I want you to know the worst part of the tour in Vietnam is over. I'm safe, and you can count on me coming home. In around one-hundred-ninety-nine days, a giant bird will sweep me from this blood-stained country and carry me home

Boy, I keep looking at the photo of you sitting on your brother-in-law's lap. He had better hide your sister when I come home, or I'll get my revenge.

Your loving hubby,
Bill

Madison
February 27, 1969

Hi Bill,

I sure was glad to get your letter today that everything is all right. Knowing you were off the hook was a relief, a big load off my mind.

I hope you stay in your office as it's safer and more interesting work than making oxygen and acetylene. What VC in his right mind would like to blow up an office, but what VC wouldn't want to blow up an acetylene plant?

There was trouble on campus again today. Windows were broken in Van Hise Hall, and stink bombs thrown into classrooms. Someone set off a fire alarm, but there was no fire. The police and National Guardsmen came and stopped it. I'm getting tired of all this, and I don't see the reason for it anymore.

Saturday is March 1, so the time is soon coming, and you'll be six months through and six months left to go. Again, I love you and miss you.

Love your girl,
Carole

We were at the halfway point, and Bill was counting the days—199 days left. As the Vietnam War escalated, the antiwar protests on campus heated up, making safety for both of us my ultimate concern. While the rockets and mortars exploded in Vietnam, so did my thoughts. The emotional stress took a toll on my physical body, causing headaches during the day and nightmares at night.

CHAPTER 12 - MARCH 1969: ROLLING IN THE MUCK

During the day, I went to class, then home to eat, rest, and study. But night terrors kept interrupting my sleep and had me rolling in the muck.

Austin rolled the vehicle up to the bridge and stopped. With the truck's tires shot out, they were sitting ducks. He crouched behind the steering wheel as a bullet whizzed past his helmet. If only he'd had his M-14 rifle along, he could have picked off that sniper, but instead, he yelled to Bill in the back, "Use the Thumper."

Bill loaded the grenade launcher mounted on a tripod in the truck bed, ducked down, and covered his ears. Thump. Bong. The grenade flew straight up and landed about thirty-five yards in front of the truck. Boom! Suddenly Bill clutched his chest and shook his head to clear the haze that filled his eyes. Bright, red blood oozed out between his fingers when he looked down.

"Austin, I'm hit, I'm hit," Bill yelled, slumped forward onto the grenade launcher, and passed out.

I began to stir from my sleeping state. *No, no, Bill. Please don't die.*

I rolled onto my side, leaned over, and held back the urge to retch.

Where am I? Is someone knocking on my door?

I thought I heard them say, "Mrs. William Wagener, I have a telegram for you."

God, I asked you to keep Bill safe. So why did you let him die?

The pounding increased.

Who's there?

I threw off my damp covers, my heart pounding in rhythm with the thumping on the door.

"Who is it? What do you want?"

"Wake up, Carole! You're going to be late for school." Janet's voice brought me back to the reality of my dorm room.

I flung open the door. "Janet, I had the most god-awful dream. Thanks for waking me."

I meant that in more ways than one.

Madison
March 2, 1969

Dear Bill,

I had two letters waiting for me today when I returned from class. I'm so glad to hear things have quieted down. I'd die if anything happened to you.

Wow, the war's horrible! How did you slash your leg? Was it bad the week of Tet? Oh, Bill, I hope the VC doesn't overrun your base.

From what I hear on the radio, it sounds like the offensive is still on. I'm so scared because of how bad it is around Saigon. Have you had action, too?

I hope you stay in your safe, snug, and busy office. I'm relieved that the Lord has answered my prayers and that you kept your job, rank, and no Article 15. I did tell Janet, but no one in our family.

Mom and I went to the hospital to see Grandpa last night. He turned eighty-seven on Ground Hog's Day, February 2, but now he's in his final stretch. All that tobacco he chewed gave him esophageal cancer even though the doctor said he had the heart of a twenty-year-old man from chopping wood. It's sad to see him die, but there's nothing anyone can do when death comes knocking.

Grandpa asked about you and when you would be home. He didn't realize you'd be gone so long.

Lover, I'm off to bed in my blue nightie. Nighty, night.

Carole

***

Vietnam
2 March 1969

Dearest Carole,

You liked my audiotapes, huh? I'll be sending you another in four or five days. By then, my tour here will be half over. Only one hundred ninety-five days left when I wake up tomorrow.

I'm off restriction, but I don't know if I'm getting a court-martial or not. The SFC [sergeant first class] said if we hadn't gone out, they would have lost the first seven of seventeen trucks in the convoy to the VC. That was his opinion, not mine. Too much happened after that, so it seems insignificant now. Don't worry. I doubt very much that I'll go to jail. I'll just take what I get, as I would do the same thing again if I had it to do all over.

They're having a real battle about forty miles north of here. I saw about twenty Air Force planes take off from Phu Cat Air Base within five minutes.

I laughed when I heard the news. Our government has finally decided it's an offensive, and maybe they'll have to start bombing North Vietnam again.

Yours,
Bill

Years later, Bill explained how he got out of trouble from that long-term event:

Our perimeter was weak that night, and two enemy soldiers had gotten onto our base, one killed and one escaped. The Battalion Commander didn't find out until the next day that I disobeyed orders to rescue the convoy. That probably made him look bad, so he forgave my error. The Sergeant from the convoy had expressed some thanks, so it was all played down.

Vietnam
5 March 1969

"And on the third day," Bill said, "Why the hell aren't I getting any mail?" Well, the day ain't over yet. I suppose there isn't much to say or celebrate anyway.

I don't work as hard as I used to. I don't see any reason to since this Dufus isn't promoting me. I'd be glad if he sent me to the gas-generating plant to work. I'd much rather be doing physical work than typing.

Just think, in six months and two weeks, I'll be out of this fucking Army, and we'll be together. It's too beautiful.

12 March 1969

Everything is peaceful for ten miles around here. So, I'm very safe now.

I was convicted in my court-martial for Disobeying Standing Orders, but the Commanding General's Assistant, Colonel Somebody, revoked it because of the lives saved, so my record's clean. It's just as if I'd been found not guilty.

I was also charged with desertion in the face of an enemy attack, unlawful usurpation of an M-79 and M-2 (50-caliber) machine gun, an accomplice to theft of a ¾-ton truck, and lying about having orders to leave. I, as well as the other two men with me, was found innocent of all charges. So we're all off the hook, and I'd be glad if it were quickly forgotten because it gives me nightmares.

I should be working at the 865th Engineer Detachment Gas Generating work area by Monday. I hope they don't put me in the office as I'd like to work outdoors for a while. You can't feel it inside an office when you get a breeze. Also, I'd get a few more chances to get off the compound, especially if I get to drive the diesel fuel truck. I don't think my replacement in Company Headquarters is too swift, but that's their trouble and not my problem.

Now I'll never make E-5, but that's all right. I know I should have gotten it and was worthy of it long before this Dufus, new 1st Sgt., got here. If old 1st Sgt. had been here, I would have made E-5 last January 13 when I was first eligible. That's the way the ball goes.

Your hubby,
Bill

Madison
March 14, 1969

Hi Honey,

"And on the fourth day," Carole asked, "Where in the world is my mail?"

I heard on the radio tonight that fifty towns got hit in 'Nam again, so I imagine you've had some action. In the last letter you sent, you said you were on 'gray' alert (whatever that means). I hope things didn't get worse.

Did I ever tell you what we did in speech class? Our teacher brought in a recording of a computer that talks. It spoke sentences, but I got a kick out of it singing, "Daisy, Daisy" (like the computer in *2001: A Space Odyssey*), to a piano accompaniment played by another computer! It sounded pretty good, too.

I got a C on that difficult physiology test I took last week. I got nineteen wrong out of fifty, but Doc Lars graded on a curve that ran nice and low. I've got an A going in Anatomy and a B in Therapeutic Exercise.

Have you had a chance to see the Hawaiian movie film yet? It made me so lonely for you, especially when I saw you playing that bamboo xylophone at the Polynesian Cultural Center. You looked so cute.

March 15, 1969

I got your audiotapes today, and now I know how annoyed you were when you couldn't decipher mine. I couldn't hear you decently. You sounded like Mickey Mouse on one speed and Boris Karloff on the other! Rats! I had to put my finger on the tape recorder's reel to slow it down so I could hear. From what I could understand, it sounded like you had left the orderly room. Such is your decision.

I'm happy you liked the Alpha Omega medallion I sent you to wear. I'll take it off of you when you return home. Hearing you open the box on the tape was just like me being there.

March 17, 1969

Did you know that two years ago, on March 21, it was the first time you told me you loved me? I remember the first time we had 3MS2QB45QR2 (intercourse). I started crying and sobbing. I was filled with so much emotion and was super excited after having sex with you. It was all new to both of us.

I love you, Sugar Bear, whether you're growling or bare,

Carole

Vietnam
18 March 1969

Hi Dear One,

You know I'd like to be home with you and miss you. I don't see any sense in saying I love you; it's better if I just show it. Words are too easy to use, but action, ah, requires effort and thought. Now being over here, of course, I can't caress you, feel you, or show you my love, so I prefer not to say it, lest I say something I don't entirely mean.

There's no doubt in my mind that I miss you, and I'd rather be with you. But I can't say I'm sure I love you more than any other girl I've ever known or known. I'm ashamed of myself for not honestly saying what I believe.

I thought it odd you should infer in your letter that I might want to see some other girl more than you. I don't believe I gave you any reason to think there is another girl, but since you are wondering, there are two. One is my ex-girlfriend, Misty (as she was two and a half years ago), and the other is a mental illusion of the perfect girl I never found and never will.

If I could do it over again, I probably would've married Misty when she asked me so long ago. But, like Aldous Huxley said, "Rolling in the muck is not the best way to get clean." In other words, don't wallow in remorse; repent, and resolve not to repeat the same error.

That's my problem. I'm always living in the past. I feel more unhappy with the "now" than with the good times I had "then."

Don't worry about things you can't compete with. Gain some weight, and let your hair grow out as it was when we married. Then, I'll try not to criticize you so much when I come home.

Goodbye, dear one,
Bill

I was crushed when I read that letter. So, Bill wasn't sure if he loved me and wished he'd marry Misty instead of me. And here I was in Madison, all alone, trying to be his perfect little wife.

What were Bill's expectations of me—to be sexy, dutiful, and understanding? Or should I be loyal and faithful like his old dog Mackie? Why was he constantly trying to change me into his "perfect girl" by asking me to grow my hair longer, change how I dressed, and gain weight?

And for some reason, Bill hadn't gotten over his high school sweetheart, Misty. It annoyed me that he still thought about her. While we were dating and Bill was in gas-generating training, he visited Misty at her Bible College near Fort Belvoir. She was studying to become a missionary and invited him to a Pentecostal church service.

After that, they wrote to one another, and maybe Bill thought Misty would give him a second chance. But by January of 1968, he wrote me this about one of her letters:

Out of fourteen paragraphs, thirteen were about Jesus and saving my soul. Misty has absolutely decided to preach me into heaven. The other paragraph was to say hi. You can see her letter if you're jealous.

Yes, I was jealous until later when I found out Misty was engaged to be married. Then, despite my ambivalent thoughts, I knew I loved Bill but suspected he still loved Misty even though their relationship was long over. Maybe Bill longed for Misty because he couldn't have her. But, on the other hand, would I have been the ex-girlfriend he obsessed over if I'd broken up with him? Would he have put me on a high pedestal and told his next girlfriend all about me?

All schoolwork and no play had turned me into one dull girl. Even Bill's brother told me, "Carole, you take life too seriously." So maybe I should take Bill up on his offer to go out every night during Easter break and try to make him jealous again.

But it was risky to go back to the Amber Grid. I hated how the guys at the bar looked at me that night like I was a piece of steak at the meat market or undressed me with their eyes. And what if Daniel was there again, told me he wanted to spend time with me and didn't care if I was married? Would I be able to resist Daniel's advances? Of course, no one would ever need to know. But, on the other hand, what would I do if Daniel was sweet to me and asked me home? With Bill gone and Daniel returning to Switzerland, it would be easy to cross that fine line, but then there would be no going back.

No, no. I couldn't hurt Bill that way and then carry the guilt with me for the rest of my life.

While walking home from class, I saw a flyer about an upcoming dance with a live rock and roll/jazz band with horns at Gordon Hall, the men's dorm a few blocks from where I lived. I knew there'd be lots of guys there willing to dance, and the music would be loud, so maybe the topic of my marital status might not arise.

I asked Janet to go, but she said, "No, I'm engaged. I can't go without Bear."

Then I asked Sally, and she said she'd love to go dancing. So, I bought two tickets to see Freddie and the Freeloaders and decided it would be best to leave my wedding ring home.

Madison
March 19, 1969

Hi Sweetie,

Yesterday, Janet and I were in the anatomy lab reviewing cadavers when I looked out the window and saw this guy and girl lying out on the grass. She was lying on top of him, and I almost got a whole new sex education. They were making out and looked like they were having intercourse, except they had all their clothes on! Students were standing on the balcony of Van Hise Hall watching them, too, but the couple didn't give a damn. I told Janet, "That would be enough to make the birds and bees blush!"

March 25, 1969

I had a lovely tape waiting for me when I returned to Madison from Grandpa's funeral. I'm so happy to hear you like your new job. Will you be safe working so close to the camp's perimeter? I hope it's well-guarded so Charlie won't blow up the oxygen plant.

My loneliness for you started last Saturday night when I went out to Rusty's Pizza Parlor with a group of friends. I dressed up and fixed my hair, fluffed it up on one side, and tucked the other side behind my right ear, but who was around to appreciate it? Not the one I wanted to be there the most—you.

No matter where I go, there are memories of you. I can't escape you, my love. The songs I hear seem sadder because I'm always thinking about you. But, when you return, that will be one of the happiest days of my life, happier than our wedding day because I know you won't be leaving anymore. Sometimes, I think these last six months will be the hardest. I'll take each day as it comes, Honey, but I'd like you to be here now.

I thought of you at Grandpa's funeral. Don't you ever come home to me in a casket. That's more than I could bear. All I ask is you come home alive and healthy.

Carole

The concept of death was like a foreign object to me. It didn't belong in my body or my mind. I was twenty and invincible, or so I thought. Death seemed a long way off until Vietnam.

Of course, I knew what it meant to be dead. As a kid, I'd mourned the loss of a cat and buried it in a shoebox. I lamented the death of a beautiful deer hanging from a tree branch during hunting season, but that was a hunter's trophy.

Although I worked on cadavers during anatomy lab, they didn't look real because they had their skin removed. Instead, they resembled something a mad scientist had devised to show off their muscles. And if we weren't studying the facial muscles, we kept their heads covered with a cloth.

Maybe seeing Grandfather lying dead in his casket triggered something in my brain. I realized death is final. I'd never hear Grandpa's voice again, see his shy smile, watch him working in his garden, or serve me a glass of his famous homemade dandelion wine at Christmastime with his shaky hand.

Watching the nightly news on the small black and white TV in the dorm's lobby and seeing the war firsthand was disturbing. Instead, I preferred to listen to it on my transistor radio in the privacy of my room. There I had a Vietnam map on the wall and could look up the towns with strange-sounding names where the fighting occurred. As the body count in Vietnam went up, I found myself sheltering down in *my* bunker, my dorm room, to study to take my mind off the war and the fear that I'd lose Bill.

But when I had another dream about my husband's death, I knew that unconsciously I had accepted the fact that I might lose him. So when the nightmare reoccurred, upsetting me to the max, I thought it might stop if I told someone. But, unfortunately, my newlywed sister, Cheryl, might not have time, and Mom was already a professional worrier. Maybe Janet could interpret the dream.

I walked into the dorm's kitchenette to the bittersweet smell of coffee and burnt toast and found Janet making breakfast.

"Janet, I need to talk."

"Coffee? Cream or sugar?" Janet asked.

"Yes, with cream." *I can't believe we're talking about coffee when Bill might already be dead.*

Janet handed me a cup, a spoon, and a napkin.

"Janet, I awoke with another horrific dream this morning."

"Oh, Carole, you're crying. I'm sorry. Come, sit down."

She led me to the table where a newspaper lay with the headlines, "Lennon and Ono Stage Bed-in for Peace." I pushed the paper aside and stirred my coffee so hard it sloshed onto the table.

"In my dream, Bill came home from Vietnam. We were at Dad's store, and Bill went downstairs to the basement for something but didn't return. I ran down to check on him and found his lifeless body hanging from an overhead pipe with a rope around his neck."[24]

"Oh, Lord, what did you do?"

"I yelled for Dad, but no sound came out. Then, finally, I awoke screaming."

"Carole, it's just your subconscious mind trying to make sense of all this."

"But why would I dream Bill killed himself?"

Janet pushed her eyeglasses up on her nose and looked me straight in the eyes like a professor. "Maybe you have a subconscious-Freudian premonition that Bill will die over there."

"Oh, Janet, don't say that. It can't be true." I buried my head in my hands as more tears welled up.

"But Carole, it could be true. In my psychology class, Freud taught us that dreams reveal our innermost thoughts. They're strategies to protect ourselves from real emotional pain. Maybe you don't expect Bill to make it home alive, so in your subconscious mind, you killed him off."

"Oh God, I was so damn mad at him when he told me he volunteered for Vietnam that I could have killed him. I get so angry sometimes and wish he doesn't make it back." I grabbed my cup, took a big gulp of coffee, and started to choke.

"You okay?" Janet patted me on the back. "Calm down, Honey. I'm sure we can figure out another reason. Maybe you're just worried about what will happen when Bill does come home. Will he be able to cope with the real world?"

I fiddled with my spoon on the table. "I hope we both can cope, but I wish Bill hadn't gone there. I'm so worried."

"You've gotta distract yourself to get through this. Keep writing your letters like you've been doing. That'll give you a positive focus. If it helps to talk, you can talk to me anytime, just not in the middle of the night, okay?"

Janet made me laugh. I was still upset, but it did help to talk. I finished my coffee, looked at the clock on the wall, stood up, and hugged her.

"God knows I couldn't do this without you. We better get our butts in gear or be late for anatomy."

During this time, Janet, my anchor, kept me grounded. So when the world became too chaotic, Janet was my go-to for a voice of reason.

Vietnam
25 March 1969

Dear Carole,

Four days ago, they made me shift leader (foreman) after Watts got all messed up on pot and booze. I think he'll be court-martialed for drugs. He's writing to his wife now, so I guess his family problems back home are getting better. Now my old CO wants me back in the 160th Command Office. I won't go there, but I made a deal to be a clerk in the shop office if everything works out here.

Thanks for the Rice Krispie bars and the book *Brave New World*, which I finally had time to read. Be good and study hard.

26 March 1969

It's 15:00 here. I've left the 865th Oxygen Plant and am in the Shop Office again. It isn't a bad job, but not as nice as being outside.

Did I tell you last week that a bunch of guys from my old office made a lottery bet on how long I'll last before I break down and go for a 'shot of leg' (middle leg—you know, the little one)? The longest estimate was June 1. Whoever wins gets $28 and has to buy three rounds of drinks for all who contributed and haven't DEROS-ed[25] yet.

These guys don't understand that gook girls don't excite me but turn me off most of the time. Besides, I promised you, and I will stick to it.

27 March 1969

I got the entire day off today because we passed our CMMI Inspection last week. So, it's the first time I've had the whole day off.

I got up and went to the pool, which was closed. No one was around, so I took a quick dip. Then I went to the beach. There were three 1st Lt. nurses there. Wow, round-eyed girls! I talked to one of them briefly, but they were all taken.

Please don't send me any more films of our Hawaiian trip because they make me homesick and remind me of you, the real world, and all I'm missing. Then I get even more depressed.

Bill

Madison

March 30, 1969

Dearest Bill,

I got your letter today saying you're a shift leader. Good work, Honey. I hope Watts doesn't hold a grudge against you. Be careful of him. I hope everything else works out for you. If you're so in demand, why won't they promote you to E-5 to satisfy your need?

Please call me in Sturgeon Bay on April 11 or 12 on Easter Break. Sweetie Pie, it has been so long since I've talked to you, touched you, or been with you that our marriage seems like an illusion. Do you know we've led a more chaste life this first year of marriage than during our courtship? What an ironic thing!

I dreamed about you again last night—you and I are finally in bed. What's wrong with you, Wagener? There aren't many guys who refuse to sleep with their wives during the first year of marriage. So I convinced you to make love to me. We both enjoyed it, and all went splendidly.

Some days I don't love you as much because you don't seem real to me, like you're a figment of my imagination. Other days I love you lots because I remember the fun things we've done, and it's almost like you're here, but then you're not.

I miss you, Sweetie. I want you home, so we can both be happy together.

Carole

CHAPTER 13 - APRIL 1969: GEEZ, LOUISE

Alaska
April 8, 1969

Hi Sweetie,

It's been five days since I've heard from you. I hope you haven't sent my letters to Madison as I told you I'd be at my parent's home. I read my parents' letters and learned things I didn't know. Why didn't you tell me that you went on a raid with the vicious Korean Tigers?

Oh, Baby. I miss you something fierce! These last few weeks have been terrible. I wish you were here with me, holding me, kissing me, and whispering in my ear. But, sadly, when I don't hear from you, I've got to wonder if you exist. You'd think I'd be used to your absence by seven months, but I'm not.

It would be a joy to see you and have your strong arms around me like that night at Christmas when you came back from basic training in Fort Polk, Louisiana. I was standing in the living room doorway of my apartment in Green Bay. You held me tight and kissed me hello—you were in your cold, wool Army overcoat, and I in my soft, warm, flannel pajamas.

I saw an Easter worship service on television Sunday evening at Phu Cat Airbase. I looked for you, but you weren't there as you probably don't go that far for chapel. However, it was nice to think you were only a short distance away.

I love you with all my heart,
Carole

Vietnam
8 April 1969

Dear Luv Bug,

I received your Easter package today. Thank you, Honey Bunny.

You can have the Dean send that letter to the CO of the 160th—the same address as mine. I don't know the earliest registration date for school, but I can get home ten days before that. Then we'll have time to set up our apartment, and I'll have time to adjust to life in the real world again.

I'm told I won't be able to shoot people I don't like, and I won't be able to piss on the side of the road anymore. If that's true, I might want to stay here as a civilian to do as I wish. Then you might disown me, claim an unconsecrated marriage, and get an annulment. So I guess I'd better come home.

11 April 1969

I was just notified that I must be a witness at Watts' court-martial at 0900 this morning. He may be going to jail for a while for dereliction of duty and endangering the lives of others.

As of midnight last night, our hepatitis epidemic is over. We had two deaths, and fifteen people evacuated in serious condition. Wow, I didn't even get a fever. What hurt me the most was the shot they gave me three weeks ago. Ouch!

Now I'm sure I'll be able to get off base and into Qui Nhon to call you. Have a happy seventh-month anniversary. Here's hoping we'll be together on our first anniversary.

19 April 1969

I got the sweet letter you wrote when you were up in Sturgeon Bay in my bed. If you only knew how few girls I had in that bed, you wouldn't think me much of a swinger.

You know, it seems like I'm not lonely, just numb. Nothing bothers me much, including not getting promoted. Though I miss your comforts and home, I can live without them.

Bill

Madison
April 25, 1969

Dearest Bill,

Mrs. Duffy, that old lady I told you about, called me last night, and I'm so excited that we have an apartment for fall. I made a $50 deposit today when I went to see the place again. We are downstairs and have a front porch, where we can sit out when the weather is nice and see Lake Mendota. It has hardwood floors in the living room, and big bay windows open up to the porch. It's a one-bedroom with a bathroom and a small kitchen. Our move-in date is September 1.

That will be a big adjustment for me next year as a wife, lover, housekeeper, cook, laundress, and ironer. But it will be fun, and I'm looking forward to having my man's arms around me, sleeping with him, and studying with him every night.

I hope all is safe and well with you. Your parents thought your area might be having a little fighting. You never tell me, but I guess you don't want me to worry. I've got a feeling Charlie Cong will try another big offensive soon. Your mom said you guys were sticking close to the base, so something must be brewing.

Be careful, Honey.
Carole

Vietnam
27 April 1969

Dearest Carole,

Wow, Darling, I'm eight days delinquent in writing.

I don't know about that $127/month apartment—with old furniture and a little old lady passionately in love with her cat. It sounds like the kind of landlady who is constantly visiting and poking her nose into our apartment. Is it twenty-five minutes walking distance from campus and a nice clean neighborhood? Be nice to the old lady, but don't make any promises.

To clear up confusion, I'm out of the Shop Office and back with the 865th, where everyone is exempt from guard duty because we work day and night, twelve-hour shifts, making oxygen and acetylene. I quit the Shop Office when they put me on guard duty one night. I got the post with the M-60 machine gun overlooking the Huey helicopter. It's a new outpost and receives a lot of sniper fire.

Thanks for the photos of you in the red push-up bra and French undies. Only two pictures? Why didn't you have Janet take more? It sure shows off your figure. It looks like you gained a little weight. You were looking thin and sickly in Hawaii.

When you cried at the airport in Hawaii, you looked horrible, like I'd been starving, beating, and whipping you. You sobbed and fussed, making such a scene everyone started to stare. I tried vainly to forget the whole thing on my way back, but I wished I'd never taken my R&R in Hawaii.

You shamed me in front of all those other couples. If we ever have to part again (and I hope not), I'll leave and bid you farewell in private. I'll bet I was ten times more ashamed to be seen with you as you were with me at UWGB—when I wore that red pajama nightshirt over my swim trunks.

I'm glad you bought the undies, but I wish you'd stop buying clothes and save money. You should be able to save at least $75 per month. I don't see where you need even $55 per month for "little things." You should be able to make it on $25 a month. Darling, all we'll have to live on next year is what you've saved and my GI bill allowance of $150 per month. I don't think we'll even be able to afford a car, so we'll have to use my motorcycle to get around.

In the *Door County Advocate*, I read that my cousin, Charles Overbeck, was awarded his C.I.B. [Combat Infantryman Badge] near Pleiku. So when I finished working yesterday morning, I put on my bulletproof vest, rifle, and helmet, hitchhiked to An Khe, and then tried to locate Chuck by phone. No one seemed to know where C. Company of the 2nd squadron, 1st Cavalry of 4th Infantry, was. Finally, on a hunch, I found Chuck at Blackhawk Firebase about fifteen miles east of Pleiku in the Central Highlands. It's nice and cool up there and a lot more beautiful.

Chuck got drafted right after he graduated from college. He's healthy and in good shape. We exchanged war stories and experiences. I realized how good I have it as he's in the infantry.

There, for the first time, I saw Montagnards [hill tribal people] who moved to the highlands for protection from the VC and NVA. They look like a cross between Negros and American Indians, except they are shorter. I think their topless women are a great cultural tradition. I hope the contact with us civilized people doesn't corrupt them. I got some great movie pictures of them.

Bye, Bye.
Bill

Four months had passed since Hawaii. Why was Bill still so upset with me for crying my eyes out when he left me at the airport in Honolulu? If it bugged him, I think he'd have gotten over it by now. But when I read his letter—damn, he made me angry—making me want to cry all over again when he said he regretted taking his R&R with me in Hawaii.

Yes, my face was as red as the nightshirt Bill wore to school one spring morning at UWGB on a bet with his friend. He'd purchased the nightshirt in Florida on Easter break. The words, I SLEPT ON A VIRGIN (island), were printed on it in big, bold letters, and he'd been sleeping with me the last time I saw him wearing it. By the end of that day, I was so upset that I warned him, "I'll break up with you if you ever do anything this stupid and embarrass me again!"

But now it was time to go to the dance at Gordon Commons. I dressed in my new bell-bottom hip-hugger pants, a multi-colored, fishnet crocheted sweater that hid my thin scarecrow figure, and a long gold medallion necklace. My hair had grown almost to my shoulders, and I tucked it behind my ears, revealing my glittering-gold hooped earrings. I slipped off my wedding band, grabbed the two tickets, and met Sally down the hall.

Madison
April 28, 1969

Dear Bill,

Sorry, I haven't been able to write too often, but neither have you. I've been busier this semester. It's been one assignment after another.

Saturday night, Sally and I went to the dance at Gordon Commons. They had a nine-piece band called Freddy and the Freeloaders. Their horns were loud but sounded great. Sally and I danced most of the night together until the end of the evening when two sophomore guys asked us to dance. We danced mostly fast ones and my quota of slow ones. When they asked to walk us home, we finally told them I was married and Sally had a boyfriend, but they insisted on walking us home anyway.

So I don't feel guilty about it as long as my guy in 'Nam doesn't mind if I go out.

April 29, 1969

You surprised me tonight when you called. Yesterday I had another phone call and heard a voice say, "Hi, Gorgeous." I thought it was you, but it was your brother. He sounded just like you, and I was disappointed that it wasn't you. It's too bad we couldn't have heard each other better, but I wrote this poem after we talked.

NOW

Now, I long to feel your warm hands,
Running up and down,
Along the sides of my body.
I long for your physical warmth,
As our bodies entwine,
Like it was the first time.
I long for your cheek against mine,
Your breath on my ear.
I long for your lips,
Touching mine,
Gently and softly at times,
Firm and strong at other times.
I long for a goodbye kiss,
And welcome-home kisses.
I long for the past,
But live in the present,
And hope for the future.
I long for you, my love,
And for all the sweet love,
You have given me.

Love,
Carole

Vietnam
29 April 1969

Hi Honey Bunny,

What do you mean my call gave you a new outlook, and you don't want to go out with the girls now? What were you doing before? I don't mind if you go out as long as you behave.

It won't be long now. Eight months of service will be gone, and only four months left. I still hope to get out two or three weeks early.

I tried to call you again today from MARS in Qui Nhon, but twelve guys were ahead of me. Only four got through. I'll try on Monday again because that's Sunday evening for you, and you'll probably be in your room studying. Long-distance rates are cheaper on Sunday, so that it won't cost so much on your end.

I wish I could put my arm around your waist and walk with you to a park right now. We could both be wearing our brown hip huggers, but alas. The night I got your photos, I came to work but felt like stripping and walking nude in the warm breeze. See you in September.

Love from Lousie Lover,
Bill

"Janet, quick, open up," I yelled, pounding on her door. Already in her bathrobe, Janet opened the door slowly and let me in.

"What's happening? Do you need to use my phone?"

"I'm so upset. It's these letters from Bill," I waved two opened letters in the air. "I think he's having an affair!"

"An affair! Whatever gave you that idea?"

"Look, he signed his last letter, Love from Louise Lover."

"Bill wouldn't cheat on you, would he?"

"He's too afraid of getting VD from the Vietnamese girls, but in one letter, he said he met some 'round-eyed' girls at the beach." I showed Janet the letter dated March 27. "Bill met these three American nurses and talked to one of them. That must have been Louise. He lied to me when he said those nurses were all taken."

"First of all, calm down, Carole. You're jumping to conclusions. Write back and find out what Bill meant by Louise Lover."

"You're darn right. I'm gonna write and tell him to ditch that bitch!"

Our relationship had many ups and downs. Sometimes I tried to better understand my husband by reading some of his old letters I'd saved.

While Bill was at Fort Belvoir, he'd written,

"It's nice to have a girlfriend to write to when Uncle Sam's Army imprisons you. That's why I seem to be in love with you when it's only self-deception needed to supply my conscience with a justification for holding a girl's love so that I won't be cut off and lonely. But, on the other hand, I remember being pretty fond of you before I enlisted."

At about the same time, he'd warned me,

"I was raised by an immature mother, oppressed by females most of my childhood, and heartbroken again and again in my teenage life. You've seen my hang-ups and how I can be. So, find yourself a God-loving man who had a normal childhood. Think about a life with this sort of man-child. Could you tolerate it?"

So, it was no wonder that, as newlyweds, we both struggled with intimacy. I had no experience with men, and lovemaking felt awkward, like learning to drive a stick-shift car. I always had a problem finding first gear, and the vehicle made jerky movements until it was time to shift into second. Eventually, I learned to skip first gear altogether and started the car in second.

On the other hand, Bill's sex drive was like a car with automatic transmission, and he expected me to be ready when he shifted into overdrive. So I'd tell him to slow down, and finally, we learned to use extra lubricant for a smoother ride.

But sometimes, I thought Bill had a disconnected circuit in his brain. For instance, he sent me five Valentine's cards for Valentine's Day, but on February 14, he got drunk and wrote,

"My buddies gave me a Bourbon and coke. I ain't sure, but I think I'm tripping. They were trying to talk me into going to a Clap Shack. They think I'm missing part of the gook world by not experiencing the atmosphere and the gook techniques."

Then he went into a highly detailed description of what his buddies told him a prostitute did to a GI. His buddies argued that Bill hadn't promised not to get a blow job but just promised not to screw. Bill assured me he didn't go to the Clap Shacks but once told me in a letter that he liked to tease the prostitutes who called him a "cherry boy."

But I was a "cherry girl" and hung up on the topic of masturbation. Finally, on February 21, I wrote Bill,

"If you want to masturbate, it's okay. According to our psychology teacher, it's quite acceptable in private. When a kid masturbates, you should ignore it, and when they reach puberty, you should ensure they have privacy. Every time I leave psychology class, I feel slightly astonished by what she says. I know masturbating does no harm, but it isn't our society's 'in' thing to do. Maybe it should be!"

Bill wrote back, "I'm sorry you don't masturbate. What do you want, a medal or a chest to pin it on? Damn, I'm sorry I offended you. I didn't know you had so little sex drive."

I wrote him back,

"Don't get me wrong. I'm not commending myself because I don't masturbate. It took me until my sophomore year in college to figure it out. But, look at it this way—it isn't as easy for a girl to figure it out as for a guy. Girls are different than guys. I get my 'sexcitement' from hearing your voice on the tapes, looking at your pictures, and thinking about you."

Growing up in the 1950s, I wasn't at all comfortable with my budding femininity. A tomboy, I watched football with Dad and went to Green Bay Packers games. Unlike my sister, I wasn't interested in boys or girly things like hair, nails, or makeup. In addition, I was a strict Lutheran, so I didn't watch sexy movies or read juicy books. And in the '60s, a double standard existed, and there was even a joke about it.

"Hey, Janet. Have you heard the latest joke going around? What's the difference between a good girl and a nice girl?"

Janet shrugged. "I dunno."

"A good girl goes on a date, goes home, and then goes to bed, but a nice girl goes on a date, goes to bed, and then goes home."

Janet laughed. "Then that makes you a nice girl and me a good girl."

I understood that some guys liked to date nice girls who had sex with them, but they still wanted to marry virgins. But nice girls in my high school who didn't have adequate contraceptives became pregnant and disgracefully "had to get married."

My professor said that when college girls obtained the birth control pill illegally and cut it in half to share with a roommate when neither girl became pregnant, doctors determined half the dosage was adequate. But in about half of the U.S., the pill was legal only for married women.

The first time I took the pill, I had mixed feelings. On the one hand, I felt powerful in controlling my destiny. But, on the other hand, part of me did want to become a mother even though I knew it wasn't the right time. So when Bill wrote in one of his letters that I should quit school, get pregnant, and have his babies, I wrote back, "You've got to be kidding!"

Meanwhile, Bill had a very different experience growing up. While he was in Vietnam, he wrote about having a wet dream:

"I haven't had one since I was a teen and believed masturbation was a sin. It was the worse sin I had to confess every Saturday, and I dreaded telling the priest. Despite all my praying and efforts, I couldn't understand why I couldn't overcome it until I gave up trying. If I could have only known other boys my age were fucking. Wow, and girls, I knew too, but I didn't find out until I was older and began to realize things."

I sent Bill many articles I tore out of *Reader's Digest* about improving our married life. Finally, Bill seemed to agree with me:

"I take it by the marriage pamphlet you sent and your letter concerning a 'heart-to-heart' conversation with no holds barred that you're not satisfied with our sexual relationship. I admit when we are together, it could always use some improvement. But, in the dark, in bed, if you want it like that, it is fine with me; any place you feel is conducive is fine.

I'm not the least opposed to an open discussion when I'm home and you're ready for it. I only ask that we both be completely honest, even if it hurts. I don't want it to be a hurt-each-other situation. I want it to be a get-to-understand-each-other session. So don't be impatient if it takes me a while to adjust to having a wife and being back in the world. I promise I'll try my best to be a good hubby. After the sweet letters I've gotten from you, I don't know that I could be anything else."

From movies I'd seen and books I'd read, like *A Farewell to Arms* and *Dr. Zhivago*, I understood that infidelity happened in wars. Bill was too handsome for women not to notice him. Like a doggie looking for a bone, I had to dig to the bottom of this and find out who Louise was.

CHAPTER 14 - MAY 1969: INTO THE SHADOWS

Madison
May 3, 1969

Dear Bill,

I don't know what set off the spark causing you to write your most recent letter about what happened to us in Hawaii. Please, Bill, the next time I do something that bothers or annoys you take me aside to some quiet place where we can be alone and give me hell rather than giving me hell four months later when there's nothing I can do about it. I'm sorry I made you lose face. I find my emotions hard to control when someone means as much to me as you do. I probably looked awful because of my short hair, and maybe I was underweight. But holding onto your anger and hurt only hurts yourself and our relationship.

We may be having trouble on campus again. Tonight there was a gathering near Capitol Square. Some kids and the police got beaten up. This time the cause was to end the war in Vietnam.

In answer to what I do with my money, Mom bought me the bell-bottom hip-huggers, and I borrowed Cheryl's fishnet sweater. I bought shoes for school since the heels on my ones were so worn down that my feet hurt from wearing them. Janet and I spend $6–7 each for weekly groceries. That takes care of about $28, and the dermatologist costs me $9 a visit, so I'm not spending carelessly.

Remember me? I'm the one who's the penny pincher. Regarding entertainment, I haven't spent a penny since I went to the bar at Birchwood Gardens one month ago. But I can't live on cheap hamburgers as you did in Green Bay and expect to feel good and gain weight.

To answer your question, Madison is the only place I can attend school next year. All my courses in physical therapy are here. None are offered at UWGB as they don't have a medical school.

By the way, I like the neighborhood where we'll live next year. It's on East Mifflin Street, two blocks from Capitol Square, and just a short walk to Lake Mendota. It's a clean neighborhood, and our living room overlooks a big parking lot, so we can see quite far as there aren't any houses blocking our view. And we might appreciate being off-campus, away from all the noise and kooks.

I don't think we'll have to worry about the landlady bothering us. Mrs. Duffy has arthritis and can barely go up and down the stairs. However, the two times I saw the unit, she always called the tenants and asked if it was okay. I think the relationship between her and the tenants depends on how friendly they are, plus she seemed to like me.

There's talk of a rent strike in Madison as rents are so high. I pay $70 per month, and look at what I've got—one 8'x10' bedroom with a chair, a desk, and a mirror above it; a single bed, closet, and shared bathroom down the hall. There's no air conditioning.

Today it was seventy-five degrees, too hot and stuffy for studying, so I put on my new swimsuit and sunbathed at Camp Randall in the afternoon. It was so beautiful outside, and after being cooped up in my room all winter, it felt good to get some sun. I wish you could have been here.

At your urging, I've tried masturbating. I thought you might like to know that I'm human, too. It's almost as good as having you around. I won't hold you to your promise not to masturbate. I think masturbation is an excellent way to relieve sexual and other tensions. So, when you get the urge, go right ahead.

This letter hasn't been very "lovey," but it sounds like you don't care anymore. I tried to say nice things to you, but I can't remember when I last got your "love letter." So if you'd rather not hear me say that I love you, okay then, but don't forget it!

You signed your last letter, "Love from Louise Lover." So, who's this girl Louise, and why the hell are you her lover?

May 6, 1969

In answer to your letter, I wasn't doing anything before that I wasn't supposed to be doing. I meant to say that I used to like to go out with the girls, but after you called, I felt more content. It didn't matter one way or the other if I went out or stayed home. That lasted for about two weeks because

I went to that dance with Sally, but it felt terrific to go there, knowing that you didn't mind.

If President Nixon lives up to his promise and you're not in combat, you could be home as early as July. So be good, and don't go too close to those clap shacks (although I know you never do).

Carole

P.S. I love you, but ditch that bitch, Louise

The 'new' Bill in Vietnam seemed to be distancing himself from me. Maybe he was in survival mode, thinking only of himself, or perhaps he had Louise on his mind. Meanwhile, I was in limbo with only photographs and memories of the 'old' Bill, whom I dearly loved.

Sitting at my desk, attempting to write yet another letter, I looked at our prom picture. I remembered how thoughtful Bill had been to invite me to a prom when he realized I'd never gone to one. That night as we danced on the gym floor, I felt so special dressed in my floor-length pink gown wearing the pink cymbidium orchid he'd bought me.

Another time Bill paid me a surprise visit at Dad's store at 2 a.m. He decided to sleep in the car until morning. I was shocked when Mom awoke me to tell me Bill was there! I was still in my pajamas when I found him sitting in his fuzzy winter leopard print jacket at the kitchen table while Mom was already busy preparing our breakfast. I remembered the smell of fresh coffee brewing in the percolator on top of the stove and the sound of sizzling bacon and eggs frying in the black cast iron pan as I put two slices of Wonder Bread into our new pop-up toaster.

It had rained that spring morning, but the sun broke through just after breakfast. So Bill and I took a romantic walk down the narrow dirt road to the West Alaska Lake behind my house. On our way back, we laughed so hard when our shoes became caked in such a deep layer of mud that we could barely walk. It felt like climbing a mountain as we trudged the last steep hill home. I hosed off our shoes and left them outdoors. Bill and I went inside and sat in our stocking feet, talking and rocking contentedly in Mom's loveseat for the rest of the morning, waiting for our shoes to dry.

Then I remembered our frequent trips to Sturgeon Bay, where I met Bill's family and learned to ride horses at his brother's ranch. Bill's nephew's job was to saddle up the horses. Usually, I rode gentle flaxen-colored Buddy, who was more my speed, but never his look-a-like, Silver.

Bill helped me to mount my horse. I was barely situated in the saddle when the stallion took off running. To my surprise, he tried to rub me off at the first fence post we passed in the apple orchard. Buddy had never done that to me before. Next, I quickly ducked down when he ran under a low tree branch, attempting to knock me off.

What the hell?

When we reached the open pasture, "Buddy" took off running at lightning speed while I attempted to stop him by pulling up and back hard on the reins like I'd seen the Lone Ranger do on TV. Unfortunately, that caused the beast to rear up on his hind legs and for me to grab onto the saddle's horn, holding on for dear life. Riding a chestnut mare named Ruby, Bill finally caught up to us and came to my rescue by grabbing onto the horse's reins, bringing him to a halt so I could dismount.

"What's wrong with Buddy today? Did a bee sting him?" I asked naively, walking away on shaky legs.

"This isn't Buddy," Bill explained. "My nephew must have switched them. It looks like you've been riding Silver all along." Seeing how shaken up I was, my hero suggested we ride Ruby double on the way back to the barn.

If only my hero were here now. I would thank him by playing the part of a kitten, snuggling up to him, and purring by his neck. I'd put my nose and mouth to his ear, lick him, and make him squirm. I'd rub my warm fur all over his body and then fall asleep in my lover's arms.

Vietnam
12 May 1969

Dear Carole,

I don't think I'll be promoted because of a long story simplified—the CO of the 865th has the ass at me. So, forget about it. My time's getting shorter. I will be promoted to Civilian First Class in less than one hundred and twenty days.

Sweet, Carole. I didn't say I don't love you, nor did I say I don't want you to say it. But I don't believe in wearing out the phrase. It's so trite, so common, and often said without meaning.

I'm not sure you love me, but I think you desire my "bod" not just sexually but as a status symbol to act as a crutch for your inferiority complex. So, you can say to yourself, "That's my man, the one who was a wrestling champ, forensics aspirant in high school, that athlete, that masculine hunk of sweetness." By telling yourself and showing your girlfriends (especially your sister) what you've got, you override your self-doubts about being feminine enough and being able to compete.

Not to be analyzing you, but I think I'm also guilty. Sometimes I think my desire to marry you was an overreaction to the feeling of Misty's loss, as I was not too fond of the thought of not having anyone if you lost interest in me while I was in Vietnam.

Sure, I'd split up with Misty six months before I met you, and it was all over for us, although I didn't accept that fact. I clung to the idea that God would bring us back together again. It was too much to admit that I'd thrown away the greatest love I'd ever experienced. I had to realize I was deceiving myself and dare to admit it.

I saw myself using you as a substitute for Misty. When I became acutely aware of my many faults, I told you I thought you'd be better off without me. It was hard, so hard, because I believe I was a little in love with you. The mere thought of no one to love, or love me, no one to confide in, or lean on when I was down, was too terrible an idea. That's when I started seriously feeling like marrying so I'd have someone.

What a fool I was! I'm over here all alone without any real friends at all. You could be cheating on me (but I doubt it), and I wouldn't know. That's why I don't pretend to be unbearably in love. I'd rather be honest if I can't be anything else of value. It hurts me to admit that I could let my emotions take me so far, as I'm sure this hurts you. That's why I don't want to make false impressions because, in the end, they end up hurting you. So, I'll just say I miss you.

I believe you to be a fine girl. My folks have said a dozen times what a fine girl you are. If anyone is lacking, it's me—I am not good enough for you, but I think we will learn to love each other. If it doesn't work out, I'm not going to cling to you just to escape being alone again because being over here has molded me (even against my will) to stand alone and to live without anyone to love or love me.

If I mentally survive these last three and a half months, I can live without anyone because I did it here and crushed my fears. I found being without anyone I could count on through thick and thin wasn't as bad as I thought, so I'm not afraid anymore.

With no fears and your pleasant personality, we might become deeply involved with one another. Don't be downhearted about me not being overly sweet and loving. I respect you, and I remember the good times we had together. I know you'll be good for me. What more can I say? Don't think I don't love you. Just give me time.

Bill

I was confused and hurt by Bill's letter. Did he want to break up with me? Maybe he was right about my insecurities, but what about his own? He still missed Misty! And due to the time it took for our letters to travel back and forth, I still hadn't heard from him about Louise.

I was on an emotional roller coaster, one day up and the next day down. Waiting for this ride to end in another three and a half months felt like forever. Yet, I had to hang in there. I had term papers to write, finals to prepare for, and letters to write my husband. In them, I hid my true feelings, attempting to focus on the positive things in my life, looking forward to summer vacation, a new job, and staying at Grandma's, who liked to cook. I was excited because I needed a break from school and would get invaluable experience working in PT. And, best of all, I'd get paid.

Madison
May 14, 1969

Hi Bill,

Guess what? I got a job this summer! I'll work as a physical therapy aide with older people at a small hospital in Algoma. It doesn't sound like the neatest job, as younger folks tend to avoid working with older folks. But I'm excited about my first real experience working with patients, and I can stay at Grandma's house rent-free.

Only nine days left of classes and then final exams. Today, Janet and I took a break, borrowed two bicycles, and rode up to Vilas Park after school. It was so much fun. Next year, we'll plan a picnic there with you and Bear.

Saturday night Janet and I are going to the Hoffman House for a PT banquet for school. It costs $5, including a steak dinner. Yummy, I haven't had steak since Hawaii. They'll have a live band for entertainment. I can't wait. I'll wear the turquoise dress from our wedding.

May 16, 1969

Okay, Smarty Pants, you've been right all along. We proved in physiology class today that I'm underweight by 2.25 pounds. I weigh 122.75 and should be in the range of 125–140. I'd be immense at 140 pounds, though. So I've got to gain two more pounds, as you said.

You know what? Since Hawaii, I haven't cried once, but I miss not having you here with me. Sometimes it's good to be alone when I need to study, but I hate being alone in my room so much of the time.

What's bugging me most is that many of my girlfriends have steady guys and are engaged. They see their fellows every week or so. Yet, here I'm, married, and I am all alone. I didn't marry you to have a security blanket, but I did want your companionship and love. We have three and a half months to wait, and nothing will make that time go faster.

I guess love doesn't fit into your hot, miserable, and sticky world, but it's still a big part of mine. You don't seem to care if you tell me how, when, or if you love me. So, what do I have—a small room and myself? I live from day to day. So, I guess we're both in the same boat.

I relieve my boredom by walking to the drugstore, washing my hair, and listening to my radio. I've got nothing to complain about because you never complain. But maybe if you did, I'd get more mail! I want more letters even if you have nothing to say. Geez, I'm beginning to sound just like my mother!

Honey, what do you do with yourself all day? You never have much to say about your life there. Do you work one or two shifts, sleep during the day, go swimming, or go to the photo lab?

I wish you were here to cheer me up, tell me how stupid I am to feel this depressed, and not let this stuff bother me. I love you, Bill, probably more than you realize. There's nothing more for me to say.

Carole

Vietnam
18 May 1969

Hi #1 Girl,

Just a note to tell you I think you're the finest—most faithful and kindest; good, better, and the best wife. A bum like me doesn't deserve you. When I get home in less than four months, I'll try to make you happy and be worthy of you.

I want you to know there is no Louise. I meant to sign that letter Lousy Lover, not Lousie Lover. My spelling and penmanship ain't so great. So how can I ditch a bitch that don't exist?

I've been faithful and haven't even been downtown teasing the whores. It's nasty—little four and five-year-old boys run up and say, "GI want blow job? My sister do number one job, five dollar, okay?" It's disgusting how war and what follows it has denigrated these people.

You can see I've been wearing my medallion in all the photos I've sent, but I lost it today in a brief fistfight with another GI. I got sick and tired of him picking on our house girls and making them cry. It isn't a good way to make friends with these people. The irony is I don't even like these girls.

How did I come out? It was a draw. I got a bloody nose and a cut. My mistake was offering him the first swing, but I accomplished what I wanted to. Though not as hard as I wished, I gave him a few good clips. Finally, he got tired and left the girls alone. He hasn't bothered them anymore. Maybe I'll find the medallion tomorrow. It means a lot to me.

Bill

Catholics often wore medallions for protection, so I'd sent Bill the Alpha and Omega medallion as a gift. In Revelations 22:13, Jesus referred to himself as the Alpha and Omega, the first and the last, the beginning and the end. The plan was Bill would wear the medallion during his time in Vietnam, and I would remove it when he came home, but now that was out of the question.

Madison
May 25, 1969

Hi Billy Boy,

There's a new song out called "Good Morning, Starshine." It makes me think of September when I'll wake up every morning with you by my side. Does it seem that a magical month called September will come someday? A Big Bird will carry you away from that war-torn land and bring you back to the people you love. Could that be possible, or is it a fantasy?

It was nice to hear your voice while listening to your tape recording today. It turned out beautiful; everything was clear and understandable. Thank you for your many kisses.

I was lonely for you again yesterday when I walked past the lit-up fountain by the library at 10 p.m. The windy night reminded me of when we drove down to Lake Michigan, parked, and made out by the rocky shoreline. I think of you more now as summer nears.

As of June 5, I will no longer be in Madison, so send my letters to Mom's address or Grandma's.

May 29, 1969

Tomorrow is Memorial Day. I doubt whether you or I will see much of a holiday as I've got to study for my final exams. I'm sure you hardly remember what a holiday is, being in the service for two years.

Great, you'll be home by September 2. I think I can wait that long. Then, you'll be a free man. Free of the Army but tied to me. I don't think you'll mind that, though!

I saw films from the Apollo 10 moon flight. Now I know why you once wanted to become an astronaut. Those films are cool, almost like you're there with them, looking back at the earth.

I don't understand why we wanted to go to the moon anyway unless to see the view, but it would add prestige if the United States were the first to land there. Even though man is so intelligent to derive a means to get to the moon, how much smarter must God be to allow a man to get there? Next, men will be fighting over the moon. It'll make a great battleground—no innocent people around to get killed.

Would you believe Helen is getting lonely for Henry? As you said, when you get home, we should take some time to reacquaint Carole and Bill before Henry and Helen get reacquainted. We can decide then in what order we want to do that. I know the first thing I want from you is a big smile, a huge hug, and a long kiss, in that order.

I'm anxious to get back home. It's two months since I've been there. As this is my last summer vacation, I plan to relax and enjoy it. Since I was a freshman, I've gone to college straight through all the summers, but there's no homework this summer. That's great!

Carole

Vietnam
31 May 1969

Hi Dum, Dum,

I still don't know if I got the fifteen days or three weeks cut off from my stay here for an early out. But, boy, I'm going to eat a lot of French fries, banana splits, and butterscotch malts when I get back. Then, after I rest a bit, I can't wait to take you dancing.

I'm getting itchy and restless after the movies I saw last night. *The Flim-Flam Man* and *Woman Times Seven* didn't help. I didn't sleep well, and I'm still irritable and tired. So far, I haven't laid anyone. I've kept my promise to you. I hope you've been good, too.

You're a swell girl, a "numbah" one girl, as the gooks say, to put up with such a cranky young buck like me who can't even speak from his heart that he loves you more than anything or anyone else. I hope I'll fall in love with you all over again when I get home and that I'm capable of giving love.

I'm so sick of Vietnam and fed up with the entire thing—the Vietnamese attitude, the GIs, and the whole atmosphere of this crazy war. Last week two VCs were caught on our compound, mapping our area.

The 173rd Airborne has opened up an in-country training school here. They also have Vietnamese troops training with them. Since they started sweeping the area around here, we haven't been mortared once.

Both the acetylene and oxygen plants broke down for lack of parts. I'm so short I don't care. We've had the spring monsoons for the last three days, so it has kept the temperature under 100 degrees but made up for it in humidity. The past two months will be horrible with heat and high humidity like when I arrived here.

I'll see you in less than three months. So be as happy as you can. I'll be home soon.

Lousy Lover,
Bill

P.S. Here's a poem I wrote for you.

CAROLE

Evening's peaceful tranquility
Calls softly to my soul,
And the confusion of the day
As starlight beckons me to follow,
Into the shadows alone to escape
The reality of my being.
Into heaven's infinity
I gaze with tear-filled eyes,
And to the chaotic regions of my mind,
The cherished memory of Carole's love
Fills my lonely heart with life as
I touch the silence of the night with a prayer.

CHAPTER 15 - JUNE 1969: ALL OF WAR'S A STAGE

Vietnam
4 June 1969

Dear Carole,

Save this thought:

> I am but a man,
> A boy at heart.
> You are my life,
> For you are my love.
> You are my fire engine,
> All shiny, red, and new.
> Yes, I cherish you.

The days and nights don't go fast enough now. I'm sick to death of this compound and Vietnam. Don't worry. Everything is fine here, and nothing ever happens to married short-timers. "See You in September," as the song goes.

Glad you're home now and away from that campus with sex-hunting males. After going without sex for so long, it would blow my mind to find out you didn't wait for me. Wow, I think of you more and more. Sometimes, I can almost feel you. I hope you're more aggressive (like a nymphomaniac, she-devil) when we get back together.

I've got a DEROS date of 26 August (unconfirmed) and a separation from the service date of 1 September. So if all goes well, which you and I know it rarely does in the Army, I'll be home late on 2 September or, for sure, by 4 September. I'm so excited about coming back to the world. I can't tell if it's a love of America, you, or both.

Watts shipped out to Japan yesterday to be cured of the clap, syphilis, and its complications. He got it bad. What can I say? He reaped what he sowed.

Love you,
Bill

Watts had been a thorn in Bill's side since they'd been in advanced training at Fort Belvoir for their MOS of gas generating. A big, burly guy who did illegal drugs and had more brawn than brains, he was also known as Horndog, the wild man.

Bill replaced Watts as the leader of the oxygen-acetylene plant after Watts was found guilty of smoking pot on duty and reduced to a PFC (E-1). Later Horndog contracted a difficult-to-treat form of gonorrhea and syphilis after he raped an elderly Vietnamese woman out in the field.

While Bill hitched a ride with a convoy rolling through the countryside, a hunched-over mama-san with her wrinkled skin and blackend-beetle-nut stained teeth smiled at them passing by. While waving her hand, she called out to the soldiers saying, "You Americans numbah one! Thank you much!" Watts was riding on the same truck with Bill, and when Watts heard the accolades, he leaped down and sprinted towards the mama-san. Horndog pulled down the woman's black silk pajama pants and raped her alongside the highway.

It happened so fast and unexpectedly that no one stopped it. Bill told me he winced at the feat, shaking his head. If he had any respect for Watts, Bill lost it that day because Watts was a married man with a wife and child waiting for him back home.

Watts refused to pay the old lady who shouted at him. "You no numbah one GI! You owe money. You numbah ten!" She shook her fist and ran after the truck as it rolled away.

As fate would have it, Bill was assigned to deliver Watts' transfer papers and be part of the wild man's escort to the Qui Nhon airport, where Watts would be flown away for special treatment. Bill drove the jeep, and an MP sat in the back seat with Horndog, who wore his handcuffs and shiny new leg irons in style, asking to stop at the next whorehouse along the way. Bill guessed the incurable venereal disease had already attacked Watts's brain and that he never made it home.

Meanwhile, I wondered what was wrong with Bill's brain after writing me a letter about his dream of being in bed with Misty. Maybe he'd watched too many R-rated movies or needed some "sexcitement" in his life, but why did he have to share his dream of having sex with his ex?

Heading back to Alaska on a Greyhound bus
June 5, 1969

Dear Bill,

I'm writing on the bus going home, so my writing might sometimes be shaky. I'm sorry I haven't written in so long. You must understand how difficult it was to study for finals. I'm exhausted from not getting enough sleep. I almost can't believe it! But I'm beginning to feel free of school, and the pressure is slowly drifting off my brain.

That's some dream you had about your ex-girlfriend and me. If you want it psyched out, then here goes. Sigmund Freud would say Misty was giving me her Bible means she has found you were more important to her than religion, so she puts the Bible aside. All the crying on my part means I think you've been unfaithful to me. All the fuss about Henry means you believe you mean more to me sexually than personally.

Here's what I say—"Never happen, GI." I'd tear Misty's eyeballs out before she'd get that close to you. I'd pound her head with that big Bible and tell her to practice what she preaches. How do you like them apples? I'm not a spineless creature. I fight for who and what I want, and usually, I get it. Bang! Pow! Boom!

Honey, please be extra careful these last few months. Don't get lax. Catching two VCs on the compound doesn't sound good. Don't go out on long hikes; you never know when Charlie might strike again.

Don't break down now and go to a clap shack. Clap shack is a big "No, no." Masturbation is a "Yes, yes." I've been as faithful to you as the Old Geyser in Yellowstone Park, so don't worry.

Alaska
June 7, 1969

Dear Bill,

I'm sorry if I worried you that my grades were going down as I initially thought they were. My final grades are Psychology-A, Physiology-A, Anatomy-A, Therapeutic Exercise-B, and Communicative Disorders-B.

Surprise! My semester average is 3.6. That's the highest grade point I've gotten in college. The A in Anatomy meant the most to me as I worked so hard for it. And with these good grades, I might get that $1,000 trainee scholarship next year.

My parents and I have been discussing having a first anniversary/welcome home party for us when you return home. We can invite 125 people for a meal at the Alaska Resort; my parents will pay for it. What do you think? It would allow you to see all the relatives once you get home. In addition, you could invite a few of your old friends—at least the ones Uncle Sam hasn't taken.

Algoma, Wisconsin
June 15, 1969

Dear Bill,

I sure was glad to hear from you today. I got your letter with four pictures. Why did you shave off your beautiful curly hair? Please have hair when you come home, or I'll threaten to cut mine shorter than it was in Hawaii!

I started my new job Friday night and worked 4.5 hours, finishing up at 9:30 p.m. Then Saturday, I worked from 8 a.m. to 5 p.m. My muscles were so sore this morning. I'm not used to lifting people in and out of bed and into whirlpool baths. Outside of the physical fatigue, I enjoy the work and get paid $1.75 an hour. Also, I like staying with Grandma, who has dinner waiting for me when I come home.

But, without you, it's gonna be a long, lonely summer—like that song goes. It's been six months since I saw you, the longest time we've been apart since we met. There are no words to describe this enduring constant loneliness. I should be happy you'll be home shortly, but the last two and a half months will go by the slowest.

I'm thinking about us being together in our new apartment and being able to take long walks to Lake Mendota, to campus, or uptown any time we feel like it—to be away from everyone we know and just the two of us in Madison. It seems like a dream that's close to coming true.

I think I'll start counting down the days like you do instead of the months—another lousy, miserable day gone by and one day closer to happiness. Do you ever feel this way? That life would be more endurable if we were together?

But I do feel more grown up now. I hope, for your sake, I'm not that spoiled, pouty little girl who always had to have her way or wasn't happy. I can even watch Grandma's corny TV show, *Green Acres*, and get a chuckle out of it, whereas before, I nearly had to leave the room.

I don't mean to criticize or pick on your family, but I wonder what caused things to be the way they are. I don't know how often I've heard your mother say she had to raise five children alone. Now she expects to be treated royally as a reward for all her hard work. Was she more energetic when she was young, or was she always this lazy?

One weekend I was at your house and could still hear your mother complaining when I went to bed. I thought, Now you don't have to listen to this. I'd have gone crazy if I'd had to go through another day there. It was awful. Even though the house was quiet, and everyone was asleep, in my mind, I could still hear your parents arguing.

Guess I've blown a few things off my chest that have been there for a while. I'm waiting for you to come home so we can talk again.

Blabbermouth me,
Carole

Vietnam
20 June 1969

Hi Honey-Comb,

I'm getting short. I mailed a package of personal items home tonight. I can ship things home for free, but if I send old letters home in an envelope, I have to pay six cents a letter. Isn't that stupid? The Army is so dumb in so many ways.

I've got less than seventy days left. I can't stand being apart much longer. I feel like I won't even know you—it's been so long. It'll be like being married to a stranger, but I don't think I could have found a better or more faithful stranger to marry.

I hope to make one more trip to the boonies for three days in the Delta to see my cousin, Chuck Overbeck. The only hitch is getting approval from this pansy-pussy CO for our detachment. Nevertheless, I'd like to see Chuck and see what this fouled-up war is like in the Mekong Delta.

I think Nixon is wise pulling out our troops, but if we can ever halt the Reds, we should bomb, destroy, and free North Vietnam and keep the Reds on the defensive. It's the only solution that no one has considered. It's the only alternative short of giving all of Vietnam to the Reds.

That will eventually happen with our peace talks in Paris[26] and our "win-nothing policy." We're just holding ground; this place will be theirs as soon as we leave. I bet two years after the last US troops leave, communist soldiers will be swimming in our pool and sleeping in our quarters.

21 June 1969

Wow, it took a full hour to read the ten letters waiting for me today. That was nice. My mission up north was cut short by a partial failure in our security. We had only three injuries despite the ambush, and those guys are okay. An Allied troop's chopper picked up the other missing man.

The only thing I didn't tell you about was the village or hamlet the VC terrorized. I'm taking the anti-anxiety medication I got in Da Nang, as it still upsets my stomach to think about this. It just makes me sick.

The VC emasculated and castrated a hamlet's[27] freely elected chief (mayor) and his three sons in front of him. They publicly raped his wife and daughters, ages five to seventeen. The youngest girl died apparently from shock and vaginal bleeding. They also took three babies, one from each of the three men who defended the village, rammed a spiked bamboo pole up into them, and placed the poles upright into the dirt like crucifixes outside the hamlet. It was the first thing I saw when we entered. After that, I couldn't get it out of my mind. The villagers told our interpreter what happened but wouldn't say how many VCs there were or what direction they went.

How could anyone be so vicious to someone of their own race and nationality? People back in the rest of the world can't realize how savage these communists are. Now, I'm all in favor of dropping the cobalt bomb on Hanoi or Peking. But those goddamned fools in the United States are clamoring about letting the Vietnamese decide for themselves after we pull out.

This was Bill's first reference to being sent up north on a spy mission. Usually, he wrote letters or postcards ahead of time and had a buddy mail them to me at intervals, so I wouldn't have to go for long periods without mail and worry.

However, he didn't have time to write postcards before this mission, so he explained his absence in his letter. This incident may have been the beginning of his posttraumatic stress disorder (PTSD).

---

23 June 1969

Yes, I intend to come home bald unless you let your beautiful hair grow long, too. But, of course, you shouldn't care because you said you'd love me hairless and toothless.

Yes, deep inside, I know you've been faithful to me. It's just that the guys keep ribbing me. I tell them, "We agreed before I left; I've been faithful, and I know she has been, too," and they chuckle. I tell them, "I'm going to be able to go home and tell my wife I've been faithful."

Then they say, "Yah, and she'll tell you about her lover—so face it, you can't know because she's ten thousand miles away—you just think she's faithful." There's not much more to say, especially when they point to the high number of GIs planning on divorcing their faithless wives when they get home. I guess I'm a lucky guy.

Two more of my coworkers got the clap really bad and may join Watts soon in Japan. These guys don't harass me anymore about not being a man because I don't go to clap shacks. I wonder why? Ha ha! It serves them right.

Our gas-generating plant has been running, and I'm working the night shift permanently. I sure hope it stays this way. I don't have to make formation during the heat of the day and listen to a lot of BS since that's my sack time.

I'm trying hard to avoid any vulgar speech, but it isn't easy. I don't think a young lady, especially my wife, should have to listen to her beau use foul language. I never said the F-word before I came into the Army, but the Army has cheapened and degraded me.

The good news is that my buddy found my medallion and chain out in the dirt. So all I have to do is have the chain fixed.

24 June 1969

Only sixty-eight days until you're in my arms. I wonder what you'll look like when we meet. I wonder how much you've changed. Can you still make that fruit salad with whipped cream and marshmallows? I often think of you and remember the good times we used to have.

As you can see from the photo, our rebuilt barracks are even better after the VC hit them with a mortar. And we got new screening to keep the bugs out, too.

Be sweet. Be you,
Bill

Algoma
June 25, 1969

Dearest Bill,

Honey, I know you've been through hell in Vietnam. It's hard to believe that the communists or people, in general, could be so cruel and filled with hate to do the things they have done in war. It's terrible, but I'm glad you told me about it. I hope you continue your writing project and round up enough notes and information to write a book someday.

I think politics would be a good place for you. You could change things because you're intelligent and a great thinker. For example, you looked ahead during the battle at your camp and planned your next move. Then, when it was time, you carried out your plan and were safe while the average GI sat in the bunker waiting for the mortars to hit.

I can see why you believe the U.S. could be taken over in fifty to sixty years by the communists. We might not be around to see it, but our children will. You are responsible for warning our fellow countrymen, especially when you see it coming.

By the way, I never received the letter you sent from Da Nang. So why were you fellows sent up there anyway? It was tough for me to go twelve days without a letter or postcard. I was so relieved to receive two yesterday and one today.

Bill, you're a sweet fellow. I'm glad we're married, and you'll be home soon. I still love you, but I'll love you so much more when you're around, and we're together. We'll start from scratch in our relationship and must build a strong foundation of mutual trust and respect. I believe you've always been honest with me.

Carole

Vietnam
28 June 1969

Hello Honey,

I've enclosed a short-timer's calendar so that you can mark off the days. I should have about fifty-eight days left when you receive it.

The swimming pool was closed for a month for repairs. The electric power is off at the photo lab, so there isn't much for me to do during the day except sleep (which it is too hot for), sweat, and study my radio electronics course.

It's been unusually quiet here lately. These past few nights, we haven't seen flares over Phu Cat Air Base.

I'm glad the Army is beginning to pull out of Vietnam, but it's terrible for the Vietnamese. The loyal ones are starting to panic. The ones with money are trying to buy their way out to France, Thailand, Japan, the United States, or any free country. The South Vietnamese fear a blood bath when a coalition government is forced on them.

How stupid to have them fight the Reds for fifteen years, then stop, and expect them to shake hands and love one another. Hundreds of thousands will die, and perhaps as many will illegally flee South Vietnam to Thailand.

Sweetie, be happy,
Bill

While Bill was completing his time in Vietnam, June was a busy month for me. I worked full-time and finally gained weight from Grandma feeding me her homemade bread, raspberry jelly, and cherry kolaches.

On my days off, I drove the five miles back to Alaska and planned our anniversary party. I wanted to save Mom and Dad money because even though I was married, they agreed to pay my senior year's tuition. So I typed postcards (mistakes and all) for invitations, designed a three-tiered cake with a spiral effect of yellow roses, and found a local farm lady to bake it. For entertainment, I hired a one-man band. Mom and Dad reserved the hall at the Alaska Resort, agreeing to pay for the buffet dinner while Bill's parents would pay for the beer bar.

We had nothing to our name except Bill's motorcycle, and next year we'd live on his GI Bill and the $1,000 scholarship I received. Nevertheless, I sincerely hoped we would receive cash and enough gifts to set up my kitchen and buy a small black-and-white TV for the furnished living room. Meanwhile, I sewed curtains for our bedroom, Mom gave me some of her old linens, and Grandma made me a quilt.

As reality sunk in, I was excited but anxious about being a wife and homemaker. Mom noticed my nervousness and said that all I ever talked about was Bill coming home, but I couldn't help myself. All that mattered was him being safe in my arms.

CHAPTER 16 - JULY 1969: A MILLION ANGELS' WINGS

Vietnam
5 July 1969

Dear Sunshine,

I'm leaving on July 30 for a seven-day leave at one of the Pacific area's ten R&R centers. Hawaii and Australia are out because R&Rs have priority over leaves. (Those are the favorite R&R spots.) So I'll probably end up in Formosa, Hong Kong, Bangkok, Japan, Okinawa, or one of the other out-of-the-way spots.

I'll have only about nineteen days left with my unit when I return. I'll spend the last five days packing, clearing out, and processing. You better believe I won't knock myself out for the Army.

Don't worry about me. This short-timer is determined not to get killed. By the way, if the news mentioned our base getting hit on July 2, I wasn't even there. I'm lucky to have missed all the action in the past months. So please don't believe the BS about NVA regiments pulling out unless it's to regroup and recuperate.

Right now, I'm on light duty because I just got out of the 67th Evacuation Hospital in Qui Nhon yesterday, July 4. I wasn't going to tell you, but the 1st Lt. nurse said not to worry when I got discharged because the hospital had sent out a form letter to inform you I was not seriously injured. You're probably worried if you got that letter already. I was in the hospital from July 2–4 and just had hairline fractures of three ribs, but I feel good now, so don't sweat it.

It'll be a few weeks before my ribs can take a steam bath and a massage. You don't seem to mind me getting the relaxing treatment I wish you were here to give me. Koreans run the place I have in mind; it's clean and fairly respectable. I haven't heard of anyone getting laid there, though. Guys say they got a blow job, but I doubt it. I can't see myself getting the clap when I'm this short after doing without man's most essential pleasure for one year.

I'll wait until I hear from you again to know that you say the full treatment is fine and okay with you, so you won't resent me or hold it against me later. The guys would say I'm pussy-whipped (same as hen-pecked) if they knew I asked your permission to get a steam bath and a massage. But, of course, they say that anyway because I don't go screwing clap-shack whores.

I'm working days now because the generator that supplies power for the oxygen plant needs repair. I've got nothing to do but sit here and write this letter unless one of the lifers catches me. They like to see us busy even if we aren't doing anything. I'm too short to care if they do see me.

Now about the *Playboy* centerfolds, I don't intend to paper the walls with them. I don't think they're out of order or unsuitable for married life. I wouldn't think of tacking them up on the walls, but I think some would look good in the proper frame. I think you'd like them almost as much as I do.

You have this old-fashioned feeling that nude photos are dirty and not respectable. I see it as an expression of the essence of womanly beauty in its simplest, basic and unadulterated form. Don't ask me to hide them in the closet. I don't give a damn what that little old lady rents to us sees.

The general idea is that a man's house is his castle, and if he can't have the castle as he wants, he isn't the king, and his queen is the ruler. Perhaps you feel you have something more suitable. Okay, we can compare ideas and talk it out later.

It's taken me about five years to break away from the cultural taboos and think freely. But, even now, I still think of God as a punishing God. Pure theology teaches that God gives us free will and doesn't interfere in our average day-to-day life but waits until we die to punish or reward us. It's contrary to what I learned as a child.

Six days ago, one night when I didn't have to work, it cooled off. I showered and felt cool, clean, and nice. The sky was beautiful, and the moon was bright. I watched *Wild in the Streets* and felt groovy. I thought about how nice it would be to be with you and make love, but here I am, and there you are.

Bill

Algoma

July 7, 1969

Dear Bill, Honey,

I'm anxious to see you back in my world. To have you home safe and out of the Army will make one of my happiest dreams come true. You won't have any problem getting reacquainted.

I feel more of a woman now than when I think of my behavior in Hawaii under different circumstances. Unfortunately, our Hawaii trip started on the wrong foot. But we needn't worry about that this time. I'll be so glad to see my husband that I won't have anything else on my mind except you.

Right now, I'd enjoy talking with you about nothing in general and everything in particular—whatever pops into our heads. What I look forward to the most is lying by your side—you with your shirt off, your arm around me, and my head on your shoulder. A simple request isn't it?

Take care, Tiger, and come safely home.

Carole

Vietnam
8 July 1969

Hi Lover,

Do you know why I'm happy? Today I got my orders for release from Active Duty on September 1. Can you dig it? I'm almost free again! In fifty-five days, when I wake up, it won't be in a bunk with some "Scruffy" yanking on my toes, but with you alongside me. Groovy. I feel so good because now I'm getting out of this Mother-Fucking Army. I'm so looking forward to seeing you.

How do you like my poem? I got inspired one night thinking about how crazy in love I used to be. I wish I could feel that way again. Now I feel empty and numb, but I still miss you.

BILL'S WORLD

Only those who have been kissed
By the morning's soft sun rays,
Could know the warmth of loving her.
Only those who have had the
Cotton-candy dandelion touch their cheek,
Could know the softness of her gentle touch.
Only those who have seen the glow
Beyond the twinkling night-sky stars,

> Could see love's shining fantasy in her eyes.
> Only those who know the voices
> Of a million angels' songs,
> Could know the beauty of her voice.
> And only those who know the joy of
> Watching children's laughter-filled games,
> Could know the joy of seeing her smile.
> Indeed, only those who have heard
> Her sweet half-child, half-womanly words,
> Breeze off her lips so tender and kind.
> And,
> You can only know them one by one,
> Seeking all in each
> But missing some.
> But I have found them all within,
> The loving arms of Carole Lynn.

12 July 1969

I still don't know what courses I'll take at Madison. I'd better take some refresher courses and general classes until I get my feet on the ground. The biggest battle will be overcoming this "I don't give a damn" attitude the Army has instilled so deeply in me.

14 July 1969

Yesterday was an exciting day for me. The 160th and the 865th had the entire day off because we were ahead of our work quota. I went to Qui Nhon heliport and caught a chopper to Long My and An Khe. We flew briefly over my compound, but I couldn't get a photo of it. We were traveling at one-hundred-twenty knots, three-quarter miles altitude.

I stuck my head and hand with the movie camera out the side door. The wind almost yanked me out of the chopper, and I almost dropped the camera. Good thing I had a safety belt on. I got a picture of the road where a convoy I was on got ambushed late in the afternoon a few months ago. Then we flew directly over the An Khe Pass so I could get a few shots of the hairpin curve.

As we were nearing An Khe heliport, an enemy anti-aircraft gun opened fire on us. We made four circles and passes at the half-hidden position. The vibrations from the two fifty-caliber machine guns were so strong that

I had difficulty hanging onto my camera to change the film. It all happened in less than three minutes. Finally, we emptied the M2 (Ma Deuce) machine guns and landed at An Khe, less than two miles away. I don't know how the film will turn out, but if it does, you'll be able to see how a ground-to-air fight looks. It's rare that the enemy attacks in broad daylight. They're getting pretty darn brave.

Then I went toward Pleiku and got on a truck to visit a Montagnard village. I hiked about a quarter-mile off Highway 19 to get some shots of village life. After that, I caught a convoy back to the base. My buddies were here from Cam Ranh Bay to scrounge parts for their oxygen plant.

You asked what Saigon tea is. It's a thimble-sized drink the bar girls expect you to buy them. It costs $2 and is usually watered-down coconut juice and Coca-Cola. That's what the girl orders while the guy pays for it. The GI can buy a beer for $0.85 or a liquor drink for $1.75. It adds up fast. GIs aren't supposed to know that Saigon tea is nothing. It's a big screw to the GI, who has to pay for it.

So, you miss me fiercely, huh? Good! It serves you right for not talking me out of the Army.

Yours,
Bill

Algoma
July 15, 1969

Dearest Bill,

Thanks again for thinking so much of me to write such a beautiful poem. It's such a tender poem. You've impressed me. I think it's grand, especially the line: "You can only know them one by one, seeking all in each but missing some." I have this uncontrollable feeling for you, and I think it's love.

In your July 5 letter, I liked the part about the cool night you described. Wow, a paragraph like that makes me hot and bothered. I wonder what I was doing that night.

Here's a joke for you. What goes in long and hard and comes out soft and juicy? Give up? It's a stick of gum.

Carole

P.S. How do you feel about September 6 for the party? You should be home by then, inso?[28]

Vietnam
17 July 1969

Hi Carole,

I finally got a letter from my cousin, Chuck. He says there's too much action down by the South China Sea and for me not to come to visit. His CO says "No." That's what I wanted, though, action in the daylight, so I can photograph it as it happens.

The summer before I graduate college would be the best time for a trip to Germany. What do you think? We may have to economize to save money. I'm tentatively planning on us going in the summer of 1971.

Henry's gone into permanent hibernation. I miss you. I miss putting kisses on "the twins" and resting my head on your lap—many a tired night. I wish I could do that now.

Love,
Bill

Algoma
July 17, 1969

Dearest Bill,

Today I put up the Snoopy short-timers calendar you sent and crossed off your forty-sixth day. I miss you fiercely, badly—these words don't even describe the feelings in my heart.

Will September ever come? When will your warm kisses touch my lips and your arms hold me tight? Will the day I meet you at the airport ever arrive? Why doesn't it hurry? I can see it all in my mind, and I long for that day.

Bill
I'm trying to express in words,
What my voice cannot say to you.
What my touch cannot reveal to you
Because of the distance separating us.
I'm trying to convey my words
On a piece of paper

A mood within me,
An indescribable, crazy warmth for you
And a tenderness that's difficult to put into words.
Maybe you'll be able to catch the mood some night, too.

Your Carole

Vietnam
18 July 1969

Dear Dum, Dum,

September 6th sounds all right to me for the party. Anytime that is convenient for your folks is fine with me. I expect to be home for sure by 3 September 1969.

Wow, I'm excited about Apollo 11. It was nice they included a token of the dead Russian cosmonauts. I wish I'd become an astronaut. Unfortunately, it's a dream that will never materialize now, but perhaps one of our sons will become one. I see why parents are interested in directing their children's lives. They want them to succeed where they have failed.

I'm glad you're fiercely horny; if one of us is, we've got a fifty percent chance. If neither of us is, nothing will happen. I hope my desire will increase as I get farther from here and closer to home.

I want you to know I'm not going to flirt (as you say) on my short-term leave. Dance and talk, yes, maybe. Flirt and screw, no. So you can stop worrying about that.

The Army is sending GIs with nine months or more of service left to Thailand instead of home. They started doing that this month. It looks like Thailand will become the new Vietnam. Twenty-one out of twenty-four guys DEROS-ing that thought they'd spent the last nine to twenty-four months of service in the States or Germany were shocked when they found out they were going straight from Vietnam to Thailand (without even a thirty-day leave). I'm so glad I didn't enlist for three years.

I shall be a free man in forty-five days, home in forty-seven. I hope you'll be able to cope with me. I may not be the same as before, but I'm determined to be happier than I was.

I'm sick of this dreary existence. All that matters is counting the days to be out and alive. I'll be delighted to sleep until 8:30 a.m. and eat a private breakfast for two instead of two hundred. I'll be glad to have a private bedroom, shower, and a kitchen I can snack from. I won't have to put up with potheads and belligerent loudmouth drunks. It's beginning to sound like a bitch letter, so I'll close.

Love,
Bill

Algoma
July 20, 1969

Dearest Bill,

Hey, know what song is playing? It's our theme, "Dedicated to the One I Love," by The Mamas & the Papas.

It sounds like you had an exciting helicopter ride. I'll bet you were surprised to see your friends when you returned to camp.

Yesterday, I bought a dress on sale for $5. It's what's called a bra dress and has a built-in bra. It's a bright orange and yellow, low in the front and back, and a short skirt. Now I'm working on a suntan to go with it. So that's what I'll be wearing when you first see me.

I like my job and am happy everything has worked out for me. I'm making good money and the days and weeks go by fast. I'm learning things that will benefit me for school in the fall.

Honey, be careful on your leave and don't run around taking chances. You've been lucky so far. I'll worry about you going to Ben Het Camp and other dangerous places because if you get hurt there, it will be your fault for nosing around where you don't belong. Promise me; you'll be extra careful. Please don't blow it all now!

Write to me when you're on leave—even postcards will be fine—so that I know all is well. Then hurry, pack, and come home to me. When you return, I'll be waiting for you with open arms and ready to get reacquainted.

Love ya,
Carole

P.S. We just saw live pictures of the astronauts on the moon—first step down and all—and can even hear them talking, "That's one small step for man, one giant leap for mankind." It's quite a thrill to think the U.S. is the first to get a man on the moon and that there are men up there right now.

Vietnam
20 July 1969

Hi Mrs. Wagener,

It's taken me an hour to decide which two laminated photos to mail back to you for safekeeping. I like them all. Your pictures sustained me through the last hard six months, without which I think I may have even started to hate you, simply for the lack of you. That's an uncontrollable built-in mechanism I have. When I'm pressed hard and can't have something I want, I begin to hate it rather than longing for what I can't have. (I'm self-analyzing.)

At least through these photos, you were here by sight, and by the audiotapes, you were here by sound. That fills two of my five senses. I hate to part with them now, but I'd hate to have to show them to some dirty-minded inspector MP when I'm processing out of Vietnam. He might try to confiscate them as pornography. I've heard many GI inspectors do that and don't turn them in for destruction but keep them for themselves.

22 July 1969

Thanks for the "okay" and "no sweat." As soon as my ribs feel better, I'll get one of those all-over massages. I hear they even pop the toes and massage the heels. I may be hen-pecked, but I'll enjoy it more knowing you don't mind. I won't be able to stop Henry from being a dick, but I'll keep him from doing his thing. Okay? Thanks!

I'm afraid you might feel that I think of you as a sex tool. That's simply not so. I may be oversexed, but you're the sweetest thing that has entered my life. It seems the only way I've tried to show you is with sex. But, since I've been over here, I realize that it probably meant nothing to you.

Love, being something hard to define, includes sexual and sentimental meanings. It doesn't show how much I admire you and marvel at how an eighteen-year-old girl could grow up so sheltered, innocent, and unblemished. I'm glad that the time I walked you home and kissed you, you didn't shun me. Even later, you didn't lose your Fanny Hill type of innocence. Now, after more than ten months of being a single wife around all those men at the U.W., you're still a faithful and caring woman who writes nearly every day. Most guys around me talk openly about their wives getting it from some "Jodie."

I admire and respect you for being that way—Carole Lynn—faithful to the smallest detail. It almost seems impossible for a girl like you to exist, much less be my girl. You are so good and never hurt or rejected me (except for the red pajama incident). Only your "maybe" answer to my marriage proposal hurt more and still hurts. But getting back to my point, you're wonderful, and your faithfulness for the last eleven months has proved it.

As you say, you trusted me so blindly. Being a sweet girl was your greatest weapon or deterrent to keep me from being unfaithful to you. I'd have resented it if you'd asked me about other girls, acted suspicious, or were jealous. But knowing you, so naïve and trusting, I couldn't corrupt or mar my relationship with you. I wanted to be able to tell you everything openly without being ashamed of my actions.

Carole Lynn, I'm fortunate to have you despite some of your imperfections and inhibitions. Even though I find it hard to say I love you the way I did that night when I rode my motorcycle the thirty miles from Green Bay to Alaska. I ran out of gas, walked my cycle two miles, and then found you all asleep, so I sacked out in your car all night. I'm not just buttering you up or flattering you, Carole, hoping that you'll wear a micro skirt when you meet me at the airport or wear a sexy tight blouse with a pushup bra like a high society starlet.

I was proud of you for holding back the tears when I left on September 12. It wasn't until Vietnam that I realized what a brave, wonderful, good woman you are. I doubt the Virgin Mary would have been as faithful as you if she had been on the UW campus. Instead, as I interpret the Bible, she led a sheltered life and had her husband with her.

I sometimes get the feeling, quite deeply, that I'm not worthy of you. You may find that hard to believe, but it's true. I suppose it strikes you odd that I carry on like this, but that's how I feel. I never said it before; perhaps I should have said it more.

I was disappointed when I saw you so thin and pale in Hawaii. I should've understood and been proud that you worked so hard in school. I should've loved you for sacrificing your health. I should've been waiting for you at the airport instead of going to a movie to lose my anxiety.

You're right. I was thoughtless. I think you got the short end of the stick. You'd have been wise to keep saying, "Maybe when you get home from Vietnam," when I asked for your hand in marriage, even at the risk of being an unwed mother.

I will try hard to live up to what you deserve, love you again, and get over Vietnam and all the hate and bitterness it's created in me. But, if I start to slip, give me a kick in the ass and whip this letter on me to remind me.

I read somewhere that a woman and a man want companionship first. A man looks for sex-love second and sentimentality-love fifth. A woman looks for and needs sentimental-love second and sex-love seventh (next to last). It just struck me that I'm not only telling you all this but also telling myself what I never admitted before because it lessens me.

I thought I told you the convoy I was on coming back from An Khe went off on the highway's shoulder to avoid a big chunk of metal and some rocks in the middle of the road. The VC had deliberately planted a mine in the soft shoulder, and we hit it. The jolt threw me up in the air. I'd been standing next to a machine gun and landed on it. That's how I cracked my ribs. I wish I hadn't told you because you wouldn't have known or worried. But, just so you know, I didn't fall out of some girl's bed!

I just watched a twenty-minute Apollo 11 Moon Walk video. The reception was poor because of the heavy rain and many mountains between Qui Nhon and us, but it was exciting to see it like it was. Now the astronauts are one-third of the way home. I hope we can watch Apollo 12 together.

I'm not sending you one of your nude photos today because I can't decide which one I like least, so I'm keeping them all for a while longer. I love how you look unabashedly, healthily, and sexily stripping your bra off. I wish you'd smiled like that in all your photos. I wish I could see you do that again right now!

25 July 1969

The 1st Sgt., who I didn't get along with in Company Headquarters, was relieved of his position yesterday for incompetence and dereliction of duty. After several months of his leadership, the orderly room was messed up and confused. The new acting 1st Sgt., whom I worked with in the Shop Office, asked me to come back and help set things right when I'm back from leave as he knows I know how to do the job.

29 July 1969

I'm staying at Cam Ranh Bay tonight and might get out for Bangkok, Thailand, or Taipei, Formosa, tomorrow. I'm so short and happy because of it; I almost can't stand it. I've made up my mind not to let Henry do his thing in Bangkok, no matter if he explodes. Besides, I'm too cheap to spend the money, so don't worry.

Your faithful and horny husband,

Bill

CHAPTER 17 - AUGUST 1969: A SOLEMN WARNING

While Bill was on his leave for Thailand, I received this letter and a few postcards from him. I didn't know who the original author was, but this type of document was most likely passed around from GI to GI, and as company clerk, Bill retyped it. The Navy had a similar Official Notice.

OFFICIAL NOTICE

Issued in solemn warning at Cha Rang Valley, Republic of Vietnam, this 7th month, 24 day of 1969, A.D.

To the friends, neighbors, and relatives of William J. Wagener:

Very soon, the above-named individual will once again be in your midst, de-Americanized, de-moralized, and dehydrated, ready once again to take his place as a human being with freedom and justice for all, engaged in life, liberty, and the somewhat delayed pursuit of happiness.

You must make allowances for the crude environment he has been calling home for the past year. In a sense, he may be a bit vulgar, uncouth, and suffering from profanity. He must be handled with extreme care. Show no alarm if he cries with terror at the sight of a child's cap gun or if he rips menus to pieces when they contain items such as C-rations, fish heads, water buffalo steaks, and other Asian delicacies. Don't be shocked if he yells, "I can't take it anymore." Refuse to ridicule him if he drinks liquids out of beer cans, forgets to flush the contraption, or faints at the sight of a tent. Be tolerant when he stands on the front lawn at 5:00 a.m. with a sour look on his face and an evil expression in his eyes. Don't get upset when he calls the kitchen a mess hall and tries to clean the oven with a brick. He will go insane at the word re-enlist and, above all, never ask him why the neighbor's son was over there for a shorter time than he was.

In making your joyous preparation to welcome him back to respectable society, you must make allowances for the crude environment in which he has suffered these past twelve months. He may be somewhat Asiatic, suffering from advanced stages of Viet Congitis, or too much Ba Moui Ba Beer.

Therefore, show no alarm when he prefers to squat rather than sit on a chair, pad around with sandals and a towel, shyly offers to sell the postman cigarettes for fifty cents, and picks suspiciously at his food as if you were trying to poison him. Don't be surprised if he answers all questions with an "I hate this place" or "Number Ten."

Be tolerant when he tries to buy everything for half the asking price, accuses the grocer of being a thief, and refuses to enter an establishment that doesn't have screens over the doors and windows. Any of the following sights should be avoided since they can produce an advanced state of shock: people dancing, television, and round-eyed women. In a relatively short time, profanity will decrease, and he will be speaking English as well as he ever did.

He may complain of sleeping in a room and refuse to go to bed without a mosquito net. Make no flattering remarks about exotic Southeast Asia; avoid mentioning the benefits of overseas duty, and seasonal weather, and ask before mentioning the food delicacies of the Far East, such as "flied lice" (fried rice). The mere reference of these particular subjects may trigger an awesome display of violence.

For the first few months until he is housebroken, be especially watchful when he is in the company of women, particularly beautiful specimens. The few good-looking girls he has seen are either WAC officers (the possession of male officers) or are just untouchables; therefore, the first reaction to meeting a round-eyed girl may be to stare. Wives and sweethearts are advised to take advantage of this momentary shock and keep young ladies out of his reach.

Keep in mind underneath his tanned and rugged exterior beats a heart of gold. Treasure this, for it is the only good thing of value he has left. Treat him with kindness, tolerance, and an occasional fifth of whiskey, and you should be able to rehabilitate this hollow shell of a man you once knew and loved.

Send no more mail to APO 96492 after 15 August 1969, for he is leaving the tropics in 35 days and heading to the land of the big PX.

Vietnam
8 August 1969
Dear Carole,

Bangkok was great. I only wish I'd had even half the money I spent in Hawaii to buy more tailored clothes and gold rings. You can't imagine how cheap everything is there. I've sent home the tuxedo that I had made in Bangkok. It should get there in about three weeks or when I get home. I caught a touch of the Hong Kong flu in Bangkok. I should be all right by the time you get this letter.

Love,
Bill

Alaska
August 14, 1969

Dearest Bill,

As I lie here and write my very last letter to you, I can't help but think of all the lonely days and nights you've spent in Vietnam. Yes, I was lonely too, but not like the heartbreaking loneliness you must have been through being away from home, family, and everything familiar.

I'm sure none of us can or will understand the agony and frustration of this war and the year you have spent there. We were all too content in our own little worlds and concerned about our own little problems. But, when you're home and the urge hits you to talk, you can tell me, and I'll gladly listen. I want to know all about your experiences there.

This year has gone by very fast and yet very slowly. Our wedding seems like only days ago; it was such a happy time for me. I will never forget how you looked at me when we said our vows. It felt like it was just you and me there in the room. It'll always be a day to remember, having had to do it all on such short notice.

We also had a few unhappy moments. Times we've hurt each other. Times I'd rather forget, but surely the happy moments have outweighed the unhappy—then all we have are happy ones. Inso?

These last eighteen days will be the hardest. We've been through it before, and they're always slow. But, we can keep busy and think about what we want to do when we're together again.

Oh, Bill, there is one thing I want you to know. I still love you and always have loved you even though I said maybe I wasn't sure that I did in one letter. I just said that because you were giving me so much static.

Give Henry a great big love pat and a squeeze for me. Tell him his Helen will be waiting for him when he gets home.

You silly boy, I'll always be your girl (not just your wife). It should be more fun that way—living together. I don't feel very married to you either right now.

No more packages to send.

No more letters to RVN.

Just a date in the back of our minds,

September 1st or 2nd

You'll be mine.

Well, Bill, it won't be long now, and we'll have completed our twelve months of waiting. The Army has had you long enough. Now it's my turn.

Take care. Enjoy your trip home and back to the real world. Call me collect just as soon as you get into Washington State.

Auf Wiedersehen,
Carole Lynn

Vietnam
15 August 1969

Hi 'dere, my faithful girl, lover, friend, companion, future roommate, mistress (i.e., wife),

How are you with only seventeen days to T-Day (Togetherness Day)?

Guess what? The guy who took over my job at Company Headquarters went home twelve hours after being notified that his wife had a nervous breakdown. That meant I was the only one left in the company who knew how to do the job of decoding, security backup, training, and re-enlistment. The two guys who work there don't like me and don't want to see me there either (and I am too short to be there), but the CO has no choice.

I made a deal since I had the CO over the barrel. All I will do is supervise for one or two days showing their remaining clerks how to do the work. I stop working tonight at midnight on the oxygen plant. I don't pull any guard duty, no reactionary guard duty, no alert guard, no extra duties, and nobody can give me any static.

Every dog has his day, but I'm having nine or ten of them until I leave here. I will "respectively" insult the top sergeant, my former senior NCO, and several other people. I started with the clerk who got my E-5 promotion seven months ago simply because the top sergeant didn't like me. I did it right in front of the CO and got away with it. Oh, the joy of joys! It's nice to have your CO and top Sgt. over a barrel. Haha! This is better (more kicks) than masturbation.

Ummm. I'd like to give you a big hug right now. I'm so happy that even though we are supposed to get clobbered with mortars, hit by nerve gas, and sapper attacks sometime in the next seven nights, I couldn't care less. I'm too short to bother with Charlie.

After eleven months in this stink hole called Vietnam, I refuse to die now. I've been stabbed in the hand, shot in the foot (really just nicked), and hit in the leg by fragmentation and stones from a mortar. I cracked ribs when an armored truck blew up under me; I was shot at in a chopper while returning through the An Khe Pass; I was ambushed, shot at, and chased near the demilitarized zone.

I was sniped at while driving to Qui Nhon, had my first Super 8 mm camera shot to pieces in my hands, and was shot at while on guard duty. I have been mortared while I slept; been up for court-martial for helping save the survivors of a convoy. Right in front of me, I had a typewriter shot up; and a hole put in my office wall in the middle of the day. I was pinned down by two more snipers near Pleiku and mortared in Cam Ranh Bay.

Blankety, blank to the NVA, the VC, and the Red Chinese NVA advisors. They haven't gotten me yet. Charlie ain't gonna get me because he had his chance. He blew it. I absolutely refuse to die. Furthermore, I laugh at stupid, sneaky Charlie. Ha, ha, ha.

You'll see me in seventeen days, about ten days after you get this letter. Know something? I think you're GREAT.

18 August 1969

I'm having a groovy time harassing everyone I can. I've had lifers threaten to "beat the shit" out of me, "break me in half," or "hang my ass" (court-martial me), but I'm careful only to provoke and not to do anything they can nail me for.

I hope some of those old SOBs do come after me because I'll kill 'em. As a civilian, they can't fuck me over. I'd take great delight in fighting 'em, but while I'm in these last days, I will be careful not to do anything to result in me staying in any longer.

I just pissed off one of the lifers. He sat at my friend's desk to write a statement of charges to get a GI court-martialed, and I said to my friend, "Gee, you mean you let lifers contaminate your desk?" Boy, (mentally) he got the ass. Good, I enjoy pissing off lifers.

Two weeks and I'll be free. Keep your spirits up. Hang on. We have tanks guarding our perimeter now. Don't worry about what you may see on TV.

My orders for Sgt. never came down, so I'll be the same Sp. 4 when I leave, the same as when I arrived. It's unheard of to wait seven months for an allocation. Soon I'll be a civilian in the Army Active Reserves or on inactive duty. Yippee!

25 August 1969

I got delayed a day here in Qui Nhon, typical of the Army. They say I can expect at least a three-day delay in Cam Ranh Bay, which means I won't get out of 'Nam till the twenty-ninth or thirtieth. At least I am out of the miserable 865th Bn. In one week, I'll be a PFC—not a Private First Class—but a Proud Fucking Civilian. How do you like them apples?

I'm getting out at a good time. I heard today that my base out in the Cha Rang Valley got hit hard the night I left. I suppose you heard of the convoy that got hit by the NVA between Pleiku and An Khe and lost fifteen out of nineteen oil tankers a few days ago.

I will try to call you tonight through the MARS station here in Qui Nhon. One thing I probably won't say over the phone is that I miss you very much.

So why am I writing? To kill time.

26 August 1969

I should be someplace over the Northern Pacific coming home to you. But, instead, I'm sitting on top of a double bunk at the 507th Return to CONUS [Continental United States] Station in Cam Ranh Bay. There's a good possibility I won't get out of here until the first or the second of September, and therefore I won't get back to the States until the third or fourth.

Remember, never trust the Army, but I'm not alone. Two thousand other GIs are waiting; some have been waiting a week or more. The confusion here is fantastic. Nine hundred GIs are sleeping in the sand outside.

Wow, Nixon's speeded-up pull-out is putting the fuck to many people—maybe me included. Boy, I'd hate to miss my homecoming party, but it would be expected because I'm always late, although it's not my fault this time.

I'm trying to call you through MARS or ocean cable, but I can't get through either way. So if I haven't called you by the fourth, you better set our dinner party back to the sixth.

Here's one of my short-timer's calendars. Keep it for me to mark off the last day when I get home. I'm glad I only have a handbag to drag around. I was smart to send almost everything home by hold baggage. Smarty me!

I'm so frustrated, irritated, pissed off, and angry at the Army. I'm disappointed, disillusioned, and disheartened that I'm still here. I can't express the depth of depression I'm in. If I don't get out of here and at least get Stateside, I'll go absolutely crazy.

Today is Tuesday, and if I'm lucky, I'll get out by Saturday. Dammit!

Be ready for me when I do get home.

Yours truly,
Bill

"I'm worried about Bill," I said to Mom after reading his last letter.

"Why's that?"

"He sounded so angry about being detained. Do you think he'll have changed much?"

"War makes men out of boys and women out of girls. Don't worry about it while you still have all these preparations to do for the party."

Mom grabbed the box of anniversary napkins for the cake servings. Then, we sat at the kitchen table, folding them into small squares.

"Will Bill even make it home in time for the party?" I asked, biting my lower lip.

"I'd better not have to reschedule it like I did Cheryl's wedding."

"I'm sure he'll make it even if he has to cancel his stop in California. But how will he adjust to being in a crowd of people after being in the jungle?"

"He'll be just fine. It's a small gathering, and Bill already knows everyone."

Then Mom asked, "Anything else you're worried about?"

"My anniversary cake! What if all its tiers fall apart, and the spiral of yellow roses comes tumbling down?" As my brain went into a meltdown mode, I envisioned my three-layered cake, like the Leaning Tower of Pisa, crashing to the floor, and as a result, my head pounded with a number ten headache.

"Mom, can you get me some coffee and an aspirin?"

Mom poured me a cup, set it down next to me, and handed me an aspirin. My hand trembled as I took the aspirin.

"Carole, you need to calm down."

I sighed. "I can't do this anymore. Can you finish these napkins for me, please?"

PART III

CHAPTER 18 -
THE HARDEST JOURNEY HOME

By Bill Wagener

When I returned from my one-week leave to Thailand in early August, we had a new second lieutenant assigned to the 160th HEM, to which my 865th GG detachment was attached. Unfortunately, he seemed a bit overwhelmed by my DEROS date of August 26, as I'd been approved for an early out to college. I'd been in charge of the office and barely had time to finish training my replacements.

I placed my discharge form in his inbox. "Sir, here are some papers for you to sign."

He barely glanced up from his work. "When I get to them."

I returned the following day to check, and although he'd signed a stack of other papers, mine was still at the bottom of the box. So, I shuffled the documents in the box and placed mine back on top. By the third day, my form still wasn't signed. So, I thought I'd sign it myself if I had to.

I was over it, really over it, and ready to return to the States. I didn't want to go home in a body bag like some of the other short-timers I'd known—a telephone guy killed on a pole while repairing a line, and a medic killed after he'd written his last letter home to his girlfriend. I'd taunted that shadow guy Charlie, who lurked around every corner, but in my letters home to Carole, I'd covered up my deepest fear of dying in Vietnam. I wasn't taking any more chances.

On the fourth morning, a signature miraculously appeared on my form. I grabbed my personnel file and my packed carry-on bag. I didn't bother saying goodbye to anyone. Instead, I told the gate guard, "I won't be back," before hitching a ride with a unit going toward Phu Cat Airbase. When they turned left, I hopped off, and picked up another ride, not to the military airbase in Qui Nhon but to the civilian airport. There I waited for a flight to Cam Ranh Bay, where I could catch a TWA flight home.

Being back in Cam Ranh Bay was a *déjà vu* experience. Fifty-one weeks earlier, when I arrived in Vietnam, I was assigned to the awful "bag and tag" duty in the morgue. My job was to tag my dead predecessors. Some didn't even have legs; I had to place their tags on their ear lobes. It was disgusting work and brought back a horrific memory of being on funeral detail in Texas after washing out of helicopter training. A distraught grieving wife grabbed onto me at one funeral, weeping, and wouldn't let go.

I realized how lucky I was to have washed out of the helicopter training school at Fort Wolters. Even though it was for a minor technicality (I signed in wrong), our warrant officer's class of 116 men needed to be reduced to 99.

While I was still in Vietnam, I picked up a copy of the June 27, 1969, *Life* magazine and froze when I read an article entitled, "Faces of the American Dead in Vietnam: One Week's Toll." Slowly turning page after page, I saw pictures of my former helicopter training classmates' faces staring back at me—all killed in Vietnam during one week of battle.

I later learned that flying a Huey helicopter in Vietnam wasn't easy. A pilot friend took me on a trial flight, and I barely got the thing off the ground. If I'd finished my training, it could've been me returning home in a body bag.

On September 1, it was finally my turn to leave. I was more than ready to board the TWA flight home. Unfortunately, it felt like a relentless wait while the plane sat on the tarmac for about an hour. I worried they'd pull me off because I hadn't even said goodbye to my superiors. Before I boarded, I'd heard rumors that the MPs were looking for some guy who'd gone AWOL and might be trying to sneak out on a flight home.

Is my second lieutenant looking for me right now? What if some sergeant escorts me off the plane and tells me I'm not going home?

I looked around and started to sweat. A slim and shapely stewardess with beautiful round eyes, perfect makeup, and reddish hair tucked under her flight hat came down the aisle.

"It's sure getting hot in here," I said, pulling on my collar.

"We're just waiting for a few more soldiers to board who are late arriving."

Whew! I closed my eyes and felt myself relax, grateful that I was on my way back to civilian life instead of my funeral.

The cabin doors closed after the remaining GIs boarded, and the plane began pressurizing. As we rolled down the tarmac, a roaring shout of sheer glee went up from the two-hundred soldiers onboard. Our flight attendants didn't even flinch at the noise, seemingly accustomed to hearing this outpouring of joy.

The seatbelt signs came on, and the co-pilot reminded us to stay in our seats. As we lifted off, I looked out the window. We were about 200 feet above the ground when I heard what I thought were the gears of the wheels lifting and then a dull *thump, thump, thump*. I glanced down, thinking something had hit my combat boot, and saw a hole in the cabin floor and then heard a whistling sound. A deformed bullet lay next to my boot.

Am I hit in the foot? Thankfully, I saw no blood and could still wiggle my toes. The plane steadily climbed, offering a beautiful view of the Pacific Ocean. I should have been ecstatic, but I felt like a human sardine trapped in an aluminum can.

What if we crash and all become shark food?

The whistling continued even after I covered the small hole with my boot. Charlie, or some other SOB, had given me one last goodbye. The other GIs looked around at each other, concerned. There were no rifles or pillboxes to jump into to take cover and no way out.

A male voice came on the intercom. "We've received some hits, but nothing critical. So, we'll continue and not return to the Cam Ranh Bay Airport."

Another hurrah went up, but the hole kept hissing like a coiled rattlesnake about to strike. *What am I to believe—the calming voice on the intercom or the shrill whistling under my foot?*

I said a silent prayer to God Almighty. Once we'd leveled off, I called the stewardess and pointed at the hole. She moved me to an empty first-class seat, where civilian contractors, a few majors, and some colonels were seated. I tried to forget the hole and focused on the beautiful stewardess serving alcoholic beverages. I asked for 7-Up and wished my wife would magically appear from behind the curtain, but I decided I wouldn't want her here if we were about to crash.

An hour later, the co-pilot's voice came over the intercom again to announce that we were making an unscheduled landing in Japan, where we'd change planes. "We'll continue to the States tomorrow." He said something had damaged an oil line and didn't want to chance flying to Alaska. Then he informed us that we would board buses and stay overnight in a hotel after we landed.

We landed without any problems. Once off the plane, I discovered I was in a large Japanese city. The bus left me in front of a beautiful modern hotel. I was shocked by the luxurious accommodations when I walked through the lobby door with my hand-held duffel bag. They didn't have fancy hotels like this where I came from in Door County.

It was another "wow" experience when I arrived at my room. I fell in love with the super-soft bed. I helped myself to candy bars and a bottle of Perrier water but skipped the complimentary wine. I wanted to be fully awake to enjoy the comforts of the bed and to be alone with no one else to share my private room.

So, to whoever that Charlie was who put those bullets in our plane, I said, "Thank you, Asshole. You got me the most luxurious bed and my first hot bath in a private shower room in eleven months."

Another GI I'd met on the plane knocked on my door and asked if I wanted to go whoring. I said, "Hell no!" I'd avoided that filth for 51 weeks, plus I was only three or four days away from being with Carole. After watching some Japanese television that I didn't understand a word of, I slept soundly through the night. The next day, someone phoned to say a bus would be waiting for me in one hour in front of the hotel. "Don't miss it," they warned.

On our next flight, the stewardess gave me complimentary hot meals and slipper socks (which I kept for years). Many hours later, the plane arrived in Anchorage to refuel in the darkness of night. When we finally landed in Washington State, it was daylight as I walked down the steps to the tarmac, looked up, and saw the stars and stripes flowing in the breeze. The air was fresh and didn't smell like 'Nam anymore. I got down on both knees and kissed the ground without even a second thought. I was so thankful to be almost home and all in one piece.

At Fort Lewis, I was treated to a huge steak dinner with fresh mashed potatoes, not freeze-dried or frozen ones. A second lieutenant walked up, sat down briefly, and asked if I wanted another steak. I hadn't eaten much in Japan, so I said, "Yes, Sir, Lieutenant. Cooked medium-well, please."

He returned with another perfectly cooked steak and said, "When you exit (pointing to a well-marked sign), stop and see me."

I finished my second steak and dessert of cake and ice cream. Only the Phu Cat Air Force Base had real food like this in 'Nam. While I poked at my second helping of ice cream, I wondered why the second lieutenant wanted to talk to me.

Why is he so nice to me? Did my second lieutenant in Cha Rang Valley send word that he hadn't signed my paper to leave the 160th? Are MPs waiting to arrest me outside the door?

I glanced back at the entrance, then at the exit. New arrivals were still coming in from another bus. Finally, I decided I'd take my chances because I was here in the U.S. I passed through the exit doorway to find happy, smiling young sergeants and second lieutenants in the room. The guy who had brought me the steak waved me over.

"Specialist Wagener, have a seat here, please."

I looked around, glad to see no MPs, and took a seat.

"Well, Specialist Wagener, I see you served honorably, but for some reason, you didn't get your scheduled promotion to sergeant in the 865th. I have the authority to fix that for you, and the Army also owes you more than forty days of paid vacation."

He grinned widely. "Just sign these papers to re-enlist, as so many other soldiers have before you."

I stared at him in disbelief. *What the hell?*

He repeated himself. I would get my E-5 promotion (my pay raise) and 40 days of paid vacation at E-5 tomorrow if I just signed the reenlistment papers.

Is he crazy? I don't care about being an E-5 anymore.

When I didn't pick up the pen, he added, "I could also ask that the promotion to E-5 as a sergeant be retroactive for pay purposes. So, you can leave for your overdue, forty-day paid vacation tomorrow with sergeant stripes on your shoulder in a fresh new uniform."

Is this offer punishment for leaving without saying goodbye to my superiors? Then it sunk in. The military wasn't disciplining me for something I'd done in Vietnam, but the Army wanted to keep me with them and away from my wife and my freedom for another four years.

Finally, I asked, "So, you want me to re-enlist?"

"All you need to do is answer 'yes,' and sign here." He pointed again to the papers where my name was already neatly typed. "Then you can see your family as a rich, newly-minted sergeant."

Why aren't I being reprimanded for not saluting when I entered the room? That could be an Article 15 punishment. Instead, my military ambushes me with steaks and happy smiles.

Finally, I asked the officer, "Have you ever served in Vietnam?"

He didn't answer and pointed at the form for the umpteenth time, repeating, "Just sign here."

"And what happens if I don't sign it, Lieutenant? Then what?"

His smile faded. "No back pay for E-5 rank. After four years of inactive reserves, you go home as a Specialist E4 with orders to be unenrolled. You are out of active service but covered by military law until the end of two years. And you better behave according to the Army regulations."

"I choose to be a civilian again, Sir. So you can keep that E-5 and sergeant stripes; I won't need them in college."

He stood up. I stood, too, and snapped a quick salute. He returned it, and we parted, never to meet again. I knew that the second lieutenant had never served in Vietnam. However, my brother, Dr. Rod, had taught me an essential life lesson, "Those in the know, take two (years) and get out." Most GIs had to enlist for three-year programs, but I'd enrolled for only two and was discharged.

I walked my file to the pay window and received my pay in real American greenbacks. I was assigned a bunk and told my military exit papers would be typed. I could leave that day or spend the night. I decided to spend the night and rest.

The next day, I flew to San Francisco Bay, where my elder sister, Pamela, lived with her husband and their children. I spent a day with them and then flew home to Austin Straubel Field in Green Bay the following day. When I arrived, I saw Father and Mother waiting for me on the tarmac with my dear brother, Rod, and his wife. Carole was wearing a halter dress and waving to me with the biggest smile I'd ever seen.

Oh my God, I'm finally home. Sheer joy filled me as I received big welcoming hugs and pats on the back. Everyone wore grins from ear to ear, and my big brother joked around just like he had on all those audiotapes he and his buddies sent me while I was in 'Nam.

Henry immediately came to my attention when I hugged my faithful Carole. I told Rod that he was right and that "those in the know do take two years and go," although the Army had tried hard to convince me otherwise. I promoted myself to civilian, the highest rank there is.

I was home in time for our first-anniversary celebration and my welcome-home party at the Alaska Resort, with about 100 family members and friends in attendance. I wore my new blue tuxedo with white embroidered flowers, hand-tailored for me in Thailand. I'd sent Carole silk fabric, but she hadn't had time to make a dress, so she borrowed a fancy lace one from her sister. It felt wonderful to mingle with the crowd and to be able to dance with my beloved wife.

Carole and I spent that week trying to relax in Sturgeon Bay with my family, who constantly reminded me to stop clearing my throat, stroking my mustache, and clicking my rings together. I wasn't even aware of these nervous habits I'd developed in Vietnam, trying to stay awake while on guard duty. Finally, Rod advised me to get counseling, seeing how anxious I was. I promised him I'd make an appointment once I returned to Madison. (Unfortunately, my counselor wasn't trained in combat trauma, and to Carole's dismay, he dismissed me after a short time, saying, "If you survived 'Nam, you're doing well.")

I drove my Honda Super Sport 90 to Madison, wishing instead that I could keep traveling across the country with my I-don't-give-a-damn attitude intact. But instead, I was headed back to the UW campus, suddenly adjusting to being a husband, a college student, and best of all, a Proud Fucking Civilian.

CHAPTER 19 - SEPTEMBER 1969: *DI DI MAU!*

A week after our anniversary party, we moved back to Madison. Bill had been home less than a month when I awoke to his screams one morning.

"*Di di mau, Di di mau!*[29] Let's get the hell out of here!" Bill's eyes were closed as he thrashed around, throwing all the blankets on the floor.

"Wake up. Wake up." I yelled, shaking him. "You're not in Vietnam anymore."

His glazed eyes opened with a blank stare.

"Bill, you're home with me, Carole."

Glaring at the corner of our bedroom ceiling, Bill shouted, "Hurry, get my rifle. The gooks are coming up over that hill. Can't you see them? Charlie's after us. No escape, man. *Di di mau! Di di mau!*"

Since returning home, Bill had nightmares and sometimes mumbled in his sleep. Usually, I'd give him a good poke, and he'd stop. But this time, he wouldn't snap out of it. I touched his hot, sweaty forehead and grabbed a glass of water from the nightstand.

"Bill, you're feverish. Sit up and drink some water."

Bill struggled to sit, so I helped him to get upright. Finally, he took a few sips of water, dropped back to his pillow, and went to sleep.

What the hell's happening?

I threw on my sweatshirt and pants, dashed into the kitchen, and grabbed a wooden spoon out of the drawer. *Clang, clang, clang!* The waterpipe vibrated as I hit it hard.

Due to the apartment not having a phone, our elderly landlady Mrs. Duffy recommended using the waterpipe as a signal if I ever needed to use her phone. Though Bill slept through the noise, I hoped it was loud enough to awaken her.

I sprinted up the stairwell, puffing when I finally reached her apartment. I pounded on the door, shouting, "Wake up, Mrs. Duffy." Every second of waiting felt like ten minutes.

"Please hurry." I banged on the door some more until the side of my hand hurt. "I need to use the phone."

I heard footsteps and the lock turning slowly. The door opened a crack, and I pushed myself through, narrowly missing a black streak with green eyes.

"Come here, kitty. Say hi to Miss Carole," Mrs. Duffy croaked.

I stepped around her cat, Mr. Biddlesworth, a severe ankle-biter almost as neurotic as she was, and made a beeline for the rotary phone.

"Goodness sakes alive, what's wrong?" Mrs. Duffy asked, concerned.

"I need to take Bill to the hospital."

I dialed "O" and waited until a nasal-toned voice came on the line.

"Operator, how may I help you?"

"I have an emergency and need a Yellow Cab."

"What's your emergency?"

"My husband's talking like he's out of his mind. I need to take him to UW Hospital."

The operator said she'd alert the hospital and connected me directly to Yellow Cab. I gave the dispatcher my address.

"I'll have a cab there in ten minutes," the dispatcher said.

I hung up the phone and headed for the door. "Thanks, Mrs. Duffy. I'll let you know how Bill's doing later."

I ran down to check on Bill and found him sound asleep.

How could he sleep through all this commotion?

Gathering a few things I might need for the hospital, I grabbed Bill's nylon camouflage blanket from Vietnam and went to the front porch to wait. Sitting there, I came up with a plan. Bill would fight me if he knew I was taking him to the hospital, so instead, I'd trick him.

Honk, honk! The black and yellow checkered taxi rolled up to the curb.

The cabbie shouted through his open window, "Hey, lady. You called a cab?"

"Yes, please wait a minute," I shouted and rushed back into the apartment and played along with Bill's perceived attack.

"Wake up, Bill! They're here to rescue us. Hurry up. *Di di mau!*"

Bill aroused half-awake. I sat him on the edge of the bed, put his slippers and robe on, and helped him walk. I covered him with the green Army blanket on the way out the door.

"Come on, let's go!" To my surprise, Bill, without a word, calmly followed me to the front stoop. "Grab onto the railing," I said, guiding him down the fourteen steps to the waiting cab.

Each step became more arduous as we descended until Bill's knees finally buckled, causing him to lean his total weight onto me. I could barely hold him up.

"Help me," I yelled to the cabbie.

It took all of our strength to get Bill down the remainder of the steps and into the cab. I swaddled his shivering body with the blanket and put my arm around him to hold him upright on the seat. Bill dozed off again as we rode to the hospital, his head resting upon my shoulder.

The cabbie pulled up to the hospital's rear entrance, where a waiting hospital attendant assisted Bill into a wheelchair and whisked him off to the emergency area. While I filled out paperwork, the staff quickly examined him. I sat in the waiting room until a nurse approached me.

"Mrs. Wagener, I started an IV to hydrate your husband. Please come with me. The doctor would like to speak with you."

She escorted me back to a curtained area where Bill was lying on a stretcher with his eyes closed. A young male resident was standing next to him. He asked me a few questions about my husband's medical history. I told him he'd just gotten back from Vietnam.

"What do you think's wrong?" I asked.

"Your husband may have contracted malaria over there."

My knees almost buckled. *Malaria? Hadn't Bill finished the anti-malaria pills the Army gave him when he came home?*

I took Bill's hand. "But he's been back three weeks already and hasn't been sick."

"I need to do a spinal tap."

"What?" Bill sprang back to life, sat straight up, and grabbed my arm. "No, no, I won't have another spinal tap!"

"Doctor, he's not going to sign the consent. He had a spinal tap in Vietnam and said it was the worst pain he'd ever experienced."

The physician handed me a pen.

Bill screamed at me, "If you sign that fucking thing, I'll never forgive you, Carole."

I felt torn between my husband's irrational pleas and the doctor's stern gaze. I grabbed the pen, signed the form, and darted out of the room. Hoping I'd made the right decision, I found a payphone, searched my purse for quarters, and dropped four in. Holding back the tears, I asked the operator to assist me with a long-distance call.

Mom answered the phone on the first ring. "Alaska General Store."

"Mom, it's me." I sniffed.

"What's wrong, Carole?"

"Bill's in the hospital. He woke up early this morning, hallucinating, and thought he was back in Vietnam. He has a high fever, and the doctor's doing a spinal tap right now."

"Why a spinal tap?"

"To rule out spinal meningitis, or maybe he has malaria. Mom, I'm so scared."

Mom told me that her neighbors had recently had the flu virus with high fevers. "Bill's probably run down from Vietnam. He might have caught the same bug."

Hearing this bit of news calmed me. "Thanks, Mom. I'll tell his doctor."

I went to the cafeteria, ate breakfast, and checked on my distraught husband. The nurse said Bill stopped screaming after she sedated him, and he tolerated the spinal tap well.

"Your husband must lie flat and rest for the next twenty-four hours. Otherwise, he could develop a spinal headache."

Feeling helpless, I told the nurse the news about the flu back home, left the hospital, and went to my classes. That worrisome afternoon I returned to check on Bill again.

When I entered the room, my husband closed his eyes and turned away. Even with the IV still going, his hand felt too warm in mine. I told him about the flu going around back home. He didn't respond. Accustomed to getting the cold shoulder when he was angry, I left. When I returned to the apartment house, Mrs. Duffy had a chicken dinner waiting for Mr. Biddlesworth and me.

The following day, the physician informed me Bill's spinal tap was normal, and his temperature was down. He was now well-oriented, talking, and eating, but the doctor wanted to keep him another night for observation.

I revisited Bill, but he refused to look at me or speak, so I told him I loved him and went home. Returning the following day, I found a smiling Bill in a wheelchair, racing down the hallway toward me doing "pop wheelies." I wheeled him back to the front desk to talk to his nurse.

She said, "He's been harassing me all morning about going home. I'm waiting for the doctor to discharge him."

The doctor told me Bill was ready for discharge, concluded that his spiked fever was likely the flu, and informed me, "Young children and some adults hallucinate with elevated temperatures. Nevertheless, keep an eye on him. Bring him back if symptoms return."

Little did I know that Bill's non-fever nightmares were associated with posttraumatic stress disorder (PTSD), a condition brought on by anxiety from traumatic experiences during the war. A monster of a demon remained buried in his psyche, yet he refused to talk about Vietnam. I understood why Bill didn't want to talk about it and relive the ordeal.

Also, on the news, antiwar protesters called Vietnam veterans "baby killers," spat on them, and gave them the finger or worse. Bill locked those memories deep inside, just below the surface of his conscious mind,[30] and didn't speak of them to anyone.

Over the years, Bill refused to celebrate the Fourth of July and would sit indoors with the TV blaring and the curtains shut while the children and I were outdoors, enjoying the neighbors' fireworks. He continued to block the memories of 'Nam for 30 more years.

But in 1998, while Bill worked as a substitute teacher near Vandenberg Air Force Base (currently Vandenberg Space Force Base) on the central coast of California, a military helicopter flew in over the green hills for a landing. Between the *chuff-chuff* sound of the helicopter blades and local Hmong immigrants speaking in their native language nearby, Bill's mind instantly transported him back to Vietnam. That break with reality caused his stress-related anxiety and the unrelenting night terrors to return with a vengeance.

This time, Bill told me what happened, and I recognized the disorder. I'd recently read an article about Vietnam combat stress in my journal, *ADVANCE for Physical Therapists*. A study estimated fifty percent of war-zone Vietnam veterans had experienced clinically severe reaction symptoms. PTSD often altered their neuroendocrine and sympathetic nervous systems, leading to various chronic and infectious diseases. I showed Bill the article and read it aloud point by point.

"This is you, you, and you. There's a number to call. I'll find you some help."

I called Santa Barbara County's Veteran's Administration office, and Dr. D., a Ph.D. specializing in PTSD counseling, was assigned to Bill's case. Dr. D. told him that only a small percentage of Vietnam veterans ever received counseling for PTSD. Unfortunately, the V.A. had no counseling or support groups available for families back then. So, we and our five children struggled with the aftermath of Vietnam on our own, causing one of our sons to leave home early at age seventeen.

With counseling Bill gradually opened up and shared stories of how he survived Vietnam. I finally understood how much he suffered and continued to suffer emotionally.

Bill told me that during a few days off, he'd hitch-hiked to a remote area to photograph the hill people of the Montagnard tribe. On his way back to his base, he was captured by the North Vietnamese Regulars and forced into a large tunnel used as a latrine and a garbage dumpster. It had a bamboo-like door and an air hole in the ceiling for ventilation. The enemy soldiers forced him to take off his boots and hand them over.

When the door opened, it allowed enough light for Bill to see a captured South Vietnamese soldier and a large battery, a piece of steel wool, and some dried leaves on the floor. Bill had learned how to start a fire using these same materials in the Boy Scouts.

Bill heard the screams of another captured soldier tortured outside the tunnel and worried he'd be next to have his toes cut off. He busied himself by starting a small fire, rubbing the steel wool against the battery terminal using friction to light the dry leaves.

While trying to find a way out of the tunnel using the firelight, he heard men yelling *"Di di mau"* and the welcomed sound of American bombers overhead. Then, the earth above him suddenly shifted from the jolt of a bomb. Afraid the tunnel might collapse and trap him, Bill figured a way out.

He boosted the other prisoner up to the air vent. The Vietnamese soldier grabbed a bare tree root that had fallen into the tunnel, climbed through the small hole, and pulled himself out. Bill grabbed onto his foot, but the freed soldier left without helping.

The U.S. bombers continued hitting their target, causing the ground to shake more, loosening the air vent dirt. Bill pulled himself up, widened the gap, and squeezed through using the same tree root for leverage. Narrowly escaping with his life, he snuck away barefooted and found his way back to camp.

In another close call, Bill was riding in the back of a half-track truck with other GIs when their vehicle hit a landmine. Miraculously, he wasn't killed but knocked unconscious when his body flew up and out of the truck bed and landed face up in a palm tree. Bill awoke to the *chuff-chuff* sounds of a helicopter's blades. It hovered while one of the crew members fished him out of the tree. The helicopter then picked up a lone survivor on the ground, who said that the Viet Cong must have assumed Bill was already dead and decided not to waste a bullet.

Bill's secondary training was in photography. Occasionally, he was sent on secret reconnaissance missions with a specialized team and dropped off by helicopter into North Vietnam. His mission[31] was to spy on strategic areas, take photographs, and bring back the film.

On Bill's last decoy mission, something went horribly wrong. The North Vietnamese were waiting in ambush for the Americans. They fired on the helicopter, which crashed, killing the pilot, the crew, and three team members. Bill and two others jumped out before the helicopter belly-flopped on the ground. They dodged bullets as they bolted to safety. The skinniest GI took a hit, and Bill carried him across his shoulders using a fireman's carry.

Eventually, the other surviving soldier told Bill, "He's dead. Put 'em down; he's slowing us down." When Bill set the body down, he noticed the GI had taken five or six more bullets meant for him.[32]

Then the two soldiers found their way to their assigned pick-up point, but no one came for them. They eventually made their way to an alternative pick-up point, but no one was there either. Finally, Bill's Boy Scout survival training kicked in, and he followed a river to the ocean. Once there, they saw a Navy ship offshore, radioed them, and a Navy helicopter came to their rescue.

That was Bill's last reconnaissance mission. He heard no one made it back from the next one, which he narrowly missed by one day due to his early out from the Army. These were just some of the close calls Bill tried to forget from but couldn't.

CHAPTER 20 - OCTOBER 1969: WE DON'T WANT YOUR GODDAMN WAR!

After that hospitalization, Bill didn't have another reoccurrence of PTSD symptoms while in college. Instead, he busied himself with schoolwork and volunteered with the Madison Police Department as a weekend spy.

Clang, clang, clang!

The annoying sound of Mrs. Duffy banging on the water pipe awoke me from a sound sleep like a gong. I yawned and looked at the clock, realizing it was already 7:30 a.m.

Darn, what does she want now? Maybe some milk from the store, or do I have a phone call waiting?

Bill moaned, rolled over, and pulled the covers over his head. "You'd better run upstairs and see what the old lady wants this time."

"It's your turn! Why don't you go?" I grumbled, wiping the sleep out of my eyes as I got up.

Bill ignored me. I glanced into the dresser mirror at my messy hair and bloodshot eyes and slipped on my pink bathrobe before heading up the stairwell. I sprinted up the cold wooden steps, two at a time, shivering in my bare feet, and then knocked softly on my landlady's door.

Mrs. Duffy opened it a crack, letting me slip in without waking Mr. Biddlesworth, curled up in a big black ball next to the knitting basket on the old-fashioned sofa. The musty room almost made me cough.

"Your sister woke me up." Mrs. Duffy huffed on the way to her kitchenette. "It must be urgent if she's calling this early."

At this hour, Cheryl was already at work, staffing the front desk of the local sheriff's department.

"I'm sorry." I grabbed the phone's receiver, "Cheryl, what's wrong?"

"I can't talk long. I need to alert you something big's happening today. The officers are ready to leave the station. I hear them clunking around in those heavy boots, getting their helmets and nightsticks."

"Oh God, I thought something was wrong with Mom or Dad."

"No, no. They're fine." Cheryl took a deep breath. "But I overheard one cop saying that the Chancellor gave the Madison police and the Dane County Sheriff's Department permission to come on campus today to break up any antiwar protests or sit-ins. He's afraid of more riots and property damage. The officers will arrest anyone who gets in their way!"

"That does sound serious. But don't worry about me. I'm taking the bus in."

"Be careful, Carole. I gotta go. There's a call coming in."

Click.

Mrs. Duffy's sickeningly sweet voice interrupted my thoughts. "Can you stay for coffee?"

"Sorry, but I'm late for my clinicals." I ran out the door. If I could make the bus in time, it would drop me off on the quieter side of campus, precisely in front of the UW Hospital. If I missed it, I'd have to walk up Bascom Hill past all the protestors.

Since Bill was asleep, I didn't awaken him but rushed to get dressed. While still dazed by what happened to me last night and Cheryl's news, I slipped into my dress uniform, pantyhose, and white nursing shoes. Then, with no time for makeup, I grabbed my purse and hairbrush and was out the door.

Notebook in hand, I ran the two short blocks up to Capitol Square to the bus stop in front of the old brick YMCA building. The National Guard troops were up early, too, already encircling the Wisconsin State Capitol, a replica of the Capitol building in Washington, D.C. The GIs stood at attention, shoulder-to-shoulder, with expressionless faces, and allowed only legislators and state workers to go inside. To my relief, the city bus was still on the corner. The driver, Antonio, originally from Long Island, opened the door for me. As I climbed the steps, Tony's eyes never came off my shapely legs.

"Hey, Mz. Legs. How are ya today?"

I smiled at him. "Running a bit late. Thanks for waiting for me. And by the way, Tony, it's Mrs. Legs."

My quarters clinked as they hit the bottom of the collection box. The bus pulled away from the curb, and I plopped down into the seat directly behind Tony, whose brown eyes sparkled as he looked up at me in the large rear-view mirror.

"Legs, how's school going for ya?"

"Fine, but I hear they're expecting trouble on campus today."

"Yup, today and every day."

I glanced out the side window while Tony made small talk—another story about his old cabbie days in New York City. I responded with an occasional nod and an "Uh-huh" to let him know I was listening, but mostly I was on the alert, looking for trouble.

The bus chugged down the half-mile that comprised State Street, Madison's most illustrious street, with the Capitol on one end and Bascom Hill on the other. Madison had never had to protect itself from rioters before, and as the bars, restaurants, and small shops boarded up their windows to prevent looting, it was almost unrecognizable.

At the Park and State Street intersection, I glanced right towards the Memorial Union on Lake Mendota's quiet shoreline. Inside, *Der Rathskeller*, decorated like an old German Beer Hall, was a great place to grab a beer, a bratwurst, and visit with friends. Occasionally, Janet and I splurged on a Bing cherry ice cream cone at the Babcock Store and then sat on those funky green, orange, or yellow sunburst chairs out on the patio, relaxing and watching the peaceful, bobbing sailboats moored to the pier.

But today, it looked anything but peaceful. Passing the base of Bascom Hill, I spotted a black windowless paddy wagon parked in a No Parking Zone. The vehicle resembled a horse-drawn funeral carriage from an old western movie.

That's strange.

On the bus's left, about twenty protestors strolled along the sidewalk carrying hand-drawn placards. No doubt, they were headed to an antiwar gathering. I read their descriptive signs, "Hell No, We Won't Go," "War Is

Not Good for Children and Other Living Things," and "We Won't Fight Another Rich Man's War!"

The marchers looked like young hippies. Bearded guys with long flowing hair wore fringed leather vests over their shirts and old blue jeans. Young gals with long straight hair, their necks adorned with long love beads, dressed in peasant blouses and long colorful skirts. Some carried "Peace" signs and chanted, "Make love, not war."

Are these students or the outside agitators Bill talked about being part of America's New Left movement?

Tony pulled over at the last bus stop on State Street, welcoming more passengers, while my thoughts raced back to last night's big adventure.

Bill and I attended an antiwar rally in the new gymnasium on the other side of campus. Bill didn't support the antiwar movement, but he wanted to check out the audience, always scouting for troublemakers. He also wanted to hear the speakers because he thought Tom Hayden from the SDS or someone from their radical branch, The Weatherman, might be there.[33]

Using the alias of B.J., Bill was on a spy mission for the Madison cops. First, B.J. could easily pass for a hippie with his long hair and goatee while wearing an old trench coat and jeans. Then, with a camera in hand, he aimed to identify protestors who damaged private property, look for people who could be paid instigators, and turn the film back into the police.

B.J. liked the excitement of going undercover, but I, on the other hand, preferred to play it safe. So, when he invited me to the rally, I hesitated.

"I need to stay home and study," I said, even though it was a Friday night.

"Aw, come with me." Bill pleaded. "You might learn something new."

I didn't want to endanger myself, but I didn't want to disappoint Bill, so I agreed to go. As we sped off on his Honda Super Sport, heading to the other side of campus, my nerves were already on edge. Recently, riding at night, we almost got creamed by a car that made a left turn in front of us.

We made it to the rally just in time to hear the speaker, someone I didn't know. His speech was informative, and the rally was orderly and peaceful. But when we left, a group gathered on the sidewalk in front of the parking lot.

I nudged my husband nervously. "Why are all these people milling around?"

"I don't know. But you wait here while I get the bike."

Bill ran, zigzagging through the parked vehicles while I watched the growing crowd overflowing into the parking lot. Then, finally, two men showed up carrying bull horns.

"Follow us," the organizer shouted. "We're marching to the Capitol for a sit-in."

My stomach sank until I saw Bill on the motorcycle, rewinding his way through the crowd. Finally, he stopped in front of me and handed me my helmet.

"Hurry, get on. Let's try and get ahead of this crowd."

I jumped on the bike, and the Honda took off. But we soon found ourselves behind a large group of students marching up the one-way street towards Capitol Square, our exact destination. The riot police, who'd been strangely absent from the rally, now lined the streets in full force. With the side streets barricaded for crowd control, no alternate routes existed to the other side of the Capitol where we lived.

The crowd soon doubled as large groups of primarily Black people streamed off parked buses and joined the protest. As the racially-mixed group locked arms to form a human chain in front and behind us, the two pied pipers shouted into their blow horns.

"One, two, three, four. What's war good for?"

The marchers shouted back in unison, "ABSOLUTELY NOTHING!"

"One, two, three, four."

Through my helmet, I heard them respond. "WE DON'T WANT YOUR GODDAMN WAR!"

Unable to pass and without an escape route, Bill and I were trapped in a sea of protestors and forced to follow the procession. My shaky knees clamped down hard on the sides of the bike while frightening thoughts came to me.

What if the police stop us, arrest us, and we get expelled from college? What if we get caught up in a riot and injured? What will my parents say then?

I hugged Bill tightly, around his waist, and clung on for dear life. Then, suddenly, three shots rang out.

Pop, ping, pang!

Gray metal canisters clanged as they hit the pavement in front of us, rolling out in all directions. The bike swerved, narrowly missing a canister with a puffy cloud of dense white smoke billowing into the air. I grimaced and pinched my eyes shut. Tears rolled down my cheeks as we rode through the white mist.

"Tear gas," Bill shouted and sped up.

The throaty growl of the bike's engine revved up, and I felt the bike lean to the left, so I leaned with it. I cracked open one eye and discovered that Bill had driven around a barricade away from the tear gas.

"Hang on, Carole."

The bike jumped over the curb, landing on a grassy lawn away from the tear gas. I held on tighter and opened my eyes to see we were heading up Bascom Hill on an empty sidewalk. Bill stopped at the top of the hill and let me off by Lincoln's bronze statue. I tapped on old Abe's foot for luck, hurried down the steps back to State Street, and stopped to catch my breath. There I watched Bill skillfully maneuver the cycle down the side of the ancient 850-foot drumlin left over from the continental glacier which once covered Wisconsin.

We hopped on the bike again and headed home on an eerily deserted State Street. We passed by a few drunken bums sitting on the sidewalk, and we were back at our apartment house in no time. Bill left me out front, drove the bike to the back, and hid it in the basement entry room. He was paranoid and worried that one of those "bums" might have followed us home.

I climbed into bed and tucked the blankets around me. My body violently shook the bed as if a California earthquake had just struck Madison. I couldn't fall asleep with swirling thoughts about what the antiwar speaker had just told us.

This war was evil, with so many killed, soldiers and civilians alike. Yet, to my amazement, American businesses with government contracts were getting wealthy from the war, causing me to wonder, What if the antiwar protestors are right?

My thoughts returned to the bus as Tony maneuvered it in a wide left turn onto Park Street. I watched helplessly as one of the male protestors stepped off the curb directly into the path of the bus.

"Look out, Tony!" I yelled.

Tony slammed on the brakes. The bus shuddered to a halt, narrowly missing the bold pedestrian wearing a cowboy hat, who turned around, held up his middle finger, and yelled, "F. U.!"

I gasped.

Tony blasted the horn, shook his fist, and yelled through the open window, "Goddammit! Watch where you're going, you stupid a-hole. You wanna get yourself killed?"

I thought about all those soldiers I had heard about last night who died in Vietnam. *How many more people have to die before this war ends?*

In May of 1970, I happily graduated cum laude from UW. We gave up our little apartment, and I moved two blocks to the YMCA women's floor while Bill moved back to his family home. I had a three-month internship to complete at Madison General and the VA Hospital, where I would work with my first veterans.

As the war in Vietnam dragged on, violence escalated on US campuses. First, on May 2, 1970, students at Kent State set fire to the ROTC building. Then, two days later, a crowd of 3,000 rowdy students protesting Nixon's aggressive air and ground strikes into Cambodia threw rocks at the Ohio National Guardsmen stationed there. The soldiers retreated but fired into the crowd in an unprecedented move, killing four students and wounding nine others. I read all the news articles about Kent State and saw the photographs of students dying in the street.

Could this happen on the UW campus too? Would even more students have to die?

As the antiwar protests continued, I no longer felt safe in Madison. I didn't walk or shop on State Street anymore but took the bus. Meanwhile, Cheryl's husband almost had a car accident when another protestor walked out, without warning, onto a busy thoroughfare during rush hour traffic. I worried when I heard a group of protestors attempted to overturn a city bus with passengers still on it.

By early August, I had completed my internship and moved back home. Fortunately, I wasn't in Madison when, on August 24, 1970, at 3:40 a.m., a massive car bomb ripped through Sterling Hall. A van filled with almost a ton of ammonium nitrate and fuel oil exploded. A blast comparable to 2,000 sticks of dynamite sent shock waves throughout Madison's East Side.

The bombing was a protest against the UW for allowing U.S. military research on campus. One graduate research student, Robert Fassnacht, was killed, and three others were injured. A group known as the New Year's Gang, which consisted of four young men (two were brothers), was implicated and went on the lam. It took the FBI six or seven years to arrest three, who ended up in prison. The authorities never found the fourth one.

At that time, the UW bombing was the worst act of domestic violence in our nation's history. It was a turning point in the protest movement and quieted Madison's nearly daily antiwar demonstrations until the war finally ended on April 30, 1975.

During the Vietnam era from 1961 to 1975, 9.7 % of Americans served in Vietnam. The U.S. lost 58,320 soldiers, while 304,000 were wounded, 1,584 listed as MIA, and 50,000 deserted (numbers vary depending on the source).

Bill lost his cousin, 1ˢᵗ Lt. Philip Overbeck (Chuck's younger brother), killed at age 22 on June 10, 1970, in Binh Dinh, Vietnam. You can find Phillip's name on panel 9W, row 40, on the Vietnam Veterans Memorial Wall in Washington, D.C. Chuck is alive and well but said many of the men from his water-purification unit died of complications from Agent Orange.

Meanwhile, the war continued to rage in Bill's subconscious mind, came to a head, and he was finally diagnosed with PTSD. With Dr. D's help, Bill applied for VA Disability in August of 1999 but was denied because he didn't include stressors from Vietnam. So, he appealed, providing the necessary information and photographs I found for him, including one of him helping put out the fire of a burning diesel tanker. Finally, on September 22, 2003, Bill received his long-awaited award letter and rating decision for fifty percent disability from Veterans Affairs. The letter stated,

Service personnel records show assignment to the 865th Eng Det (USARV) from September 1968 to August 1969. We concede stressors based on your being in-country during Tet 1969. You reported being exposed to incoming enemy mortar, rocket attacks, and occasional sniper fire and were required to accompany convoys from Qui Nhon to Phu Cat. Miscellaneous photos were submitted, one of which showed a burning tanker truck, likely hit by enemy fire. Statements from Dr. D. provide a substantive diagnosis of posttraumatic stress disorder associated with experiences in Vietnam. Symptoms may include flashbacks, nightmares, sleep impairment, intrusive recollections, avoidance of stimuli, anxiety, anger, irritability, loss of control, difficulty with concentration and memory, social isolation, social and occupational impairment, paranoia, and delusional thinking.

The Hardest Year continued for over fifty more years, with us celebrating our fiftieth wedding anniversary in 2018. Bill's symptoms improved with counseling, and our marriage survived by us agreeing to disagree with one another. For example, when we didn't want to continue a discussion, one of us would say, "*Verstehen Sie?*" [Do you understand?], which ended that discussion and a potential argument.

Grandpa said it best: "The hardest part of being married is the first fifty years. After that, you run out of things to argue about."

EPILOGUE

March 17, 2007
Voices of the People's March
Santa Barbara, California

It's been 38 years since Bill and I attended our first antiwar rally held in Madison, Wisconsin. Today we head to another antiwar rally, and this time it's on a different State Street, and it's a different war—the war in Iraq. It's crucial that my fifteen-year-old twin daughters become aware of the detrimental effects of war. So I tell them they must go with us to Santa Barbara for the day. Santa Barbara is a cool place to hang out, so they don't even put up a fight or give me an attitude.

After an hour's drive along the gorgeous Pacific Coast, we arrive at the gathering area. Bongo drums fill the air, giving a sense of excitement. Bill carries his video camera as he takes the lead, skillfully maneuvering us through the crowd. I hold up my homemade placard on which I've drawn a large pink flower with four petals and the words, "WAR IS NOT GOOD FOR

CHILDREN AND OTHER LIVING THINGS." I notice other people carrying signs, too, such as "Stop War," "War is Not the Answer," and "Impeach Bush, He Lied." Meanwhile, the twins tag along behind us.

Multiple flags flutter overhead in the morning breeze like giant colorful butterflies—a bright orange one embossed with a gold peace symbol, a rainbow flag bearing the word "PEACE" in large black letters, and the red, white, and blue of our own stars and stripes.

Two motorcycle cops roar in, joining the bicycle police patrol already present—a shrill whistle blast cues the drummers to lead the procession. We follow along and march in step to their beat, loudly chanting an antiwar slogan.

"What do we want?"

"PEACE!"

"When do we want it?"

"NOW!"

Random photographers dodge in and out of the crowd, taking photos of the marchers. I wonder if these pictures are for media use or will be stored and used for other purposes, such as facial recognition. Finally, when it's my turn, I pose for the camera.

Go ahead. Take my picture. I'm not afraid anymore. Holding my placard up high, I smile sweetly. *I'm proud to be here today.*

After the march ends, we eat lunch at Rusty's Pizza. Then we walk the short distance to the Sunken Gardens lawn in front of the Santa Barbara Courthouse to listen to the speakers. My girls and I sit on the grass while Bill roams around with his camera filming for his local TV show, "On Second Thought."

A man from Veterans for Peace informs us that 3,210 American soldiers have died in Iraq, 24,042 are wounded, and the U.S. has already spent 417 billion dollars on this war.[34] Finally, the rally ends, leaving me thinking.

Did we learn nothing from the war in Vietnam?

Bill returns and tells me that a group of veterans is having a vigil at sunset on the beach. The girls and I will stay as long as we can go shopping at the downtown mall.

At dusk on Santa Barbara's pristine shoreline, my family gathers with other veterans at Leadbetter Beach. Earlier that day, Steve Sherrill and the Veterans for Peace had erected three-foot-high wooden crosses in the sand.

Walking down to the ocean, I see the 60 perfect rows of white crosses and feel a lump forming in my throat. "Arlington West"[35] is an impressive sight of 3,000 crosses with small US flags waving in front of them. Some crosses bear soldiers' names, but most are left blank—un-named soldiers—gone but not forgotten.

"Taps" blasts from a loudspeaker, drowning out the sound of the ocean. It's my cue, as a volunteer, to light one row of the forty-eight candles set in red plastic cups on the sand in front of each cross. The candles will burn for two hours, making the cups glow reddish, symbolizing the blood shed by American soldiers—men or women who gave their lives in Iraq to be free of tyrants.

After I light my row, I walk back to my family, waiting for me near the Stearns Wharf Pier. We join a group of fellow veterans, holding hands and forming a large circle on the beach. Someone says a prayer. In solidarity, we sing "Kumbaya" ("Come By Here") followed by Pete Seeger's rendition of "We Shall Overcome," the influential 1960's Civil Rights Movement song.

As the blazing sun sets into the Pacific Ocean, peaceful waves lap the shoreline, and a slight breeze causes the 3,000 candles to flicker. Tears roll down my cheeks as I think of all the lives snuffed out too soon by yet another war. *Will war never cease?*

Then I recall what Jesus said in Matthew 24:6:

And you will hear of wars and rumors of war; see that you are not alarmed.[36]

Finally, I think of Pete Seeger's other song, "Turn! Turn! Turn!" written from the words of the Bible, Ecclesiastes 3, beginning with verse 1 and ending with verse 8:[37]

For everything, there is a season and a time for every purpose under heaven . . .

A time to love and a time to hate;

A time for war and a time for peace.

After educating myself for thirty years as a Libertarian, I now understand the connection between wars, politics, and our country's foreign policies. I know that the best US foreign policy would be one of nonintervention. I believe our government shouldn't involve itself in other countries' affairs or get entangled in foreign wars but should maintain a strong national military defense at home. Some might call me a pacifist who believes that war and violence are unjustifiable, but I call myself an antiwar activist, standing here strong on the beach.

Night falls, and a full moon rises on the horizon as the vigil ends. It reminds me of the last night on our honeymoon in Oahu nearly forty years ago—that moonlit night when Bill and I walked arm-in-arm back to the Hilton Hawaiian Village. Then, we were both so young, and I was scared that the war might take my husband's life.

But Vietnam did claim a part of my happy-go-lucky guy. I didn't know Bill's lack of patience when driving and unexpected angry outbursts resulted from PTSD. Thirty years after the war, the VA counselor told Bill he may have to return to Vietnam "to face your fears," but Bill said he would never return. So instead, we plan to visit the Vietnam Traveling Memorial Wall (The Wall that Heals) when it comes to our area.

Back on the beach, I squeeze Bill's and my daughter's hands. A warm wave of cleansing love washes over me, putting my fears to rest. Our memories of the Vietnam War are tucked away in handwritten letters in shoeboxes buried in the garage. And they remain collecting dust, to be read again when the time is right to tell our story, this story, of *The Hardest Year*.

THE END

GLOSSARY OF TERMS

Bn. Battalion

Charlie Viet Cong or North Vietnamese Army; also referred to as Victor Charlie

CIB Combat Infantryman Badge

CMMI Command maintenance management inspection

CO Commanding officer

CONUS Continental United States

DEROS Date Estimated Return Oversees; date eligible for return

GG Gas generating

HEM Heavy Equipment Maintenance

KP Kitchen patrol or kitchen police

MARS Military Auxiliary Radio System

MOS Military occupational specialty

MP Military police

NCO Non-commissioned officer

NVA North Vietnamese Army

NVN North Vietnam

PFC Private first class

PT Physical therapy or physical therapist

PTSD Posttraumatic stress disorder

R&R Rest and relaxation; rest and recuperation (leave)

RVN Republic of Vietnam

SDS Students for a Democratic Society

SFC Sergeant first class

SVN South Vietnam

TAA Teachers Assistant's Association

TWA Trans World Airlines

UW University of Wisconsin

WAC Women's Army Corps

WOC Warrant Officer Candidate

VC Viet Cong

VD Venereal disease, sometimes referred to as "the clap"

German Words & Phrases

auf wiedersehen Until we meet again

bier Beer

danke Thanks

ein bisschen A little

frau Woman, wife, lady

ja Yes

kummel klops German meatballs

sehr gut Very good

Sprechen Sie Deutsch? Do you speak German?

Verstehen Understand

Was wollen Sie? What do you want?

Wie geht es Eihen heute? How are you today?

Vietnamese and French Words & Phrases

beaucoup or *bookoo* A lot

déjà vu A feeling of having already experienced the present situation *di di mau* Hurry up

gook Foreigner

hootch girl. Promiscuous female

Montagnards Vietnamese tribal hill people

Tet Vietnamese Lunar New Year

xin loi Sorry about that

ENDNOTES

[1] Alaska was an unincorporated village located thirty miles south of Sturgeon Bay where Bill lived and thirty-five miles east of Green Bay where Carole went to college. It consisted of Carole's parents' Alaska General Store and Texaco gas station, a golf course and supper club, two taverns, an old schoolhouse, and of course a cheese factory.

[2] Tom Hayden was a civil rights and antiwar activist who founded the Students for a Democratic Society (SDS) in 1969. He and other protestors were charged with conspiracy after the riots at the 1968 Democratic National Convention. His high-profile trial is the subject of the movie, *The Trial of the Chicago 7*. He was married for seventeen years to the actress and antiwar activist, Jane Fonda. (In 1988, "Hanoi" Jane, who was seen in the eyes of many Vietnam veterans as a traitor, apologized for her outspokenness during her 1972 two-week visit to Hanoi) After their divorce, Tom Hayden served in the California legislature. He died in 2016.

[3] An Article 15 was a means of NJP [non-judicial punishment] and was the least severe of NJP's.

[4] In 1965, the birth control pill became legal for married couples, but it was still illegal in twenty-six states to prescribe the pill to unmarried women until a Supreme Court decision in 1972.

[5] The rabbit or Friedman test was the only pregnancy test available. The initial pregnancy test involved injecting a woman's urine into a female rabbit, then sacrificing the rabbit, and studying its ovaries to determine if the woman was actually pregnant.

[6] One year was the required amount of time for GIs to serve in Vietnam unless they re-enlisted for a second tour.

[7] Before Bill met Carole, he attended UW-Madison in 1964-1965 during his freshman year.

[8] See front matter map of South Vietnam.

[9] Carole later learned that Dr. Tom Dooley had close ties to the CIA. His books were used to spread disinformation, which helped to further popularize U.S. involvement in Vietnam.

[10] Bill was in Camera Club while in high school and enjoyed taking and developing black and white prints. In Vietnam, due to his photography skills, he was sometimes

assigned to dangerous spy missions, dropped off by helicopter into North Vietnam to take photos, and then picked up and flown back to his base. He was not allowed to write home about this as U.S. troops were not supposed to cross the demilitarized zone.

[11] Bill worked hard to complete a forty-page family genealogy book before he went to Vietnam. While in Vietnam, he corresponded with a Catholic priest from Kröv, Germany, and Carole helped translate their letters. Father Binder found Bill's distant cousin, Frau Schnitius-Lauxen, who they planned to visit when Bill returned.

[12] According to the U.S. Department of State publication P-4442 September 23, 1970, "Frequently US forces encounter elaborately built bunkers, tunnels, and trenches protected by overhead layers of logs and earthworks from which the enemy can fire with relative immunity… Napalm is the best weapon to penetrate these heavily fortified positions. If the use of napalm were withheld from them, U.S. troops would unnecessarily be exposed to far greater risks of injury or death than they now face."

[13] According to *On Wisconsin*, "The first Black Cultural Center had in 1968–1973 born and died amid protests and demonstrations" when the regents eliminated the center's budget. It took forty-four more years for a Black Cultural Center to have a home on the Madison campus "to acknowledge the specific and particular realities of black communities at UW-Madison" (Fall 2017, p. 13).

[14] A civilian ham operator in the U.S. picked up a high frequency radio wave which bounced off the earth's ionosphere from a military operator in Vietnam. The ham operator then telephoned Carole collect for the long-distance phone charges from wherever the ham operator was located. Then Carole spoke to Bill over the phone and the radio using a 'phone patch.' Calls were only three to five minutes long, as other GIs waited in line for their turns.

[15] The NOW [National Organization for Women] began in 1966 to end sex discrimination but there were still societal expectations of a wife's responsibilities in the home. Carole was invited to a NOW meeting by my friend, who was breaking through societal norms by becoming a single mother. Carole didn't agree with NOW's philosophies as she recognized the probability that she would be expected to work double-duty: have a career and run a household. Also, she didn't think Bill would approve, so she declined joining the NOW movement.

[16] Disc jockey and Air Force Sergeant Adrian Cronauer popularized this saying in 1965, inspiring the 1987 film, *Good Morning, Vietnam*, starring Robin Williams. After Cronauer left Vietnam, other DJs copied his salutation.

[17] The Sacred Falls Trail was closed indefinitely on May 9, 1999, after a fatal rockfall near the waterfall killed eight hikers and injured many others.

[18] According to reporter, Sara Rose, for *The Washington Post Magazine*, "During the Vietnam War, Pan Am had an exclusive contract with the Department of Defense to run R&R flights for soldiers on leave throughout the Pacific. The R&R flights were a key part of boosting troop morale for a rapidly unpopular war. By the latter half of 1970, about 17,000 soldiers would take R&R every month."

[19] Austin Straubel, a lieutenant colonel in the U.S. Army Air Corps, was killed in the Pacific in 1942. The Brown County Airport was renamed after him.

[20] *The Bob Hope Christmas Special,* January 16, 1969, can be viewed on YouTube. Go to time code 51:55 to hear what Hope had to say about the college campus uprisings.

[21] *Reader's Digest*, January, 1969, pp. 59–62 (condensed from *Redbook*, June 1968).

[22] Tet or the Chinese Lunar New Year celebration began on February 17, 1969. Over 1,140 Americans and 1,500 South Vietnamese were killed in three weeks of fighting. The bloody siege of Hue and the assault of the US Embassy in Saigon occurred during TET of 1969. (https://www.vietnamwar50th.com/1969-1971_vietnamization/Mini-Tet-1969-Begins)

[23] The TAA represented all graduate-student workers at UW-Madison and formed the first graduate employee union in the world. Organized in 1966, their first contract with the university was in 1970.

[24] Veterans dealing with mental health issues should call the Veterans Crisis Line at 1-800-273-8255 for help. The Department of Veteran Affairs estimates 17–18 veterans a day commit suicide, and according to the *Military Times*, 6,435 veterans died by suicide in 2018.

[25] DEROS was the estimated date of departure as to when a GI would be discharged home.

[26] According to the US government publication P-404 October 8, 1970, in May of 1969, President Nixon had advanced a comprehensive program for peace which was presented at the Paris Peace Talks. "This detailed program laid out basic principles for settlement of the conflict, including our essential objective: the opportunity for the South Vietnamese people to determine their own political future without external interference." A month later, Nixon announced the first withdrawal of US troops from Vietnam. The troop ceiling at the beginning of 1969 was 549,500 men. The President reported on October 7, 1969 that "In the past twenty months, I have reduced our troop ceiling in South Viet-Nam by 165,000 men." He also announced a

major new initiative for peace in Indochina and proposed a "cease-fire-in-place" throughout Indochina but it wasn't until 1973 that our troops finally pulled out of Vietnam.

[27] According to the US publication P-4442 September 1970, "Conversely, the enemy often attacks hamlets and villages defended only by farmers who care for their crops by day and become militia at night. The enemy also sets booby traps which often claim civilians as victims. Throughout the war, the Viet Cong have assassinated village and hamlet officials, kidnapped persons of all ages, and forced young men and even boys into their ranks."

[28] Northeastern Wisconsin slang, a contraction for "Ain't that so?"

[29] *Di di mau* is a Vietnamese phrase meaning "go, go, fast" or "move, move faster."

[30] It wasn't until the controversial movie, *The Deer Hunter*, came out in 1978 that a serious public debate began about the morality of the Vietnam War. It opened the door for Vietnam veterans to speak freely about the war.

[31] Years later, Bill learned that his TDY missions were actually decoys used to keep enemy soldiers from finding the Army Rangers in the same area who were on separate covert missions. Bill was livid when he heard Secretary of Defense McNamara state this on a TV documentary.

[32] Bill carried the guilt of leaving that dead American GI behind for 52 years. Carole told him the dead soldier probably saved his life by shielding him by taking those extra bullets. In February 2021, he retold this same story to his half-sister, broke down, and cried for the first time. Carole explained the concept of survivor's guilt to him, and he decided to return to the V.A. for more counseling.

[33] The Weathermen (Third World Marxists), named after a line in a Bob Dylan song, were white revolutionists allied with the Black Liberation Army. From October 8–11, 1969, The Weathermen worked to organize thousands of young people in a direct assault on the police called "National Action," to coincide with the trial of the Chicago 7. In 1970, the Weathermen went underground to build bombs. They targeted banks, the US Capitol, and the Pentagon.

[34] From 2003–2011, there were 4,400 US casualties and tens of thousands of Iraqi's killed during the Iraq War.

[35] Arlington West was set up by members of Veterans for Peace at various California beaches, including San Diego and Santa Monica. Santa Barbara's Arlington West, which began on November 2, 2003, measured almost the size of a football field at 141 feet wide and 310 feet long. When Carole and Bill were there in 2007, it had met its

full capacity of 3,000 crosses placed three feet apart in rows spaced five feet wide, allowing visitors to walk through as if in a cemetery. The crosses, flags, and candles were put in place on Sunday and then taken down that same evening.

[36] New Revised Standard Version Bible, ©1989 by the Division of Christian Education of the National Council of the Churches of Christ, published by Zondervan, p. 966.

[37] Ibid p. 648.

www.ingramcontent.com/pod-product-compliance
Lightning Source LLC
Chambersburg PA
CBHW040251090526

44586CB00041B/2747